There When We Needed Him

Wiley Austin Branton, Civil Rights Warrior

JUDITH KILPATRICK

There When We Needed Him

THE UNIVERSITY OF ARKANSAS PRESS   *Fayetteville*   *2007*

Copyright © 2007 by The University of Arkansas Press

All rights reserved
Manufactured in the United States of America

ISBN-10: 1-55728-848-8
ISBN-13: 978-1-55728-848-6

11   10   09   08   07   5   4   3   2   1

Designed by Liz Lester

♾ The paper used in this publication meets the
minimum requirements of the American National
Standard for Permanence of Paper for Printed Library
Materials Z39.48-1984.

LIBRARY OF CONGRESS CATALOGING-IN-PUBLICATION DATA

Kilpatrick, Judith, 1946–
    There when we needed him : Wiley Austin Branton,
civil rights warrior / Judith Kilpatrick.
        p.   cm.
    Includes bibliographical references and index.
    ISBN 1-55728-848-8 (cloth : alk. paper)
    1. Branton, Wiley Austin, 1923- 2. African American
lawyers—Arkansas—Biography. 3. Civil rights
movements—Arkansas—History—20th century I. Title.
    KF373.B68K55   2007
    340.092—dc22 [B]

                            2007016709

CONTENTS

ACKNOWLEDGMENTS

Many people helped with locating and collecting information and documents about Wiley Branton's life. My apologies to anyone I omit from the list. The most significant help came from the Branton family: Leo Branton Jr., Sterling Branton, and Julia Branton Jones (Wiley's siblings); and his children, Richard Branton, Wylene Branton Wood, Wiley A. Branton Jr., Beverly Branton Lamberson, and Debra Branton. They were very generous in providing me with their memories, photographs, and papers. All took the time to sit and talk with me about Wiley Branton; for most, more than once. Wiley Branton Jr. entrusted me with twenty-five boxes of his father's personal papers.

Branton's friends and colleagues, too, were willing to give of their time and recollections in interviews and telephone conversations. Some are cited in the text, and others provided background and context. These were Derrick Bell, Roderic V. O. Boggs, The Hon. William Bryant, Joseph A. Califano, Ramsey Clark, William T. Coleman, John Crump, Geleve Grice, George W. B. Haley, George Howard Jr., Elaine Jones, George W. Jones, Vernon E. Jordan Jr., Warner Lawson, James W. Leslie, Cecilia Marshall, Christopher C. Mercer, Marianita Porterfield, The Hon. Constance Baker Motley, Weldon Rougeau, Eckel and Marge Rowland, Mildred Bond Roxborough, Gina Shropshire, Ozell Sutton, The Hon. David Tatle, The Hon. Paul R. Webber III, Eddie Williams, Miller Williams, Patricia Worthy.

Historians David Appleby, Taylor Branch, Evan Bukey, Dennis C. Dickerson, Tom Dillard, Tony Freyer, Elizabeth Jacoway, Grif Stockley, and Daniel Sutherland all contributed facts and guidance to me. The law firm of Sidley & Austin (now Sidley Austin Brown & Wood), through Michael Nemeroff, Nancy Williams, Carter Phillips, graciously provided me with copies of the tapes created at the firm's annual luncheon held in Branton's memory.

Librarians and libraries were wonderful sources of information and help: Sally Kelley of the University of Arkansas School of Law performed several web searches for me. JoEllen Elbashir of the Moorland-Spingarn Research Center and the Civil Rights Documentary Project at Howard

University, Allen Fisher of the Lyndon Baines Johnson Library and Museum, Kathryn C. Fitzhugh of the University of Arkansas at Little Rock/Pulaski County Law Library, and Anne Pritchard in Special Collections, University of Arkansas, Fayetteville, Mullins Library, were helpful hosts when I visited and kind enough to provide additional information afterward. Other contributors were the Library of Congress, National Archives; Wisconsin Historical Society Library Archives at the University of Wisconsin–Madison; Pine Bluff–Jefferson County Public Library; John F. Kennedy Presidential Library and Museum (Sam Rubin); Butler Center, Little Rock Public Library; Auburn Avenue Research Library/Atlanta–Fulton County Library System (Constance Carter); Henry Hampton Archives, Washington University Film and Media Archive, Special Collections; Butler Library, Columbia University, Rare Book and Manuscript Library (Whitney M. Young Jr. and Oral History Research Collections); Civil Rights Documentary Project, University of Virginia (William A. Elwood); Minnesota Historical Society; Arkansas History Commission; Manuscripts Department, Wilson Library, University of North Carolina at Chapel Hill; and Mississippi Department of Archives and History

Over the years, a number of students provided research assistance: Kristin Thompson (UA History '01), Tiffany Armstrong (UA Law '02), Gina Smith (UA Law '02), Rhonda Williams-Henry (UA Law '02), Peggy Lloyd (UA History '03), Johnnie Lee Miller (UA Law '04), Scott Cashion (UA History '000), Ashley K. Ragsdale (UA Law '05), and Calysta Johnson (UA Law '06). Jacque Fifer spent hours transcribing interview tapes.

My own friends and colleagues also must be thanked for contributing time, energy, and encouragement: Connie Dove, Julie E. McDonald, Cynthia E. Nance, William E. Nelson, Betty Luber, Mack Bullard, and David Rinehart. Last, but not least, heartfelt thanks to Beth Motherwell, whose original question introduced me to Branton's life and legacy. This has been a wonderful journey.

INTRODUCTION

When Wiley Branton agreed to represent a group of Little Rock, Arkansas, parents and their children to force the Little Rock public schools to integrate, he had no idea that the case would change his life. He was thirty-two years old, married, with five children. Branton had become a lawyer in 1952, and conducted a solo law practice in his hometown of Pine Bluff, Arkansas, with his wife as his secretary. He had begun to build a small reputation for successfully handling local civil rights matters. He also continued to run the taxicab business started by his father and grandfather in 1915. His future as a prominent lawyer in his small-town community seemed settled.

But Branton also was a black man in a southern state that practiced segregation. While he could live a comfortable life, segregationist laws and attitudes would limit him. All his life, he had observed, and been subject to, discrimination based solely on his color. He knew that such comfort as he enjoyed was not the lot of the majority of black men and women. A student of his country's history, he was proud to be an American, yet he recognized that America was not living up to its ideals. He joined hundreds of other black men and women who worked to change discriminatory practices in this country through the National Association for the Advancement of Colored People (NAACP) and other organizations. The law would be his vehicle, but his best results were not always achieved in a courtroom.

Branton's involvement with *Cooper v. Aaron,* the formal name for the Little Rock integration case, began almost by chance following the United States Supreme Court's 1954 decision declaring public school segregation unconstitutional in *Brown v. Board of Education.* When Arkansas governor Orval Faubus defied the Court's decision and forced President Eisenhower to send federal troops to protect nine black high school students, allowing them to attend Central High School in Little Rock, the world's attention focused on that city. *Cooper v. Aaron* became the first contest of the new law. Branton was catapulted onto the national scene and wound up becoming a national figure in the civil rights movement. He devoted the rest of his life to fighting discrimination, taking a number of jobs in which his efforts improved access to civil rights for thousands of people.

Wiley Branton died on December 15, 1988, at the age of sixty-five. Eleven hundred mourners attended a funeral service at the Washington (D.C.) National Cathedral on Monday, December 19. Those present reflected Branton's life in civil rights. They included Supreme Court justice Thurgood Marshall; Jack Greenberg, General Counsel of the NAACP Legal Defense and Education Fund; District of Columbia mayor Marion Barry; and a host of other prominent civil rights activists. The eulogy was delivered by his protégé and close friend, Vernon E. Jordan Jr., who praised Branton both as a devoted lawyer and as a "friend who would go the second mile, lend a helping hand, share and care and come when needed." A more intimate "viewing" had taken place at his church, the Nineteenth Street Baptist Church, the previous evening.

Branton's body was flown back to Arkansas, where a ceremony was held at the family's place of worship, St. Paul's Baptist Church, in Pine Bluff. A memorial service was held at his alma mater, the University of Arkansas at Pine Bluff (formerly AM&N College). Almost two hundred people attended that program and Arkansas governor Bill Clinton delivered the closing remarks. Wiley Branton was buried near his parents and grandparents in the family plot at Bellwood Cemetery in Pine Bluff.

Within the year following his death, many individuals and organizations honored Branton. The National Bar Association and the Washington Lawyers Committee for Civil Rights Under Law each established annual symposia named for him. His law firm, Sidley & Austin, began an annual lunch celebrating his life and work that has become a symposium at Howard University's School of Law, where Branton served as dean. On August 31, 2003, an eleven-mile section of Interstate 530 near Pine Bluff was named in his honor, the first time Arkansas has honored a black citizen in this manner. Other, less grand, organizations also created memorials to him around the country.

Yet, during a program commemorating the Little Rock case just ten years after his death, Branton's name was hardly mentioned. His achievements are today unknown to many in the black community and to the general public. While the same is true of many who labored in the civil rights field during the twentieth century, Branton's life should not be forgotten. It demonstrates the positive effect that one man can have on a society and serves as an example and encouragement for those who follow.

CHAPTER 1

Character-Building
The Early Years

IN THE BEGINNING, Branton was lucky. When he was born in 1923, colored citizens[1] comprised one-third of the population in Pine Bluff, Arkansas.[2] It was a bustling, prosperous community, with a railroad center established during the late nineteenth century, a lumber industry, and other, smaller, businesses. Cotton plantations surrounded the town. In addition to its substantial numbers, the colored community had benefited from a number of fortuitous events.

First, Pine Bluff had a history of colored leaders, dating from the Reconstruction period that followed the Civil War. A colored attorney, Richard A. Dawson, was elected a state senator from Jefferson County in 1871. Another colored attorney, S. J. Hollingsworth, became deputy collector of Internal Revenue in 1883. Wiley Jones, a colored entrepreneur, built and owned the first streetcar line in Pine Bluff in 1886. Jones also owned a popular racetrack in the 1890s that catered to both colored and white citizens. A colored assistant prosecuting attorney, John Grey Lucas, was appointed to that county position in 1887. Lucas was elected to represent Jefferson County in the Arkansas General Assembly in 1890. Ferd Havis, a colored businessman, owned a large general store and a popular saloon in Pine Bluff. In 1894, colored attorney Alexander Burnett was appointed United States commissioner for the Post Office.[3] Pine Bluff's colored citizens built the first Lodge to house Arkansas's colored Masons. Located downtown, right across from the train station, it was one of the most prominent buildings in town.

Second, the colored population of Pine Bluff was highly educated for its time. Although they were segregated, there were public schools for colored children when Wiley Branton was born. In 1918, the city had adopted an education plan that provided six years of elementary schooling, three years of junior high, and three years of senior high for all students.[4] Pine Bluff's colored high school was one of only six that existed in Arkansas in 1920, all in urban areas.[5] Eighteen counties in the state had no high schools for either race.[6] Pine Bluff also was home to the only institution of higher education for colored people in Arkansas, established in 1875 after they petitioned for a school that would train "colored teachers." First called Arkansas Branch Normal, the school provided only a two-year teachers program for many years. By 1921, however, the school had been renamed the Arkansas Agricultural, Mechanical and Normal College (AM&N) and offered a four-year degree. Thus, there was an educated colored middle class in Pine Bluff.[7]

Third, while Arkansas was legally segregated, it had never, unlike other southern states, fully disfranchised its colored citizens. They could vote, and they did, preventing the worst restrictions on their lives. For example, colored voters were instrumental in preventing imposition of a "grandfather clause" and other educational requirements for voting in 1911.[8] Colored residents also owned property and, in some instances, their homes were mixed among those of white citizens. This group was able to maintain a certain amount of dignity and influence in their hometowns, despite the existence of segregation. Pine Bluff's colored community was not isolated from other communities across the country. The railroads allowed for travel and an influx of visitors. AM&N College brought important colored politicians and performance artists into town to speak on campus. The colored press was in its heyday and copies of the *Chicago Defender,* the *Pittsburgh Courier,* and the *St. Louis Argus* were circulated throughout the town.

While conditions for Pine Bluff's educated colored residents may have been better than the average in the South, they were never easy. Public transportation was segregated. The public library was closed to colored people, except for a small space in the Masonic Temple Annex where a few books were located. Only a few restaurants served colored people, and only in separate areas accessible through separate doors. None of the retail stores allowed colored customers to try on clothes before they purchased them. Neither the stores nor the restaurants had bathroom facilities available to colored citizens. Those who came into town on Saturdays to shop were required to use the facilities designated for colored people in the bus or train stations. The movie theaters in town had separate balconies designated for colored people and the drive-in refused them admittance entirely.[9] There were no public parks where either colored visitors or residents could relax in the open air.[10]

The town's newspaper would not use courtesy titles (Mr., Miss, or Mrs.) for any colored person mentioned and no colored social events were covered. Even space for colored obituaries had to be paid for and they were required to carry the notice "paid advertisement." Colored people were not allowed to use the city hospital until after World War II and, even then, there was a separate wing for them. Of course, none of the city or county law enforcement personnel were colored. Even though an active NAACP chapter was established in 1919, it operated within the confines of segregation. During a national campaign for federal legislation against lynching, the local chapter had to return 150 campaign buttons to the national office because "[i]t was found in some cases to be dangerous to display them in some parts and places of our city and county. The wrist bands and large placards we could not handle at all on account of prejudice here among the whites."[11]

These advantages and disadvantages required the colored community to consolidate in self-defense. The churches had been a center of power and influence within the colored community since the Civil War.[12] Fraternal benevolent groups like the Prince Hall Masons and others came into being after emancipation and joined the churches in strengthening the community. Some of these groups provided life insurance and burial policies not available from white insurers. Others provided networking and social outlets for those denied membership in existing white groups. One of these groups built a small hospital in the late 1920s in Pine Bluff, when hospital care was otherwise unavailable.[13] Some groups also helped to provide loans for the purchase of real property, which could not be obtained from white banks, aiding many in the community to become homeowners. The National Negro Business League, begun by Booker T. Washington, had a branch in Pine Bluff.

Wiley Branton was lucky in his family, as well. His paternal grandfather, James L. Branton, had come to Arkansas with his wife, Estelle, from Grenada, Mississippi, around 1915. At that time, James Branton was about fifty years old. Little is known about his Mississippi background. Family history says that James Branton had adopted the name "Branton" from a stepfather, and that the original family name was of American Indian origin, "Wise" or "Wiseman." Family lore also states that James L. Branton once was married to a woman named Julia LeFlore, through whom the family is descended from Greenwood LeFlore, a wealthy French-Indian plantation owner, who was a chief of the Mississippi Choctaw Indian tribe.[14] Although this link has not been documented, Wiley Branton recalled that, in 1963, he had refuted charges of being an "outside agitator" in Greenwood, Mississippi, by claiming LeFlore as his ancestor.[15] To an interviewer, Branton described the suspicion that met him as he entered a Greenwood courtroom and its dissipation as the audience saw his features and began nodding in acceptance.[16]

James Branton first earned his living by selling real estate. However, he owned one of the few cars in the colored community and soon found he could make more money shuttling people around town. Ownership of an automobile in 1915 was remarkable for anyone, and particularly so for a colored man. Pine Bluff had seen its first auto only in 1900. By 1906, there were only nine members of a white Pine Bluff Automobile Club. Branton's taxi business quickly became so busy that James Branton urged his son, Leo Andrew, then twenty-eight and working in the oil fields of Louisiana, to join him. At first, the taxi business operated out of a barbershop in the colored Masonic building next to the train station, using a street-side telephone on the corner outside the building. The business's first real office was located at 318 State Street, off one side of the Masonic building.

Wiley Branton's maternal forebears are more easily traced. His grandmother was the daughter of Mary Robinson, born about 1850 in Georgia, and Wesley Stewart, of Knoxville, Tennessee. Stewart was a farmer and became a Knoxville alderman during Reconstruction.[17] Effa Louise Lavinia Emily Rosetta Armstrong Stewart was born about 1875 and moved to Arkansas to live with her mother's brother, George Robinson, in the early 1890s. Family lore says that Effa had been sent to Pine Bluff to get her away from a young man who was courting her at home.[18] George Robinson was a Baptist minister who helped found St. Paul Baptist Church in Pine Bluff, after having been assistant pastor of the town's integrated First Baptist Church. Robinson also played a role in creating the Arkansas Baptist Convention.[19]

Branton's maternal grandfather, James Austin Wiley (called "Pap" by his grandchildren) was born in Hamburg, Arkansas, in 1872, the son of Ellen, a Black Cherokee born in Alabama about 1855, and a white man named Wiley.[20] The term comes from the fact that, like the Choctaw Tribe of which Greenwood LeFlore was a member, many prosperous Cherokee Indians were also slave owners and produced mixed-blood offspring. As the Cherokee were pushed from Georgia into Alabama and Arkansas, they took their colored slaves with them. Marriages also occurred between free coloreds and Indians, both before and after Emancipation. Children born of relations between Cherokee Indians and colored people were known as "Black Cherokees."[21] The family moved to Pine Bluff after 1880, where Ellen Wiley ran a boardinghouse on State Street.

Effa Stewart married James Austin Wiley on June 13, 1893, in Texarkana, Arkansas, far from Pine Bluff. The location suggests a runaway marriage. Effa was educated at the Branch Normal teacher's college in Pine Bluff and taught in the colored public schools. James worked for the Cotton Belt railroad, where he eventually became a foreman in its Pine Bluff repair shops. Later, he became holder of a private contract with the U.S. Post Office to provide parcel post service. The Post Office created an internal parcel post service about 1929 and hired James Wiley to handle it. "In the mid-1930s, a prejudiced postmaster re-assigned a number of black employees to less important jobs and my grandfather was ordered to start walking a postman's route as a letter carrier if he wanted to remain employed. He decided to continue to work . . . to accumulate sufficient retirement benefit and . . . retired in 1940. . . ."[22]

Together, the couple had eight children. In 1920, through hard work and the benefit of several parcels of real estate given to Effa Wiley as a wedding present by relatives, the couple was able to purchase a city block in Pine Bluff for $12,500.[23] The property contained several existing structures, one of them a rambling wood-frame Victorian at 1301 Alabama Street into which the family moved.

Both the Brantons and the Wileys were light-skinned people, a mixture of the African, white, and American Indian races. They benefited from the fact that the shade of a person's skin has had a profound effect on the acceptability and progress of African Americans in the United States, among both communities. During slavery, light-skinned colored people often received special vocational training and were not put to heavy physical labor in the fields. Some were acknowledged and educated by their white fathers, despite laws forbidding it, and given support toward a career. Some were given their freedom and others were able to buy themselves out of slavery.

Even without such help, though, it was often easier for a light-skinned African American to support him- or herself. White people seemed less averse to the lighter shade of color.[24] During the Reconstruction period following the Civil War, many of the colored Americans participating in local and state government appear light-skinned and census records refer to them as "mulatto."[25] One of the consequences of this more favorable treatment was the appearance of a Negro middle class around the 1890s that contained a predominance of those with lighter skin. The Wileys were part of this development.

Favored or not, however, light-skinned Negroes still suffered from racism and were aware that segregationist laws could be used to strip them of what they had acquired without much recourse. However they might try to differentiate themselves from poorer or less-educated Negroes, as far as white society was concerned, they were virtually identical. Two very different men, Booker T. Washington and W. E. B. Du Bois, were influential in convincing the Negro middle class that it had a responsibility to "uplift" the rest of its race, to help those who were unable to obtain education or who were mired in the bonds of sharecropping. Unless they did so, their own gains would be ephemeral.

The Wiley family, better educated than many of their neighbors, followed the teachings of Booker T. Washington. They believed in the benefits of education and sent several of their children to attend Washington's Tuskegee Institute in Alabama, including their daughter, Pauline Angie, who was the third of Effa and James's children.[26] The Wileys also helped to send other promising students to attend Tuskegee Institute.

Effa Wiley was a strong, disciplined woman and an activist in her community. Her obituary states that she served on numerous committees that met with public officials, including the state's governor, to complain about the denial of civil rights for African Americans. She also held a number of different state and national offices in the Eastern Star

(Arkansas Jurisdiction), the Women's Department of the United Brothers of Friendship, and the womens' body of the Arkansas and National Baptist Conventions.[27]

Effa Wiley was described by a contemporary as able to "carry her point and sway the judgment of many in the things she thought were right. . . . She was dynamic, she could be a powerful friend or a dangerous foe. She had a love for the old customs and principles . . . [and was] sought by both races in many of the vital issues that affected our people."[28] In a less complimentary manner, the secretary of the Pine Bluff NAACP said she "is the greatest Cain raiser . . . so I mean to have her help the [women's] auxiliary."[29] Effa Wiley once "waged a fight to get black people to vote against funds for a new library because city officials announced that only whites would be able to use it." Years later, Wiley Branton would say, "[e]ven though [my grandparents] knew that white folks were in control, they would by and large give them a run for their money."[30]

Members of the Wiley family were early supporters of the NAACP. The patriarch, James A. Wiley, was a charter member of the Pine Bluff Chapter begun in 1919, and he appeared regularly thereafter in its records as a continuing member.[31] Later, Effa Wiley served on the Executive Committee of the NAACP Women's Auxiliary. In 1930, their daughter, Julia, and son, Joe Wiley, became members. A second son, Frank Wiley, and daughter Pauline Branton joined in 1937.[32]

While James Branton and his son, Leo, did not join organizations, they worked on behalf of the race in their own way. "The Branton taxicabs transported sick people to hospitals when the public ambulances would not serve blacks, and they picked up children from school on inclement days. The cabs connected people on the outskirts of town with friends and relatives in the city at a time when few black people in Pine Bluff owned automobiles. On more than one occasion they provided a radio-dispatched fleet of cars descending on the scene of potential racial violence to remove black people from possible physical danger."[33]

Between Effa Wiley's community activism, James Wiley's railroad and post office work, and the efforts of the Brantons' cab company, the Wiley and Branton families were well known and respected by both races in Pine Bluff. The Wileys lived a life of some privilege, near the middle of town, with white families living across the street. The respect in which both families were held benefited the Negro community as a whole. The families occupied a kind of "middle ground" in the town. Being successful, light-skinned, and industrious made them more "acceptable" to some whites. Yet the families also were "race conscious," standing up when civil rights issues arose, which counted for much in the larger Negro community. The Wileys often were called upon to help straighten out the problems others were having with members of the white community.[34]

Daughter Pauline Wiley became a public schoolteacher in Pine Bluff after her graduation from Tuskegee Institute. She met Leo Andrew Branton, a friend of her brother Joe Wiley, and married him in 1921. Leo Branton, although he had received a basic education as a child, had not attended high school or college. His good looks and bon vivant manner, as well as his success with the cab company, likely were what attracted Pauline Wiley.

After marrying Leo Branton, Pauline Wiley Branton remained very close to her family. In the first few years of their marriage, they lived with the Wileys in the Victorian at 1301 Alabama. The first of Pauline and Leo Branton's five children, Leo Andrew Jr., was born there in 1922. Later, they moved a block away, to 1401 Alabama Street, where Wiley Austin Branton, named to honor Pauline's family, was born in 1923. Sterling and Paul Branton were born, respectively, in 1926 and 1928. In 1928, Leo and Pauline purchased one of the lots on the Wileys' property for $1,000.[35] The last of their children, Julia, was born in 1932 in the house they built at 1307 Alabama Street.

At home in the midst of a large, prominent, family, with the cab company office never far away, the worst effects of segregation did not have much impact on Wiley Branton's generation while they were young. The families living across the street were white, and the Branton children played with them throughout childhood without consideration of color. These facts, and the community service lessons he learned from Effa Wiley, had a strong impact on Wiley Branton's personality and life principles.

He seems to have been born with an interest in serious matters. As a child, although he played with his brothers and other boys in the neighborhood, Wiley spent much of his time with his grandparents, particularly his grandmother, Effa. He later recalled that "[f]rom my earliest memories, she was hauling me all over the state to various Baptist conventions and associations . . . [which gave me] early training in leadership responsibilities and public speaking."[36] There, he also learned about the issues that concerned Negro activists of the day. He observed that education could lift a person out of poverty and give him or her some control over their lives.

Given Effa Wiley's involvement in race matters, Branton absorbed the intricacies of operating safely within a society tilted toward white privilege. When Effa Wiley was called to help a family that had illness, death, or some other difficulty, Wiley accompanied her and learned how one deals with people in trouble. He saw the value of "community solidarity," as represented by the church and other Negro organizations, and he developed a preference for working within membership groups. From these experiences, Wiley Branton developed confidence in himself. He knew that one could always do something to better any situation. He absorbed a sense of responsibility and duty to his community. He learned that one could not turn a blind eye to the restrictions and hardships faced by others.

Growing up in the "boom" period of the 1920s and the "Great Depression" of the 1930s, Branton also was taught Booker T. Washington's love of this country and his belief that hard work would result in success for any citizen. These attributes led Dr. Jane Smith, president of the National Council of Negro Women, later to say that "Wiley Branton . . . was prouder than anyone . . . of being an African American in America. . . . Because he loved America, he wanted to do what he could, not only for the people of his color, but for people of all colors."[37]

Wiley attended a private kindergarten or "day school" before beginning public school. Christopher C. Mercer, Jr., a friend from those days, who became Wiley's law school classmate much later, commented, "you were considered to be SOMEBODY if you went to Miss Hattie Benson's school. She taught you manners, . . how to say 'yes sir, yes ma'am, and no ma'am,' that sort of thing."[38] Wiley then attended the segregated public schools.

Missouri Street Elementary School was not far from his home. After sixth grade, he was transferred to Merrill High School. At that time, Merrill housed junior high and high school classes and served the colored population of both Pine Bluff and adjoining school districts. Branton later recalled, "[i]t had no gymnasium nor playing field and was not accredited by the North Central Association of Secondary Schools."[39] Branton was a good student, although he did not have the academic success of his brother Leo. Wiley "was always the business manager in his class."[40]

Despite its limitations, the education he received at Merrill was more than was available to many colored teenagers in Arkansas at that time. Branton always believed that "a student at Merrill can look forward to achievement with the same degree that a student can from any other area of the country."[41] At school, Wiley always was eager for new experiences. Dr. Henry Foster, President Clinton's nominee for surgeon general of the United States, recalled that he and Wiley had their first plane ride when Foster's schoolteacher father took his science class to Toney Field just outside of Pine Bluff. There, they would learn about the properties of "air" by flying in an airplane. Some students were afraid to get into the plane for the thirteenth ride, but Wiley said, "I'm not superstitious, I'll get in," and Foster joined him.[42]

It was about this time that Wiley Branton had his first contact with racism. It occurred while he was working part-time at the cab company, something all the Branton boys did from their earliest memories. Around 1934, Wiley was given a twenty-dollar bill in exchange for some service at the cabstand. There was not enough money in the office to make change, and he went across the street to the railroad station office for it. Suspicious of a colored child possessing that large a bill, the white stationmaster questioned him accusingly. When told that Wiley was Leo Branton's son, the man stated, "Oh. Yeah, you can get change. Leo's a good nigger."[43]

Another incident that occurred while Wiley was in high school gave him his first opportunity to take a stand against discrimination. One summer, the school building burned down. While repairs and renovations were ongoing, the school board refused to allow the school to operate from the "white" Pine Street School, although it was vacant at the time. Instead, for nearly two years, classes were spread out among several Negro churches. New equipment ordered for the rebuilt Merrill school was transferred to the white Pine Bluff High School and that school's used equipment was installed at Merrill. In protest, Wiley led a group of students to meet with the school superintendent. As he reported, "Mr. Allen received us in a very polite and friendly manner and promised to look into the situation, but nothing further came of our protest. This was just another example of the fact that even though we were living under the 'separate but equal' doctrine at that time, things were always separate—but never equal."[44] Unfair transfers of this sort were not uncommon during segregation.[45]

Wiley began driving taxis for the family business when he was fifteen. Leo Branton Sr. was a taciturn man with a short temper who worked all the time, but he was fair. When the boys were old enough to drive cabs, he paid them exactly the same wage as the other adult drivers and did not expect them to repay him for any of their personal expenses.[46] Wiley later said he had performed every type of job such a business offered—from shoeshine boy, through dispatcher, radio operator, taxi driver, baggage truck driver, gasoline attendant, mechanic's helper, assistant office manager, to manager.[47]

Wiley was the only one of Leo Branton's sons to show "any interest in actually running the cab company, or . . . any interest in it at all."[48] His curmudgeon grandfather, J. L. Branton, appreciated that interest and was known to say things like, "He don't stand no foolishness. Got a business head on him."[49] Involvement in the business was where he honed many of the administrative and "people" skills that stood him in good stead and "helped to cultivate the natural wit and humor that would one day make him legendary."[50]

His interest in serious matters did not prevent Wiley from having a sense of humor, which exhibited itself at an early age. One example is an incident that took place in his early teens when an automobile salesman was attempting to sell a new car to his father. Wiley asked how the car handled and the salesman kiddingly responded, "Why don't you take it for a spin and see for yourself?" Wiley surprised the man by hopping in the car and taking it for a short drive. Wiley's brother Sterling recalls the salesman running down the street after the car. On Wiley's return, he tossed the key to the salesman and said, "That drives pretty good, you know."[51]

In 1940, Wiley and his brother Leo were jolted out of their relative innocence by an encounter with a Pine Bluff store clerk that illustrates the operation of southern racism, even on middle-class and educated Negroes. It began when Wiley and Leo were shopping for school clothes. Leo was about to begin his third year of college at Tennessee A&I State College, and Wiley was entering his first year at Arkansas AM&N. Wiley was looking for a particular style of suit, but could not find it in his size. As he worked on needed alterations with the clerk, Leo found the suit in Wiley's size. The salesman told Leo not to interrupt, probably not wanting to redo the paperwork. Leo refused to back down and the salesman hit him. Leo fought back. When others separated them and Leo was explaining the situation to the store's owner, the clerk went into the back and came out with a gun. After dodging around clothing racks, Leo ran out the door. Police were called to the store and, after hearing the story, were not inclined to pursue it further.[52]

The clerk was insistent that Leo be punished, and the sheriff's office suggested to Leo's father that he bring the boy into the station and they would grant bail so he would not spend time in jail. The next day, James Wiley, Leo's grandfather, accompanied him to the station where he was charged with disturbing the peace, fingerprinted, and released on bond. Five days later, trial was set in the municipal justice court. On the day of trial, the family's white lawyer informed them that he could not represent Leo because of "social pressure." The lawyer told them that trial would be delayed while they found another attorney. In court, however, the judge refused a delay and Leo learned he was being charged with several additional crimes, including assault with a deadly weapon. The trial took place without a lawyer to represent Leo.

The store clerk testified that Leo had beaten him with the blunt end of a knife. Despite Leo's testimony, and that of his brother and another customer, who all denied seeing a knife, Leo was convicted on all counts and sentenced to consecutive periods of incarceration. According to Leo, it added up to over one hundred days on the county farm. The sentence was appealed to the circuit court and, since trial could not be set for several months, Leo went on to school in Tennessee. Wiley Branton later commented that there were only two Negro lawyers in Pine Bluff at the time. One of the two did not practice criminal law, although he was willing to file the notice of appeal for Leo. The other was relatively new in town and was considered too much of a firebrand for safety, as he was known for "speaking out loudly against segregation and discrimination."[53]

By the time of the circuit court trial, the family had hired a white lawyer. Before trial, the lawyer did his best to "tone down" the family's middle-class status, asking both Leo and Wiley to wear old clothes. The prosecutor asked few questions, most of them intended to show that Leo was an "uppity nigger." During closing argument, Leo recalled that the prosecutor's argument "went something like this: If this was an ordinary cornfield nigra, I'd say you'd just fine him because fining would be enough. But this is no ordinary cornfield nigger, this is a nigra that's got money—got enough money to go away to college, and in another state. So fining this nigger would be insufficient, but I want to see him spend some time on the county farm." Leo was found guilty and sentenced to thirty days at the county farm.[54]

An appeal of the conviction was filed with the state supreme court, but the circuit judge suggested to the family that if they could find some reason the sentence would be a hardship, he would suspend the sentence. A doctor at the Tennessee State medical school, Meharry College of Medicine, wrote that the condition of Leo's lungs were such that incarceration would be dangerous to his health. The sentence was suspended and the family decided that it would be best if Leo did not return to Arkansas.[55]

The circumstances of Leo's arrest led Dr. John Watson, president of AM&N College, to urge a boycott of the clothing store by the Negro community. As reported in a later publication, Watson circulated word that "if he saw any faculty members coming out of that place of business, they should tell him where to send their final check, and if he saw any students coming out of that store they should tell him where to send their final transcript."[56] President Watson thereafter wrote to Dr. W. J. Hale, president of Tennessee A&I State College, commending Leo Branton and noting, "I have congratulated the boy on his pluck and he goes away with my best wishes."[57]

The author George Lipsitz later observed that, "[w]ith no central organization or public meetings, all the important black groups in Pine Bluff, including the NAACP and the Prince Hall Masons, spread word of the boycott. The removal of black business cost the Henry Marx store thousands of dollars, and when Leo Branton's case finally came to trial before the jury, black people filled up their designated area of the courtroom to demonstrate support."[58]

Pine Bluff was a community in which the more vicious outward manifestations of racism were minimal. Yet the enhanced charges against Leo for disobeying the clerk's order to shut up and for fighting back when struck, the family's difficulty in finding a lawyer (and their concern that the available Negro lawyer might make things worse for Leo), the nature of the trial (and the belief on both sides that the family's standing would have an adverse effect on the jury), the inability of the judge to properly perform his role (and his willingness to "arrange" an appropriate outcome), all create a depressing picture of life for even the most prosperous Negroes.

At the age of nineteen, Wiley was both a full-time manager of Branton's 98 taxi company (named for its telephone number) and enrolled at AM&N College. By this time, he must have felt the beginnings of conflict about the way things were. His family and teachers had taught him patriotism, and to believe in the American dream, yet he also had been exposed to segregation, unfair treatment, and the suffering caused to Negro citizens by white attitudes and laws. He was realizing the dissonance between the words of the country's founding documents and the treatment meted out to some of its citizens.

His grandmother's example had taught him to stand up for what was right. Although his own circumstances protected him from the most blatant forms of racism, Wiley could not turn away from responsibility and duty. In his high school protest, Wiley had been measured and deliberate in his actions. That common sense would become a trademark of his advocacy. He would push the traditional limits of protest, as did his grandmother, but would remain within the law from which he expected fairness, justice, and protection. Many times that expectation was not fulfilled, but Wiley never lost hope. He had absorbed principles that would carry him through perilous times. He was taught to think independently, which would test those principles. Wiley Branton acted when he saw unfairness and injustice. He does not seem ever to have wavered in his effort to do what was right in any situation, even when the action threatened negative consequences to him.

CHAPTER 2

Racism during World War II

WILEY BRANTON MANAGED to attend about two years of classes at
AM&N College before he was drafted into the U.S. Army in early 1943.
At the time, he was managing the family taxi company, which was operating six cars and had nine employees. Branton must have been appre-
hensive about his situation. Aside from the normal concerns about
fighting in an overseas war, Negro soldiers had realistic concerns about
the treatment they would receive in the military. The armed forces were
segregated. Although Negroes had fought in American wars since the
Revolution, President Woodrow Wilson had granted requests of southern politicians to impose segregation in the military during the First
World War. This official segregation continued in World War II, resulting in Negro units under the supervision of white officers.

Initially, military planners for World War II discounted the usefulness of Negro soldiers for any duties beyond the most menial.
Experience with Negro soldiers in World War I, particularly those from
the South, had revealed a lack of education that reduced their performance in a modern, mechanized army. Some military units, like the
Engineers, objected to having Negro troops assigned at all, fearing they
would not have the technical skills required and could not bear up under
the stresses imposed on the job.[1]

Continued segregation of the armed forces was opposed by organizations like the NAACP and the National Urban League. They were
well aware of the terrible experiences that segregation had imposed on
Negro soldiers during World War I. In addition, those soldiers had
returned from their experience in that first world war expecting better
treatment and more democracy at home.[2] Men who felt they had proved

their mettle in battle were unwilling again to submit themselves to the demands of segregation. When they stood their ground, there were riots and attacks on Negro soldiers in cities and towns across the country.

Negro activists were determined not to let that happen again, and kept close tabs on military planning to try and prevent their reoccurrence. The Negro press argued for a "double victory"—in the war overseas and the racist one at home—even before Pearl Harbor.[3] Negro leaders knew that their votes were valuable to Franklin D. Roosevelt's 1940 reelection and put pressure on the administration in an effort to assure that unequal treatment in the military did not continue in World War II. Presidential politics were such that Roosevelt believed he must respond to the pressure in some measure. The president tried a compromise. Negro soldiers would be taken into the service in proportion to their percentage of the U.S. population, about 10 percent at the time, and they would be assigned to every type of service.[4]

The resulting Selective Training and Service Act of 1940 made all men ages twenty-one to thirty-five eligible for duty and contained two provisions prohibiting discrimination in the selection process. However, the membership of local draft boards was left to the discretion of each state's governor, leading to "the virtual exclusion of blacks from Southern boards." Local boards' use of "discriminatory deferment criteria, [and] separate induction calls ... prove[d] that racism had not been eliminated."[5]

The Act did not eliminate segregated facilities within the military, and it also gave the individual armed forces final decision over individual eligibility. This allowed personal discrimination to prevail. Secretary of War Henry L. Stimson was not in favor of acceding to Negro leaders' demands.[6] The secretary of the navy, Rear Admiral Chester W. Nimitz, stated that "the policy of not enlisting men of the colored race for any branch of the naval service except the Messmen's branch was adopted to meet the best interests of general ship efficiency," and he refused to change naval practices.[7] Just before Pearl Harbor was attacked, General George C. Marshall rejected a proposal to abolish racial separation by responding that "the settlement of vexing racial problems cannot be permitted to complicate the tremendous task of the War Department."[8] Other officers felt the same way and little actually changed during the first two years of the war.[9]

By 1942, only 5.9 percent of military forces were Negro. While they were drafted with the same frequency as whites, the "lack of separate facilities for Blacks, [meant that] young men called to service were told to go home and wait for orders of induction."[10] Once they were inducted, army classification tests placed many Negro men into the categories of "semiskilled soldiers and laborers."[11] Most of them were assigned to noncombat units and were used as manual laborers.[12]

This effort to maintain segregation negatively affected military operations and led to unrest in the States. Young Negro men who had been told to wait were in limbo, unable to go back to work or school since they didn't know when they would have to leave, while married white men were being sent to the front lines. No one was happy and the policy of segregation hindered United States' efforts in the war. Negro activism was heightened by reports home, reprinted in newspapers and periodicals, that spoke of racist officers and unfair treatment on bases and in nearby towns. Negro troops fought back. The year in which Branton joined the army "witnessed the most widespread race-related military violence in US history."[13] Most of this occurred in the South, where many training camps were located.

By 1943, efforts were being made by the military hierarchy to reduce the tension and to demonstrate its good intentions—all without actually eliminating segregation. Specialized training was opened to Negro soldiers, a pamphlet refuting the idea of racial superiority was distributed to conscripts, and a film documenting Negro soldiers' contributions to the military "was shown in training camps and commercial theaters."[14]

Branton had read of the discriminatory treatment meted out to Negro soldiers by the military and in communities surrounding the bases where they were stationed when, on March 4, he reported for active duty at Camp Joseph T. Robinson near Little Rock, Arkansas. Wiley was assigned to Jefferson Barracks, Missouri, where he received his basic training. His brothers followed him into the service. Wiley's older brother, Leo, was drafted later in 1943 after his college graduation. Having done well in college, Leo applied for Officer Candidate School, but was rejected because the quota for Negro officers was full. Leo was transferred to the army infantry and wound up in the Ninety-second "Colored" Division at Fort Huachuca, Arizona. His unit later fought in Italy. Wiley's next younger brother, Sterling, was drafted in 1944. Sterling entered the service at a time when the navy was given priority for new recruits. He volunteered for submarine duty and was assigned to the submarine Gabilan. He was the only African American on the roster. While navy records indicated his race, his shipmates apparently did not know or did not care. His ship served in the Pacific.[15]

Wiley's own military experience was relatively benign. He did well on the army's AGCT aptitude tests and was sent to Franklin Technical Institute in Boston for three months of special training. After the course, at the end of July 1943, he was sent to join a white unit in New Hampshire.[16] Apparently, his light skin and an Arkansas twang that sounded "white" caused the assignment officer to classify him as white without asking. When Wiley told them he was Negro, he was promptly sent to a segregated unit at McDill Field near Tampa, Florida. There, he was put to work as a general draftsman with the 1888th Engineer Aviation Battalion (EAB). By the end of 1943, Wiley had been promoted to sergeant.[17]

Although benign, his experience was not without some exposure to racism. In February 1944, Wiley received training as an intelligence specialist and was made an Operations NCO. He was assigned to escort a group of Italian prisoners-of-war by train from Florida to Seattle, Washington. In St. Louis, the prisoners were fed in the train station's dining room, which "would not serve the black soldiers who were guarding them."[18]

Wiley received a "Good Conduct" medal on March 27, 1944. Three weeks later, he was being investigated for "Disaffection." The army investigation began on April 18, after an allegation was made that Branton might be affiliated with the Communist Party.[19] Branton and a friend had collaborated on a letter and pamphlet titled "Waste of Manpower," in which they complained about the discriminatory treatment of Negro soldiers within the military. They mailed the documents to the Department of Public Relations of the War Department in Washington, D.C., and to several Negro magazines and newspapers.

The investigation was intense, involving more than seventeen interviews with people in Pine Bluff and across the country. Investigators were told that Branton was "race conscious" and had once interrupted a lecture by "loudly asking the reason for racial discrimination in the army." They noted that this treatment "was the subject of most of his discussions with other men." The investigation report also included some statements that Branton was "not proud of his race" and had "passed" as a white man on occasion.[20] Investigators seemed to believe that Branton resented being Negro and that his actions against racism were an effort to overcompensate.

Historically, some light-skinned Negroes have left their families, cutting off all contact, in order to "pass" as white. For many others, however, temporary "passing" was a convenience and demonstrated a kind of "black humor" and bravery that dared discovery by racist whites. Sterling Branton recalls that, as teenagers, he and Wiley occasionally drove around to obtain service at white-only restaurants, with Sterling wearing a chauffeur's cap and Wiley in the back seat.[21] The game was a competition between the two brothers. Another story from Sterling describes the day he saw Wiley "all dressed up." Asked where he was going, Wiley said, "I'm going around to Olan Mills [Photography] to have a picture made." Sterling decided to go along. They entered the store and Wiley was taken first. When he came out, Sterling asked, "Are you ready for me?" and was told that "due to the war, there's a shortage of film and we're reserving all our film for our white customers." As Sterling sputtered, "But, . . . but . . . ," Wiley said, "Didn't you hear what the woman said, boy?" Sterling responded, "Yes, sir." They both left and burst into laughter before they had gone very far.[22]

To be caught "passing" could mean severe punishment, even death, in the South. If Branton was bragging about those exploits, and others, in the company of his peers, it indicated, not hatred of self, but both personal daring and an exposé of the ridiculous nature of a system that awarded respect based on the color of a person's skin. A similar sort of joke occurred when their uncle, Frank Wiley, registered for the draft and stated he was Filipino. Since the military was not drafting Filipinos, Frank Wiley was never called up for service.

Army investigators finally interviewed Wiley himself on July 4, 1944. Their summary of his responses to questions indicates the brashness of youth. He denied actual membership in the Communist Party, but admitted that its policy on racial equality made it more attractive to him than any other political party. Branton also said that "if the Communist Party solved the racial problem he was not particularly concerned with any other economic or political changes that the party might effect." While he affirmed his loyalty to the United States, Branton said that he was becoming more concerned about racial discrimination and "would not say what his feelings or reaction might be in the future in the event of a war between this country and Russia."[23]

In the 1930s and 1940s, the Communist Party was attractive to many African Americans and working whites in the United States. It was an offshoot of the American Socialism movement of the nineteenth century, whose goal was "a desire to protest obvious injustice."[24] Some of its members ultimately formed the Communist Labor Party that, in May 1920, was recognized as a legal organization by the United States secretary of labor.[25] The party supported its own candidates for political office, including president and vice president of the United States, in the elections of 1928 where they polled 48,228 votes[26] and 1932, where votes totaled 103,000.[27]

When the Depression began, the Communist Party was aware that African Americans suffered more from unemployment and poverty than other groups. The party made a serious effort to include them in its goals. As one author put it, "Other movements which had given some cooperation to the Negro masses in their fight for justice almost always dodged and hedged on the matter of social equality. But not the Communists."[28] Its decision to support the appeals of the Scottsboro Boys, nine young African American men arrested and convicted in Alabama of raping two white girls in 1931, brought the party into prominence within the African American community.[29]

Also in 1931, the Communist Party issued a "Resolution on the Negro Question in the United States," which set forth the arguments supporting the party's struggle "for the *equal rights* of the Negroes" and for the right of self-determination of the Negroes in the Black Belt [of the South].[30] The historian Philip Foner states that this position, plus the Scottsboro defense and the fact that one of the party's candidates for vice president was a Negro, James W. Ford, helped the party within the community.[31] Another evidence of the truth of its convictions regarding the equality of Negroes was the Party's participation in a drive to organize a sharecroppers' union in Alabama, which was repressed by white violence and received wide publicity.[32]

Anyone who hated segregation and "Jim Crow" laws would have been interested in an organization that promised to help with that struggle, and Branton was no exception. Despite that curiosity, as he stated, he never became a party member and, when he returned home, his civil rights beliefs were directed through the efforts of the more orthodox NAACP.

The pamphlet Branton helped write, and which led to the army investigation, was aptly named "Waste of Manpower." It complained about the failure of the military to make good use of Negro soldiers by providing them with training relevant to the war effort and putting them into jobs for which their skills were fitted. The pamphlet warned that this treatment and the discrimination on army bases and in nearby towns were hurting morale.[33]

The pamphlet's last paragraph called for an end to segregation and castigated the negative effects caused by inadequate education for Negroes and unequal pay for their teachers. It ended with a quote from the educator John Dewey: "Democracy must be born anew every generation and education is said to be the mid-wife."[34] Wherever he first encountered the statement, Dewey's thought stuck with Branton. He used the quote again and again in future speeches. The pamphlet's final sentence may have been Branton's own: "This is a new generation and we are fighting for democracy. Then let us educate."[35] Once the war ended, Branton carried this theme forward over his lifetime through his actions and choices.

The army investigation was closed without any formal action against Branton, but he was transferred from Intelligence work to a drafting assignment sixteen days after he was interviewed. There were no other apparent consequences. His official service record contains no mention of the investigation, and his children never heard anything about the event. Four months later, on November 25, 1944, Wiley was transferred to the 1908th Engineering Aviation Battalion at Greenville Army Air Base in Greenville, South Carolina. His service record at that time notes his character as "Excellent." Before he left Greenville in March 1945, Branton was again awarded the "Good Conduct" clasp.

The 1908th was one of 48 "Colored" EABs, comprising one-third of 157 separate EAB units operating during World War II.[36] An EAB consisted of 33 officers and 744 enlisted men. It was "the basic engineer construction unit of the Army Air Forces" and able to construct, maintain, and defend an operational airfield almost anywhere.[37] EABs primarily served on the Pacific front and provided some of the logistical support that kept the combat troops moving from island to island during that phase of the war. Forty years later, Branton would recall that even on the battlegrounds, there was little mixing of races, and he never had a commanding officer who was other than white.[38]

On March 2, 1945, Branton's unit was ordered to the island of Okinawa. En route, they spent one month on the island of Saipan. Sterling Branton's ship happened to arrive on Saipan in July 1945, and he knew from comments in a letter that Wiley's unit also was there. Sterling, who had not seen his brother since he had enlisted, described spending most of one day in an effort to reach the part of the island where the 1908th was quartered, only to learn that the unit had shipped out to Okinawa two days earlier.[39] Not knowing he'd missed a visit with his brother, Wiley Branton arrived at Okinawa on August 12, 1945. The unit arrived a month after the fighting with the Japanese over possession of the island was "declared officially ended."[40]

Okinawa is deemed the last major battle of World War II. Located south of Japan, the island was to be the base from which the United States would invade Japan. The army prepared to build thirteen airfields, along with roads and other facilities to keep them operating once the fighting was minimized.[41] From the day he arrived in August 1945 and until he left Okinawa on April 24, 1946, Branton was engaged in surveying and serving as a construction foreman and technician in helping to build those airfields. During this year, he received steady promotions. He had been made a staff sergeant on June 1, before they arrived on Okinawa. He rose to the level of tech sergeant on October 4 and to master sergeant on December 18. Returning to the United States on the troopship "Admiral Mayo," Wiley Branton was honorably discharged on March 17, 1946.[42]

Following the war, finally recognizing that its segregationist practices had resulted in an ineffective use of available manpower, the army sponsored a study by a group known as the "Gillem Board." The board did not recommend full integration, but did urge more fair and equal treatment. President Harry Truman's Executive Order 9981, signed on July 26, 1948, did not, as is believed by many, require integration of the military. It merely mandated equal treatment.[43] The army did not integrate its units fully until the Korean War.[44]

CHAPTER 3

Citizen Activist
A New Era

UNLIKE MANY SERVICEMEN who found they liked the wider world they had seen in the service, Wiley Branton gladly returned to his hometown of Pine Bluff, Arkansas. He was ready to settle down. As was the case with most veterans, there had been many changes in his life. He had fallen in love for the first time and become engaged to a girl he met while he was posted in Boston. Unfortunately, the romance did not survive the war.

His Pine Bluff family was reduced. His beloved grandmother, Effa Wiley, had died in March 1945, while he was on his way to Okinawa.[1] The two brothers closest in age to him, Leo and Sterling, survived the war but never returned to live in Arkansas. Wiley's third brother, Paul, remained in Arkansas until the early 1950s, but then moved his family to Chicago, where his daughter could obtain special education classes. Paul Branton was a teacher and, ultimately, became a high school principal of some note.[2] Wiley's baby sister, Julia, attended a boarding high school in North Carolina and then obtained her B.A. at AM&N College in Pine Bluff after three years at Taladega College. After marrying, she spent most of her life in Mississippi, returning to Pine Bluff in 1987.[3]

Only the taxi business seemed the same. Although his paternal grandfather, J. L. Branton, was long retired and would die within two years, Wiley's parents, Leo and Pauline Branton had been able to keep the business going due to some farsighted planning before war was declared. They anticipated the likelihood of war shortages and stocked up on tires and other automobile supplies. In addition, they made a point of carrying soldiers and officers stationed at the Pine Bluff Arsenal to and from Little

Rock during the war. As a result, they were able to obtain access to scarce gas rations.[4]

Wiley plunged into improving the business rather than returning immediately to college.[5] He had been thinking about expanding the taxi business while he was still in the service. By 1949, a newcomer to Pine Bluff would be told that Branton cabs "[took] care of the Blacks around here."[6] That care took on meaning beyond simply providing transportation from one place to another. On at least one occasion, one of his drivers was in an accident and being threatened by a group of whites. Wiley apparently grabbed his service revolver, jumped into a cab, drove it into the middle of the mob, stepped out holding the gun, and took the driver away. No one attempted to prevent Wiley from leaving.[7]

Wiley's personal desire to settle down and just live his life competed with the fact that segregation and discrimination against Negroes meant he never could live normally within the existing system. He was determined to carry on his grandmother's example and make changes in "the way things were." The Negro press that had kept him informed during his service about discrimination against soldiers, the "double-V" demonstrations for equality, and the pressures brought by Negro organizations in all aspects of American life continued to provide information following the war's end. Branton recalled reading local and national publications like "the *Pittsburgh Courier,* the *Chicago Defender,* the *St. Louis Argus,* the *Oklahoma City Black Dispatch,* and of course later, the *Arkansas State Press*."[8]

Branton immediately joined the NAACP, which had been vocal and active in pursuing civil rights and equal treatment for Negroes throughout the war.[9] Branton was convinced that education and the ability to vote were the best vehicles available to the Negro community for achieving self-determination. Branton had learned to hate segregation. While these limitations had not seemed like hardships to a child, they were anathema to the returning army veteran. Having risked his life for his country, he was not willing to continue as a second-class citizen. His wartime politicization was not unique. In Arkansas alone, there were at least two postwar organizations created by Negro veterans—the Veterans Good Government Association in Little Rock[10] and the Veterans and Citizens League for Better Government in Pine Bluff. The Pine Bluff group nominated a slate of reform candidates for office in the 1947 elections and won all but one of the offices.[11] Nationally, there was similar activity.

Branton knew that those who voted held significant power and could force change in state and federal laws if they acted in concert. Officials and legislators who made the law were, after all, elected by the voting public. In 1940, it was estimated that only 5 percent of Negroes were able to vote in the eleven states of the former Confederacy.[12] In 1944, while Branton was still in military service, the United States Supreme Court decided the case of *Smith v. Allwright*,[13] brought by the NAACP against the state of Texas. In *Allwright,* the Court recognized that the Democratic Party, which previously had been treated as a private association that could bar Negro citizens from membership, controlled the selection of candidates in many southern states. Selection as a candidate in the party primary was tantamount to election in the Democratic South. If Negroes could not become members of the party, then thousands of eligible voters were effectively denied their right to vote. The Court decided that the Democratic Party primaries had the same effect as if they were part of the state's governing process and should be subject to constitutional and federal franchise laws. It struck down membership barriers and the "white primary."

The *Allwright* decision opened the door, but it did not immediately dissolve decades of discrimination that kept Negroes from voting. While organizations like the NAACP increased their voter registration efforts, southern states and local political organizations immediately acted to subvert, avoid, or defy the Court's decision. In Arkansas, for example, the Democratic Party exerted authority over primaries in the same manner as did the Texas Democratic Party, and the immediate reactions of Arkansas political figures to the *Allwright* decision were negative. In addition to rhetorical challenges, the State Democratic Committee appointed a committee of lawyers to study the decision and recommend methods for evading compliance.[14]

The committee's first step was to institute a loyalty oath for party members that would eliminate anyone who had ever voted for a Republican candidate in past elections. Since many Negroes still were loyal to the Republican Party that had supported them during Reconstruction, this eliminated a portion of that population from consideration. A second action was to allow Negroes to vote in Democratic primaries, but continue to deny them membership in the party. Thus, they would be denied any participation in the selection of party candidates. A third action required an oath to support Arkansas's 1874 Constitution, which had instituted segregation in the state, to which they felt Negroes would not agree.

Two bills were promulgated in the state legislature that would continue the pre-*Allwright status quo* by other means. Passage of these measures led to such electoral chaos that a newspaper editorial stated, "If Negroes are interested in laughing at white people, there is a fine opportunity currently available."[15] This was the state of voting affairs when Branton returned to Pine Bluff.

As noted earlier, voting in Arkansas was theoretically available to Negroes. There was no literacy test, unlike the situation in many southern states. However, the procedures for registering and voting were cumbersome, especially to those with little education. First, as was the case in other southern states, Arkansas had a poll tax. Payment of the tax was required to cast a vote. That requirement can be stated simply, but it was not simple in practice. A potential voter was required to pay the tax each year and to retain the payment receipt for display before entering the voting booth at the next election, which might be a year away.[16]

Even if one had the means to pay the tax, and managed to keep track of the poll tax receipt over the period between its payment and Election Day, the choices of sharecroppers and farm laborers frequently were subject to coercion from white landowners. Plantation owners and large farmers could buy blocks of poll tax receipts for their workers. They would hold those receipts and, on Election Day, collect the workers and take them to polling places after telling them how to vote. In some instances, the employers would have the men walk through the polling place while somebody else actually marked the ballot.[17]

The second procedural knot for unsophisticated voters was the Arkansas ballot form. The paper ballot stated the title of each office to be filled. Below each title appeared a list containing the names of all candidates for that office. A voter was required to cross out the names of all those for whom he or she was not voting, leaving the name of their selected candidate untouched.[18] Without education in the process of voting, even those Negroes who could vote without employers' restrictions might be confused.

Arkansas's procedures were not the worst then in existence for African Americans. At least, they were not denied the vote entirely. Wiley Branton was born and raised in a community where his educated middle-class family had voted without hindrance. They and other Negro voters in Pine Bluff exercised that right.[19] It was primarily in the rural areas of the state where a lack of education and an oppressive white power structure prevented free use of the vote. Although Branton came home intending to work for change in the treatment of Negroes, he recognized that segregation would not disappear voluntarily. The Negro community itself must show that it no longer would stand for such treatment. The only real way of making their voices heard was through the vote.

In the first elections after his return from the army, Branton demonstrated his intentions in several ways. He worked actively with the Pine Bluff NAACP on voter registration drives, scheduling meetings throughout the county that provided information on how to exercise the right to vote. He also worked to advance the campaign of white mayoral candidate George Steed, who impressed Branton with his "plea for 'good government.'" Branton never allowed segregation or racism to limit his vision of what was possible. Though subject to discrimination, he never allowed himself to hate all those who discriminated. He looked past the labels placed on him and made his own decisions about what was worthy of his effort. Steed passed Branton's test for worthiness.

We know about Branton's work for Steed because, when he saw notice of Steed's death in the *Pine Bluff Commercial* in 1980, Branton wrote to tell the story. "It is easy for people to forget," he said, "the contributions that people make, particularly after the passage of time." Continuing, he noted that Steed not only accepted Branton's help during the campaign, but also attended every meeting Branton arranged in the Negro community and he treated his audiences with courtesy. Steed also had allowed Branton to call him by his first name. "These may seem like small things now," Branton admitted, "but they meant a lot to me and my colleagues in 1946."[20] Branton's concern about giving Steed credit for behavior that was unusual among the white community in the late 1940s demonstrates another trait that can be seen throughout Branton's life. In many of his speeches and letters, Branton would make a point of giving credit where it was due, particularly to people who had not received much attention for their work.

Steed won the election and, in creating the first municipal park commission in Pine Bluff, carefully complied with the law by creating two separate commissions. He named Branton as chair of the Negro commission and allowed Branton to select the others in the group. Steed also assured funding for Branton's commission, which allowed it to create the first park available to Negroes in Pine Bluff. Branton's commission went on to construct a field house and the first swimming pool for Pine Bluff's Negro citizens.

Branton then began a practice he continued throughout his life, that of promoting opportunities for other people. In early 1947, he worked with a Polish man named Ziegman Mayevski, a pilot and airplane owner who had settled in Pine Bluff, to provide flight training for Negro veterans. Financing was needed and Branton agreed to go with Mayevski to make the proposal to a banker. The banker did not know Branton personally and apparently thought he also was a white man. The banker assumed the flight school would operate through the white Monticello A&M College, repeatedly substituting A&M for AM&N College during the conversation. When Branton and Mayevski made it clear that the program would be established at the Negro college, the banker still assumed the students would be white. When he realized the student pilots would be Negro, the banker's reaction, as recalled later by Branton, was astonishment: "'Nigras flyin' airplanes?' 'Over Pine Bluff?' 'Over the heads of white people?' 'Maybe someday, but not in my lifetime!'"[21] The loan was denied.

In the summer of 1947, Wiley attended the NAACP's national convention in Washington, D.C., a meeting that would become an annual ritual in his life. At this convention, he met and shook hands with the attorney Thurgood Marshall for the first time. Branton had read in the newspapers during the war of Marshall's courtroom victories and was honored by the privilege. Branton heard Marshall speak at meetings over the next five years and took every opportunity to reintroduce himself.[22]

In January 1948, Branton was a member of the Arkansas NAACP State Conference Board, which coordinated NAACP efforts across the state. His work with voting drives continued, and he developed workshops that taught people how to vote. That work was effective. The 1948 state primary elections resulted in the largest number of votes cast by Negro voters in Arkansas since the end of Reconstruction.[23] In Pine Bluff, out of 2,767 votes, Democratic Party officials estimated that at least 500 (or 18 percent) were cast by Negro voters.[24]

The winner of the Democratic Party's gubernatorial primary run-off that year was Sidney S. McMath, one of a group of white war veteran candidates who had had their ideas liberalized by wartime experiences.[25] Although civil rights were not an issue in the campaign, McMath would make several efforts in that direction once he was elected. He tried, but without success, to pass a constitutional amendment repealing the polltax law and to obtain enactment of an anti-lynching law. Governor McMath was, however, instrumental in changing the rules of Arkansas's Democratic Party, finally ending the exclusion of Negro citizens from membership, only eight years after *Allwright*.

The Democratic Party's Old Guard did not approve of McMath's 1948 primary victory, and they assumed there had been fraud at the polls. A grand jury investigation was conducted. Branton's participation in the voter drive must have been prominent because he was subpoenaed by investigators to testify. Branton refused to speak about his registration efforts on the advice of his attorney, a firebrand who had been a radical Negro activist in Arkansas since 1935.[26] That firebrand was W. Harold Flowers, admitted to practice in Arkansas in 1935, who believed that "aggressive Negro attorneys can render a vitally needed service to Negroes in the South and at the same time build a profitable practice." He created a "virtual one-man campaign" with "an assembly-line succession of law suits to force [authorities] to provide better schools for Negroes."[27] The historian John Kirk observed that Flowers "proposed the creation of an independent mass black political organization, representative of the whole of the black population, as a way of tackling the common problems which they all faced."[28]

Angered by Branton's refusal to testify, investigators charged him with violating Section 4873 of the Arkansas Penal Code, which prohibited the duplication of election ballots "for the purpose of instructing voters how to vote."[29] The action that had resulted in Branton's arrest was his distribution of mimeographed ballot replicas for use in demonstrating the mechanics of voting to his audiences. Branton was convicted. The case was appealed to the Arkansas Supreme Court where his conviction was affirmed. In the only dissent, Chief Justice Griffin Smith stated that "[a] casual glance at the photographs [of the distributed papers] is sufficient to show there was no attempt to reproduce a ballot in the sense that the term is ordinarily used."[30]

The United States Supreme Court refused to hear a further appeal in 1949.[31] Branton was fined three hundred dollars, which was paid through a collection made on his behalf by the local community that felt "what he'd done, he'd done for them."[32] Section 4873 remained on the books until 1969. Wiley Branton apparently was the only person ever convicted under it.[33] Although Branton was angered by the conviction, he did not let it inhibit his continuing struggles against racism.[34] He was determined to help eliminate segregation and racism and was convinced that education and the exercise of voting rights provided the way to do it. His devotion to the NAACP increased and more of his life and energy were poured into its work.

The kind of voter registration work in which Branton was engaged in 1946 and 1948 was duplicated across the south, although Branton's focus on uneducated Negro sharecroppers and unskilled workers was unusual. Most registration drives were aimed at the educated middle class. Between 1947 and 1952, the number of registered Negro voters increased from 12 to 20 percent of those eligible.[35] It still was not much. As a comparison, the percentage of registered white southern voters averaged 65 percent in 1952. In the years following, voter registration efforts continued, but the postwar energy flagged and progress slowed, while white resistance remained strong.

The NAACP was pushing for civil rights in a number of areas. In addition to its voting rights work, Branton was aware of the organization's plan to eradicate segregated education through the courts. As early as 1926, the NAACP had realized that the federal courts were the most likely source of protection concerning the rights of Negroes.[36] Segregation was authorized by the United States Supreme Court's 1896 opinion in *Plessy v. Ferguson,* which had allowed it as long as "separate but equal" facilities were available to Negro citizens.[37] The NAACP hired Charles Hamilton Houston, a prominent Negro lawyer and dean of Howard University School of Law, to implement a campaign for equal access to education.[38]

Houston favored starting with graduate education, believing that college graduates would be less likely to be intimidated by economic and other pressures than parents of younger children. There also were fewer graduate programs available to Negroes in southern states, so the "separate, but equal" argument was not as strong. At that time, some southern states were providing their Negro residents with scholarships to out-of-state schools, thus avoiding the need to construct separate facilities. At the

CITIZEN ACTIVIST

graduate level, the issue was not unequal education but rather "nonexistent" opportunity.[39]

Houston hired a young attorney, Thurgood Marshall, who recently had graduated from Howard Law School, to lead the effort. Houston then returned to Washington, D.C. Marshall, who had wanted to attend the University of Maryland's School of Law but knew he would be rejected, chose that school for the test case. In 1936, *Pearson v. Murray* was decided in the Maryland Court of Appeals, with Marshall and Houston as the plaintiff's lawyers.[40] That court held that the state's provision of scholarships to Negro students for graduate study outside the state was inadequate compliance with the students' constitutional right to equal educational access. The court required the University of Maryland to admit Donald Murray to its School of Law.

In 1938, the *Murray* case formed the basis for the United States Supreme Court's decision in *State of Missouri v. Gaines*,[41] which challenged the University of Missouri's refusal to admit Lloyd Gaines to its School of Law. Houston and Missouri attorney S. R. Redmond represented Gaines on appeal. The Supreme Court adopted the *Murray* reasoning and held that Gaines "was entitled to be admitted to the law school of the State University in the absence of other and proper provision for his legal training within the State."[42]

Wiley Branton may not have been aware of these earlier cases, but he was following two cases concerning graduate education that were wending their way through the state courts of Oklahoma and Texas in the late 1940s.[43] The first suit was brought by Branton's former AM&N classmate, Ada Sipuel, who wished to enter the University of Oklahoma School of Law. The Oklahoma Supreme Court affirmed the school's denial of her admission in 1947.[44] Sipuel's appeal to the U.S. Supreme Court was handled by Thurgood Marshall and Oklahoma attorney Amos Hall, and resulted in a one-page decision announced on January 12, 1948, reversing the Oklahoma court on the basis of *Gaines*.[45] The Court did not order Sipuel's admission, but left it to the state to take further action. Oklahoma promptly created a law school for one student. It lasted eighteen months before Sipuel finally was admitted to the university's School of Law in fall 1949.

The second case, against the University of Texas, was ongoing at the same time as Sipuel's and presented a slightly different argument. Texas had responded to the *Gaines* decision, as had five other southern states, by creating a separate law school for Negroes. In *Sweatt v. Painter,* Thurgood Marshall and Texas attorney W. J. Durham argued that the state's action was unconstitutional for two reasons: the physical inequality of the facilities, and the inherent inequality of separating races educationally when they would have to practice together thereafter.[46] Anticipating the later *Brown v. Board of Education* cases, Marshall used both legal and sociological evidence to support a direct attack on the "separate but equal" doctrine. The Supreme Court's 1950 decision in favor of Herman Sweatt, while failing to expressly overrule *Plessy v. Ferguson,* held that the separate facilities provided by the state lacked "those qualities which are incapable of objective measurement but which make for greatness in a law school."[47]

These cases were tremendous victories and received widespread coverage in the Negro press. Although his own exposure to the justice system had not been positive, Branton was convinced by the NAACP's success with these cases that challenging segregationist laws through the courts was the best method for dismantling segregation. Marshall's success with the law school cases piqued a personal interest in the law. Branton decided to enter law school himself, but had to return to college to earn enough additional credits for admission. In the meantime, he began paying attention to the opportunities for law school within Arkansas.

Arkansas governor Ben Laney was reacting to legal events, as well. He believed that the way to avoid school integration and arguments about unequal facilities was to create regional graduate schools for Negroes in cooperation with other southern states. He began an effort to convince AM&N College and the Negro community to expand that school's offerings to include graduate degree programs. This effort culminated in a "Conference on Graduate and Professional Education for the Negro Population of Arkansas" held January 20, 1948, on the AM&N campus. All prominent Negroes in the state were invited. At that time, AM&N was not accredited even as an undergraduate institution, and Laney's suggestion that it promise graduate degrees did not receive a positive response from the school's president, Lawrence Davis.[48]

Wiley Branton attended the governor's Pine Bluff conference as a delegate of the NAACP State Conference. The tenor of the discussion at the governor's conference, particularly the concurrence of some Negro members of the audience to the governor's idea, raised his ire.

Branton stood up in the meeting and announced his intention to register in the undergraduate school of business at the University of Arkansas and, if he was not admitted, to sue the school. He stated that the business courses at AM&N were not equal to those available at the university because AM&N was an unaccredited school and, thus, he was disadvantaged in dealing with white businessmen educated at the university. This argument was adapted from the *Gaines* decision. Branton's declaration did not receive notice from the local press for over a week, but the *Arkansas Gazette* published the information after a Negro newspaper had printed an interview with Branton.[49]

On January 30, 1948, the University of Arkansas announced it would admit qualified Negro graduate students.[50] The announcement stated that Clifford Davis would be admitted to the School of Law if he appeared on the first day of classes. Branton may have known that Davis, who had been negotiating with the school administration about his admission, would not take up the offer, because Branton had already talked with Harold Flowers, the Pine Bluff attorney, about whether they could find someone to meet the school's requirements.

Branton's friend, Silas H. Hunt, who graduated from AM&N in 1947, had been accepted at the University of Indiana's School of Law for the spring 1948 semester. Branton and Hunt, when they first heard about Ada Sipuel's Oklahoma state court action, had "wondered if we could not do something in Arkansas."[51] On his return from military service in 1946, Hunt had applied to the University of Arkansas as an undergraduate transfer student and been rejected. Branton decided to talk with Hunt about switching to the School of Law at the University of Arkansas.

They discussed the situation by telephone. Hunt was interested, but he was concerned about money, since the transfer of his G.I. Bill paperwork at that late date might cause it to be delayed. Wiley, whose taxi business was doing well, offered to provide Hunt with any needed money until the records were transferred.[52] Hunt and Branton agreed that they both would go to Fayetteville on Monday, February 2, and attempt to enroll for the spring semester, Hunt in the law school and Branton in the undergraduate division. If both were rejected, Hunt would continue on to law school in Indiana, while Branton would file suit against the university.[53]

Hunt was a perfect candidate to be the first Negro law student. He had been president of the AM&N student body, editor of its student publication, and an honor student. He had been salutatorian of his high school class in 1941, where he was involved in sports, politics, and debate. Hunt also was a World War II veteran and had fought in the Battle of the Bulge. He knew how to withstand pressure. Years later, law school classmates recalled his wonderful personality and his social skills. "He was neither militant nor subservient. Always dignified, his intelligence and sensitive nature invariably guided him to the perfect response in critical situations."[54]

There was one hitch in their plan to visit the university on February 2. Wiley was scheduled to be married on February 1 in Memphis, Tennessee. He would have to delay his honeymoon. While it could not have been a welcome interruption to her, Lucille McKee Branton fully supported Wiley's decision, as she would continue to do throughout their marriage. This would not be the last time that civil rights work took precedence over Branton's personal life. Their partnership began as it would continue over forty years of marriage.

Wiley met Lucille in 1947 while on a driving vacation with friends. Wiley was then twenty-four years old, a slim, compact man who may have sported the pencil mustache he grew for a short time after his discharge from the army and which made him look like one of Hollywood's romantic actors.[55] The group stopped to visit a mutual friend, an insurance salesman, in Memphis, Tennessee. There, they also met his secretary and office manager, Lucille Elnora McKee. Lucille was born in 1919, in Memphis, Tennessee, and, although neither of her parents graduated from college, Lucille won a college scholarship after attending Booker T. Washington High School. She graduated in 1941 from LeMoyne College in Memphis with a B.A. in Sociology. Thereafter, she married a man named Leo Zinn and had a son, Richard, in 1946. The marriage did not succeed. When she met Wiley Branton, Lucille was separated and a single, working mother. She was also beautiful. Wiley fell hard.

Lucille was an independent soul and could be stubborn and opinionated. She played the piano and wrote and sold songs "to folks" before her marriage. After they married, however, her sense of identity would come from being Mrs. Wiley Branton. She was certain about what was appropriate to that role. Wiley never saw her in curlers and was required to give notice when he was coming home so that she was sure to look her best for him. She became the perfect hostess and a first-class cook.

Wiley never had to worry about bringing unexpected company home for dinner. Lucille became a life partner to Wiley and gave him the support that would allow him to devote his life to civil rights.[56]

Lucille also would follow Wiley's lead in civic affairs, becoming active in numerous organizations. She was a founding member of Pine Bluff's chapter of Jack & Jill of America, Inc., an elite social and networking organization for Negro children.[57] She also became a member of several national Negro women's organizations: Delta Sigma Theta, The Links, Inc., and was a founding member of the D.C. chapter of The Doll League.[58]

Their romance caused a temporary rift in the Branton family. Wiley's mother was not at all pleased that her son wanted to marry a divorced woman, much less one who had a child. His brother Leo recalls writing a letter of advice to Wiley, cautioning him on the obligations he was undertaking. But nothing stopped Wiley once his mind was made up. He was determined that this was the woman for him. Eventually, he was proved to be right.

Once Wiley and Lucille decided to marry, Wiley wrote to Leo Zinn, introducing himself and declaring his intent to take care of Lucille's son and to treat Ricky as his own. Wiley did such a good job at this that their subsequent children frequently forgot there was any distinction between them. When Ricky reached his teens, Branton suggested a formal adoption so that nothing could ever disturb the relationship.[59] At that time, about 1961, Branton may have been worried about the increasing potential violence surrounding his civil rights work and wished to ensure equal treatment of Ricky under inheritance laws.

While Wiley was fighting the election fraud charge and working to get Silas Hunt admitted to the University of Arkansas, he was also supporting an expanding family with the taxicab business. Their first child, Toni, was born in October 1948. A second daughter, Wylene, was born in December 1949. They lived in a house on Watson Boulevard in Pine Bluff.

CHAPTER 4

Desegregating the University of Arkansas School of Law

IN 1948, WHEN Branton and Silas Hunt planned their mission to desegregate the University of Arkansas School of Law and Governor Laney was attempting to avoid it, related activity was taking place at the university, which housed the only state-supported law school in the state. The university, founded in 1871, was located in the extreme northwest corner of the state, about as far away as one could get from the majority of the state's Negro population. Despite this distance, several Negro men had appeared to attend classes during the school's inaugural session. Since the school "was a Federal Land Grant College under the Morrell Act of 1862," its charter could not exclude nonwhite students.[1] The men were not dismissed. However, some faculty members were unwilling to instruct them, so the university's chancellor did the teaching. The atmosphere must have been forbidding, though, because they did not return after the first semester. Thereafter, for a time, the University of Arkansas educated only white students.

Pine Bluff's Branch Normal school was opened in 1875 and drew most of the state's Negro college students. One history of the university suggests this result was intended.[2] About 1887, it is said that Scipio Jones, a Negro resident of Little Rock, attempted to enroll at the university in Fayetteville.[3] He was not admitted. Jones later became a prominent lawyer in Little Rock and handled a number of civil rights cases there.[4]

When the *Murray* case was decided in 1936, J. S. Waterman, then dean of the university's law school, brought the case to the attention of then-university president J. C. Futrall, who dismissed the Maryland state court's

37

decision as unlikely to occur in Arkansas.[5] Two years later, in 1938, probably in response to the U.S. Supreme Court's *Gaines* decision, Edward W. Jacko Jr. applied to the university's School of Law. When he was rejected, Jacko did not persist.[6]

There was no further testing of *Gaines* in Arkansas until 1941, when Scipio Jones contacted the university on behalf of Prentice A. Hilburn. Jones did not ask that Hilburn be admitted, only that the university pay tuition for Hilburn's attendance at an out-of-state school.[7] Jones must have known of the *Gaines* decision, but his letter only hinted at the possibility of a suit. Either he or his client was unwilling to engage in the legal fight that would have been required to force the university to open admissions to Negroes.

Unlike other southern states, Arkansas had not developed a formal policy of paying out-of-state tuition for Negro graduate students in order to avoid integration. Hilburn's request was the first and, although the university initially rejected the idea that such a cost should come from its budget, it ultimately granted Jones's request. Perhaps this was done to avoid a lawsuit. When the legislature enacted a statute in 1943 that provided funding for out-of-state graduate tuition for Arkansas's Negro students, it was after a conference sponsored by the university.[8] This was the very action prohibited in *Gaines,* and both the state and the university had to know they were defying the Supreme Court. Adding insult to injury, the legislature stated that the sums paid for tuition were to be deducted from the budget of Pine Bluff's AM&N College, reducing already limited resources for Negro undergraduate education in Arkansas. Three years later, approximately $20,000 was being devoted annually to out-of-state tuition for over one hundred students.[9]

In March 1946, Clifford Davis applied for admission to the University of Arkansas School of Law. By this time, the dean of the School of Law was Robert A. Leflar, who recognized the power of *Gaines* and believed that desegregation was inevitable. Leflar stalled on Davis's application while he discussed his conclusions with the university's president and its board of trustees. These men left the decision to Leflar, but hinted that action should be "postponed as long as possible." When Davis pressed for an answer, Leflar suggested that Davis apply for out-of-state tuition and attend law school at Howard University. Leflar explained that he was working on the issue of Negro admissions, but that Davis should talk with J. R.

Booker, a Negro Little Rock lawyer, about pressing the question.[10] Leflar clearly expected Booker to advise caution. Davis accepted the advice and enrolled at Howard University School of Law. That gave the university another year.

Leflar knew it was only a matter of time until the school would be forced to desegregate, but he hoped to avoid a lawsuit or court order, fearing the negative publicity for the school and the state, and the bad feelings between citizens that would arise. In thinking about the problem, Leflar formulated a list of the options available to him, none of which included simply admitting Negro students along with others. Leflar believed there would be massive resistance to that idea. He decided the only viable option was admission under conditions of segregation.[11] This would mean setting aside a room in which the Negro students would be taught their classes and would be expected to study. While they would "attend" the School of Law, they would not be mixed in with the rest of the school's population.

The board of trustees had washed its hands of the decision, leaving it to Leflar, but there were others who needed to be persuaded. Leflar contacted the incoming university president, Lewis Webster Jones, who joined in the board's abdication of responsibility. Leflar then orchestrated a meeting with Arkansas's governor, Ben Laney, in June 1947. After hearing the arguments, the governor indicated he was not happy with the idea, but said he would not interfere with any decision made by the university.[12] Leflar's proposed admission under conditions of segregation became the plan.

In the midst of Leflar's negotiations, in April 1947, Clifford Davis again asked for an application packet. There was more delay on Leflar's part but, given the authority Leflar had received from the board of trustees and the chancellor, Clifford Davis's application was completed and he was admitted. However, his admission was not for the fall 1947 semester. In an August letter, Leflar explained that the school needed time to remodel and provide for segregated facilities. Davis did not respond immediately.[13]

A second letter from Leflar in November stated that Davis also would have to pay a nonrefundable advance deposit to attend "the law classes for Negroes." Davis responded in mid-December, objecting to the fee as discriminatory, since other law students were not required to pay it, and also objecting to the "special facilities" as "failing to fulfill the [Court's] requirement of equal opportunity." Davis did not pay the advance deposit. That ended any further communications between the School of Law and Davis.[14] As of late December 1947, then, no Negro student actually was expected to appear on campus.

The university board of trustees, meanwhile, intended to announce that it would accept Negro students in its graduate schools after its January 1948 meeting.[15] Although a snowstorm prevented the meeting, the board's announcement appeared in the January 30 edition of the *Arkansas Gazette*. In addition to the general announcement, the article said Clifford Davis would be admitted to the university's School of Law if he appeared for classes on February 2. It noted that Davis would receive "regular instruction from faculty members but in a separate classroom." Responding to Branton's statement that he would seek admission to the university's undergraduate college, Jones, the university president, stated that Branton's admission "as an undergraduate raises another issue." Jones announced that the university would "cooperate with the governor, the state Department of Education, the General Assembly, [and] the Board of Trustees of A.M.& N." to improve that school's offerings. If he applied, Branton's application would be referred "to the University's Board of Trustees for their decision."[16]

Asked his reaction to the segregated conditions under which Clifford Davis and other Negro graduate students would learn the law, attorney Harold Flowers was quoted as saying that he believed "the university 'eventually will be shamed into letting Davis attend classes with the other students.'"[17] Forty years later, Wiley Branton commented that the Negro community believed the board's announcement was made only after it knew that Clifford Davis had dropped his application and there would be no Negro law student that year.[18]

At the time Branton announced his intention to apply for undergraduate admission to the university in mid-January 1948, there were no federal court decisions involving undergraduate education. Branton could have had little hope that he would be admitted to the university's undergraduate college without litigation. In fact, he was quoted in a January 30 article as saying that "it would be needless for me to go to Fayetteville."[19] Discussions with Flowers and Hunt over the weekend led him to change his mind. It is likely that Branton accompanied Hunt and applied for admission in order to put additional pressure on the university so that it would adhere to its January 30 announcement and admit Silas Hunt to the School of Law. Much later, Branton told how grateful he was that the university did reject him, since his brand-new wife was waiting in Memphis to be escorted on her honeymoon.[20]

The original plan was that Branton would fly to Fayetteville after the wedding ceremony and meet Hunt there. Instead, they met in Pine Bluff at the suggestion of Harold Flowers and, together with Flowers and an *Arkansas State Press* newspaper photographer named Geleve Grice, they drove to Fayetteville. Branton later said that Flowers had decided to accompany them because he was worried they might have trouble and need legal help. Conversation in the car on the drive across the state assumed that Hunt would be admitted and was concerned mostly with speculation on "what life would be like for the only Negro on the campus."[21]

The four arrived in Fayetteville about noon on Monday, February 2, and ate lunch at the "colored school."[22] They then went to the campus where Wiley Branton applied for admission to the business program. As anticipated, his application was denied.[23] They proceeded to the School of Law, where Dean Leflar had been warned of their arrival and intentions. Branton recalled that they heard the local radio broadcast the news that "four unidentified Negroes were seen walking across the campus."[24] Leflar reviewed Hunt's transcripts, found they were acceptable, and sent him to the registrar to complete the paperwork.[25]

It is not clear precisely when Leflar spoke with Hunt about the conditions under which he would attend classes, but it presumably occurred during this meeting. Hunt would be taught each subject individually by the appropriate professor in a separate classroom, after they had taught the same subject to the rest of the class. Hunt could borrow books from the law library but had to use them in his separate study room rather than being issued a study space within the library with the rest of the class.[26] He could not use the student restrooms, but had to ask permission of the dean's secretary to use the dean's facilities.[27] To accomplish their goal, Hunt, Flowers, and Branton were willing to accept the restrictions. Silas Hunt became the first African American student admitted to the University of Arkansas School of Law.

The new student then asked about dormitory housing. Branton

recalled that the question seemed to make the dean nervous, and "[he] pleaded with us to try and find housing in the colored community and not saddle the University with the problem of housing at that time."[28] As they left the dean's office, they were subjected to some "curious stares" from students, but there were others who "venture[d] out and [shook] hands and offer[ed] a word of encouragement." Branton did not recall any catcalls, "or any other unfavorable incident."[29]

The four quickly learned that locating appropriate housing for Hunt would be difficult. As of the 1950 census, there were only 422 Negro residents in the entire county, the majority of whom lived in substandard housing. The first night, Hunt stayed with the minister of the Negro Methodist church. He moved to the home of Mr. and Mrs. Labe Joiner the next day. The Joiners, whose children were grown and had left home, had room for Hunt. The couple ultimately would provide housing for four of the first six Negro law students. Branton, Flowers, and Grice then left Hunt at the church rectory and headed back to Pine Bluff. Long after, Branton recalled the poignant scene as he waved goodbye to the solitary figure of Hunt.[30]

Although Hunt anticipated receiving individual instruction in a separate classroom, the plan apparently was not followed for long. In 1948, the School of Law was crowded with war veterans anxious to get on with their interrupted lives. Some of those white students soon joined Hunt in the smaller classroom where they could receive more attention from the professor.[31] These students were more concerned about getting a good education than whether they sat in the same room with a Negro. Bill Penix was one of those classmates. He and his wife, Marian, recalled that there were eventually eight students who attended classes with Hunt.[32]

A few other individuals made a point of spending time with Hunt during lunch or between classes, but it otherwise was a lonely time for him. Bill Penix said he gave Hunt a key to their apartment so Hunt would have a quiet place to eat lunch and rest between classes. The Penixes also played bridge with him at night. Hunt attended classes for the full spring semester and part of the summer session. He then became ill and withdrew from school. Silas Hunt died in a veteran's hospital in Springfield, Missouri, in the summer of 1948.[33]

Jackie L. Shropshire of Little Rock followed Hunt. He was admitted to the School of Law in fall 1948. Shropshire began school under the same "separate" conditions as Silas Hunt.[34] However, classes at the school still were crowded and frequently exceeded one hundred people.[35] When other students complained about the one-on-one instruction Shropshire was getting,[36] Dean Leflar decided that Shropshire would share two classes with the other students.[37]

He was required to sit in a front row seat that had been surrounded by a wooden railing, while other students sat wherever they wanted.[38] The barrier was a single wooden pole, about twelve to fifteen inches off the floor, which surrounded the chair in which he sat. Christopher Mercer, who with George Haley would join Shropshire at the school the next year, recalled Shropshire describing how he could lean back in his chair and rest his foot on the rail.[39] Forty years later, Shropshire joked about how happy he was with the change since it meant he would not be the sole focus of every professor in every class and would share the duty of recitation with others.[40]

The railing that separated Shropshire from other students lasted only a day or two. Shropshire recalled that Professor Wylie Davis led several of the faculty and presented Dean Leflar with an ultimatum demanding its removal after news of the barrier was publicized across the country.[41] Even after the barrier disappeared, however, Shropshire was required to remain in the same seat.[42]

There were no repercussions to Shropshire's joining the rest of his class and, by the time George W. B. Haley and Christopher C. Mercer of Pine Bluff arrived in fall 1949, some of the conditions had been modified. The three shared all classes with white students, although they were assigned specific seats in the classrooms and remained relegated to a separate study room.[43] Shropshire and, later, Mercer resided at the Joiners, while Haley found a room with Mr. and Mrs. Funkhouser, another of the families in the community. When Haley and Mercer arrived, matters improved considerably for Shropshire. He now had companionship.

Mercer recalled that the Negro students were treated pretty much the same as other students by the law professors.[44] However, when they were given membership cards for the Student Bar Association, but told they could not participate in the association's social activities, Mercer objected, refusing the "honorary" card. That action led to a debate among the students on whether they would be "full-fledged" members. Mercer recalls that he, Shropshire, and Haley threw themselves into the argument, which they ultimately won, gaining full membership.[45]

Wiley Branton arrived at the School of Law in February 1950 after having returned to classes at Pine Bluff's AM&N College and earned enough credits for admission. For a twenty-seven-year-old father of three, that decision seems almost irresponsible. The taxicab business was doing well, but taking three years out of his life at this point would require a good deal of change and sacrifice on the part of his family. It is clear that his decision was heartfelt. Branton attempted to reduce the potential strain by applying to a private law school in Little Rock, thinking he could commute between there and Pine Bluff, but was rejected. He believed the rejection was because of his race.[46] Branton then applied to the School of Law in Fayetteville and was accepted.

Wiley Branton became the fifth Negro student admitted to the school. As noted, by the time Branton arrived, the separate classroom had been eliminated. Assigned seating, too, had been eliminated. The four sat wherever they wanted in the classrooms. The social segregation Hunt experienced had subsided a bit. Shropshire recalled attending football games.[47] Chris Mercer, a good athlete, played on the school's softball team.

George Howard Jr., arriving in fall 1950, became the first Negro student admitted to campus housing a year later, during spring 1951.[48] Haley and Mercer joined him there the next semester. The change allowed them to have private rooms among other students, mostly veterans. Howard was asked to run for president of the dormitory in his last year of school.[49] He won, and became Lloyd Hall's representative to the university's student government.[50] That event received media coverage and Howard received a congratulatory letter from Bill Penix, Hunt's friend who was now an attorney in Jonesboro.[51] The changes initiated by the integration of Lloyd Hall and the war veterans do not seem to have become institutionalized, however. More than ten years later, George Howard Jr. would represent two Negro students in a suit to again desegregate the university's housing.[52]

Housing issues were settled, but other difficulties remained. Although all except George Howard Jr. were light-skinned, their presence was so publicized that they could not "blend" into any crowd. George Haley recalled the stress of walking into a classroom of chattering students and have the talking stop. "[T]he tenseness was there, you could just feel it.

...I felt almost like a defendant who was charged with a crime."[53] Despite the fact that he had served three years in the U.S. Air Force, this visibility was hard to take. Chris Mercer, too, recalled the stares, and also the derogatory comments made just loudly enough for the Negro students to hear them.[54]

Shropshire, Haley, Mercer, Branton, and Howard all believed that the purported anonymity of grades did not exist for them. They had some reason for this belief. Somehow, when grades were posted, other students knew which were those of the Negro students. George Haley recalled that once, when grades were posted, he and Mercer heard some white students reviewing and discussing the grades. Someone asked, "Who's number 212?" No one knew, so the student went away, then returned to say "that's one of those nigger students."[55] When Haley made the best grade in one class, he says that some of the white students couldn't believe it and insisted they go and read his paper. Later, one of them told Haley that he'd written "a damn good paper."[56]

When Jackie Shropshire graduated in 1951, his was the last group of law graduates admitted to practice in Arkansas under the "diploma privilege," which did not require graduates of the University of Arkansas to take the bar examination. The others believed that this change in admissions procedures was intended to make things more difficult for them.[57] The restroom situation had not improved, either. They still were using the dean's restroom rather than that assigned to the students and, when the dean's white secretary complained about having to negotiate with them about the restroom key, the men were asked to use a faculty restroom.[58]

The student religious groups, for the most part, shared the aversion to integration. The men should have been eligible to join the Baptist and Methodist groups, but they were rejected. Instead, with the encouragement of the Reverend William Gibson at the Presbyterian Student Center, and after an affirmative vote of the white student membership, the five were invited to join Westminster House in February 1951. Wiley Branton later said they had to be Presbyterians if they "wanted any religious experience on campus," because it was the only group that would admit them.[59] Miller Williams, the white son of a Methodist minister who befriended the law students, was mortified at the action of the Methodist students group and joined the Negro students at Westminster House.[60] This refuge became the one place on campus where they could act normally and not feel on public display. Mercer, who had been raised in the African Methodist Episcopal Church, became so comfortable that he later became an active Presbyterian and raised his children in that faith.[61] Another friend was the sociology professor A. Stephen Stephan, who, Mercer recalled, "went out of his way" to provide them with a small reception after a campus talk by Negro Nobel laureate and assistant secretary-general of the United Nations, Dr. Ralph Bunche.[62]

Although their situation was often unpleasant, there were no serious racial incidents or violence while the five were students on campus. The fear of serious violence was ever present, however, and there were deliberate efforts at personal intimidation with which they had to contend. George Haley recalled one particular event that occurred when he was walking along a street in downtown Fayetteville. As he came to an intersection, several white boys in a car stopped to let him cross. As he did so, the driver revved the engine, as though he was going to run Haley down. The others in the car laughed. Haley says he just kept walking and breathed a sigh of relief when he reached the other side.[63]

Another incident occurred in his third year, when he and George Howard Jr. were walking on campus. As they passed in front of Razorback Hall, a dormitory for football players, they heard someone say "that's some of those nigger students." Howard began "to tighten up" and Haley was impelled to say, "Now, George, we are going to continue to walk. We're not going to run. Just continue to walk." As they passed the building, someone threw a golf ball at them. It missed. Then, a Coke bottle was thrown and broke on the sidewalk. Haley says he just kept saying, "we're *not* going to walk any faster. Just completely ignore it." They reported the event to Dean Leflar, then went to the law library, from which they saw Leflar leave the building and head for the chancellor's office. Haley said, "They discovered, and they knew who the boys were, and they talked a bit about it, and we discussed it, but nothing ever really happened. I wasn't expecting it."[64]

The men all made efforts to avoid confrontations. Eckel and Marge Rowland, white students who befriended the five, recalled that when Haley was to graduate in 1952, his father arrived by automobile to attend the ceremony. When Haley used that car to drive Marge to her home, he made her sit in the back seat to avoid any trouble.[65] Miller Williams recalled his wife's shock at seeing her parents coming up the street once when they were walking with George Haley. Knowing they would be horrified, she began to say something, then saw that George had turned and already was fifteen feet away, heading in the other direction. As Williams put it, "just, whoosh, he just wasn't there."[66]

Williams also reported that he gained "two good knives" that were used to post pictures of a skull and crossbones and some other threatening images on the door of his dormitory room. He recalled that leaving a drink on the table in the student union could be dangerous, because "something" was likely to have been added to it before your return.[67]

Though these incidents were individually more irritating than dangerous, there were enough of them to induce an energy-draining constant alertness and apprehension in the Negro law students and their friends. The fact that there was no actual violence does not mean that these harassing incidents were easily ignored. The law students and their friends knew there were people whose beliefs could impel them to violence. Mercer estimated that about 5 percent of the law students were in this group. Perhaps another 10 percent of students were friendly or civil, and the rest simply ignored them. Mercer referred to himself and George Haley as "scared puppies" who "hadn't been close friends, but this brought us closer together. And we usually would make arrangements to go to school together. . . . We walked home together. If we'd stay at the Law School and study, we'd walk home together, and this sort of thing. So we kind of sat together in class. He didn't sit on one side of the room and I sat on the other—we usually just sat next to each other in class."[68]

How much of this harassment was known to the administration of the school or the campus is not clear. Even when incidents were reported, as noted above, no formal reaction was forthcoming. Was the administration trying to ignore them? Quite likely. Indeed, it is hard to think of any official response that could have been successful in ending the random attacks without increasing resentment and potential retaliation. It is probable that, since the more serious events came from outside the School of Law and no physical injuries were caused, the administration preferred to hope matters would improve without intervention. Within the school, racist actions were more subtle and harder to control. As Haley said, the men really didn't expect complete protection from harassment.

Wiley Branton began his career at the School of Law in January 1950. That he arrived only six weeks after Lucille Branton had delivered their third child is a basis for supposing his decision had her whole-hearted support. He would not have left Pine Bluff at all without it. Wiley joined Shropshire and Mercer in boarding with Mr. and Mrs. Joiner during the week, but headed back to Pine Bluff on weekends during that first semester, a journey of at least six hours each way in 1950. Although Branton was eligible for the G.I. Bill, it wasn't sufficient to support a growing family. They remained near his parents in Pine Bluff, and he continued to support them by managing the taxi company. These demands may be the reason he received two of the three "D" grades he earned during that first semester.

The strain of commuting, and his loneliness, quickly led Branton to move his wife and children up to Fayetteville. Married student housing was segregated and he could find nothing suitable in the Negro community so, on August 5, 1950, Branton purchased a vacant lot on East Center Street for something under $100. It was located just down the street from the Joiners' home. Branton then purchased a barracks structure that had been used during the war by military trainees on the university campus and hired someone to move it onto the lot and modify it to make a four-room house. His son Richard recalls that they were "either military trailers or boxcars" and the men "put them together" with some kind of connecting hallway.[69] The G.I. Bill and income from the cab company allowed him to live in relative luxury, compared with the others. It turned out to be a good investment. When he graduated, he sold the house to Fayetteville's St. James Baptist Church for $4,500.[70]

Branton spent most of his spare time with his family and studying.[71] He and Lucille occasionally attended the married student dinners at Westminster House but, unlike Haley and Mercer, who enjoyed the ping-pong table, he did not spend much time there.[72] His light skin color made him a less likely subject for hazing when he was alone. At a 1988 reunion, the others joked that whites on campus never could find Wiley and, instead, focused "on some poor Iranian student."[73]

Wiley did, however, face problems not shared by the others. In August 1951, his son Wiley Jr. was born. Lucille Branton, also light-skinned, initially was put into a private room at the Washington County hospital. At some point, the hospital authorities learned she was Negro and moved her to a colored ward. On returning to visit his wife, Wiley learned of the transfer. He threatened to file a lawsuit to integrate public facilities in town, particularly the swimming pool, if they proceeded with that plan. The hospital backed down and Lucille was returned to her private room. Wiley Jr. recalls being told that the hospital even gave Lucille flowers for her room, hoping to soothe Wiley's anger.

Wiley's home, and his growing family, enabled him to provide a refuge for the rest of the group. It was more comfortable than the boardinghouse, where they were the guests of strangers, however nice. It also would have been more comfortable than the Presbyterian Center where they were surrounded by a different culture, however friendly. Wiley and Lucille Branton liked to entertain, and she was a good cook. Their home at 404 East Center Street became the place for gatherings of the Negro law students, who often were invited to lunch or dinner on Sundays.[74]

In addition to becoming a haven for the Negro law students, Branton's home also became the "resting place" for any Negro notable who visited the area. There was no hotel in Fayetteville that would accept them and no other family in the community had the room or the same social status as the Brantons. When United Nations activist Ralph Bunche came to speak at the university on May 1, 1952,[75] he stayed overnight with the Brantons.[76]

Aside from their race and their determination to become lawyers, Shropshire, Haley, Mercer, Branton, and Howard were a very disparate group, thrown together by circumstance. They certainly were aware of the importance of their presence on the campus, although challenging the status quo was only one of the reasons they came to School of Law. All had been touched by racist incidents that made them recognize the law as a vehicle for change. Other reasons for attending the University of Arkansas were more practical. The tuition for state residents helped their money go further, they could remain closer to home and family, and they learned the law alongside those against whom they expected to practice after admission. Despite their differences, the five bonded through adversity in the same way as do soldiers thrown together by war.

Through a "veterans preference" provision, Branton was able to take the bar examination in his second year. He decided to do so, as practice for the one that would follow graduation. To his surprise, and pleasure, he passed and was admitted to practice on March 31, 1952. He began performing legal work for family and friends, but decided to continue law studies and obtain his law degree. In May 1953, Branton became the third Negro man to graduate from the University of Arkansas School of Law. The five graduates—Shropshire, Haley, Branton, Howard, and Mercer—plus Hunt, have become known in the school as the "Six Pioneers" and a meeting room has been named in their honor.[77]

In the years since Hunt's admission, questions have been raised about the segregated conditions that came with admission and about the acquiescence of Hunt, Branton and Flowers to them. A later generation would see their actions as "accommodationist." George Howard Jr. has suggested that the three may have regretted that decision and wished they had initiated a lawsuit instead.[78] But there is no evidence of any regret. Branton spoke proudly of his involvement in this event for the rest of his life. He was a pragmatist. Admission was admission, and the university could have resisted any integration for many more years, as did the universities of Mississippi and Alabama. Branton also knew there was little likelihood that the NAACP would take up the cudgels for Hunt in 1948 when it was occupied with fighting the issue of admission for Ada Sipuel in Oklahoma. The U.S. Supreme Court did not speak on the issue of "admission with conditions" until June 1950,[79] two years after Hunt's admission and just after Branton's own entry to the School of Law. By that time, the restrictive conditions were no longer being imposed at the University of Arkansas.

Dean Robert Leflar's 1972 history of the university noted the changes in attitudes about integration since 1948 but did not attempt to defend his actions, believing he did as well as could be expected at the time.[80] Leflar enthusiastically endorsed Branton's 1987 suggestion to Ray Thornton, president of the university, that the university commemorate Silas Hunt's enrollment with some special observance.[81] In January 1988, four of the five living "Pioneers" appeared on campus to participate in a two-day program titled "The Legacy of Silas Hunt."

The four recounted their experiences while students on the campus, including many that had not been pleasant at the time. Their recounting bubbled with humor. When Miller Williams, also participating in the program, commented on the fact that they remembered almost everything with a funny twist on it, Christopher Mercer responded, "We can laugh about it now, but I don't know that it was funny THEN!"[82] Jackie Shropshire said, "I've forgiven everything that happened to me. I haven't forgotten, because I can't, but I understand."[83] A member of the audience later recalled the laughter as, "the way people do when they've come out on the other side of something traumatic. It was a survivor's laugh, and Branton indulged in it heartily."[84]

All four noted that they felt grateful for the education they had received at the School of Law and felt it had prepared them well for their subsequent careers. Branton had become an active member of the Alumni Association as soon as he was eligible, and been invited to speak at the University several times prior to 1988, but it may have been the first visit back for the others. Branton's University of Arkansas yearbooks for 1951 and 1952 were found among his papers after his death, indicating his sentimental attachment to the school.

CHAPTER 5

Arkansas Practice

SOON AFTER HIS 1952 admission to practice, while he was still in his third year of law school, Branton received an invitation to join the Arkansas Bar Association. The Bar Association is a voluntary group that provides social, educational, and networking opportunities for its members. Knowing that the association was segregated, he asked one of his professors, Edwin Dunaway, whether he thought it was a serious invitation. Dunaway thought the invitation probably was sent in ignorance of Branton's race but suggested that Wiley send in his application anyhow. Dunaway and another faculty member would stand as the two required sponsors.

When the association's next annual meeting was announced, Wiley decided to attend. Arriving at the Hot Springs, Arkansas, location, he saw no Negro faces at first. At a scheduled black-tie dinner, he was relieved to see another Negro man in the room. As Branton told it, "I walked over and I held out my hand and I said, 'Hello, I'm Wiley Branton from Pine Bluff.' He said, 'I'm Charles, the maître d'!'" At the dinner, Wiley sat down next to a circuit court judge who said, "I understand you all got a nigger in law school from up in Pine Bluff, who might be going back there to practice." Wiley's response was, "Yeah, and I think he'll make a darn good lawyer, too."[1]

Apparently, the association realized its mistake. The next year, Branton did not receive a notice for membership renewal. Deciding to pursue the issue, he sent a check for the yearly dues, a grand total of $6.50, to the association. There was no response. Three months later, his check was returned in a plain blue envelope. Branton said he kept that check for years as a souvenir. It was clear that Arkansas's white legal professional organization was not ready to associate with Negro lawyers. Membership in the Arkansas Bar Association was not opened officially to Negro lawyers until 1964, after passage of the Civil Rights Act, when it was threatened with the loss of federal officials as speakers at its conventions.[2] When association membership was available, Branton joined even though he was not practicing law regularly in the state by then. It must have been satisfying to take advantage of the newly opened door.

After receiving his law degree, Wiley Branton returned to Pine Bluff. Although he had gained some practical experience in handling legal matters during his last year of school, Branton's choices for law practice were very limited. The options of Negro lawyers had changed little from those of earlier generations. There were no jobs for Negro lawyers in major law firms or in government. The only alternative to practicing on your own was the possibility of associating with one of the few other lawyers of your race. There were fewer than ten of those in Arkansas in 1953. Most Negro lawyers were located in the larger towns and cities and few were willing to travel outside their home territory.[3]

Similarly, the clientele of Negro lawyers came almost entirely from their own community. However, those Negro businessmen and private citizens with the ability to pay frequently hired white lawyers, believing that their chances in court would be better.[4] Branton's own family had hired white lawyers, as Leo Branton noted when describing their difficulty in finding a lawyer to represent him following his dispute at the Henry Marx store. A few white people did choose to hire Negro lawyers when they had a dispute against what they considered "the establishment," knowing that the lawyers would not be influenced by that.[5] But there were few such rebels and a law practice could not depend on them.

Branton was not interested in joining with another Negro lawyer. He decided to open his own office. In making this decision, Branton followed a pattern created by attorneys Scipio Africanus Jones, who was located in Little Rock between 1899 and 1943, and W. Harold Flowers, who practiced in Pine Bluff between 1935 and 1990.[6] As a young lawyer trying to build a practice, and imbued with an activist spirit, Wiley took every opportunity to try a case in court. Branton's law school classmate, George Howard Jr., later said of Branton, "He was an aggressive adversary. But if he told you something, you could rely on it. He was sincere and he was concerned with people who were impoverished and voiceless, . . . Money was secondary to him."[7]

Unlike some lawyers, Branton was not afraid to travel to unfamiliar places to represent clients.[8] Since there were few Negro lawyers outside the larger towns in Arkansas, Branton frequently spent long days away from home. With little public accommodation available to him in the 1950s, Branton often would spend the night with a family in the Negro community where he was involved in a trial. In other situations, when the client's case was locally controversial and it might have been dangerous to involve a local family, Branton would drive the miles back home for the night.

Partly because of his family's reputation and partly as a result of his own efforts, Branton's law office was almost immediately successful. He later said, "I opened my practice in Pine Bluff and never knew what it was like to sit around waiting for clients to come and see me."[9] Initially, he carved out a small room at the back of the family's cab company office to serve as his office, but he soon was able to move to separate quarters at 119 East Barraque Street, near the county courthouse. Lucille Branton's prior office management experience came in handy, and she served as his office manager and secretary, as well as taking primary responsibility for the children and their home. She would continue in this role until the birth of their youngest child in 1957. Thereafter, Lucille would help out as needed, but her major efforts became focused on the family.[10]

The files from Branton's Arkansas practice are no longer available, but a handwritten list of matters made as he was closing his Arkansas office in 1962 indicates that most of the matters Branton handled were the ordinary stuff of lawyer's work—divorces, adoptions, wills, and minor criminal matters.[11] However, Branton was anxious to take on civil rights issues, which were easy to obtain since an ever-present racism made a fair jury trial unlikely when a white opponent was involved. Branton also resumed his activities with the local NAACP, which would provide him with several of the most significant civil rights cases of his career.

In spring 1953, he attended a two-day meeting concerning civil rights held in Mound Bayou, Mississippi. This event, sponsored by Dr. T. R. M. Howard, a Negro physician, was held every year and brought together local Negro professionals from Arkansas, Mississippi, and Louisiana.[12] The year Branton attended the meeting, the attorney Thurgood Marshall was the keynote speaker. Although Branton had heard Marshall speak at prior NAACP conferences and had shaken hands with Marshall a number of times, on this occasion he was able to spend time talking and exchanging information with Marshall. He always felt the Mound Bayou meeting was the beginning of their friendship.[13]

Marshall must have been impressed with Branton, as well. By this time, Marshall had been active in civil rights issues with the NAACP for almost twenty years. Branton must have seemed like a younger version of himself. They came from similar backgrounds—both children of "proud, politically-active, African American, middle-class famil[ies] that owned successful businesses and lived in an integrated neighborhood." Like Branton, Marshall's "family was full of strong people who were not intimidated by the violent segregation that had spread across much of the country at the turn of the century."[14] Marshall would have seen an energetic, handsome young man who was impressed with Marshall's work and had a similar passion for the same goals. Marshall would have learned quickly that Branton's sense of humor mirrored his own. They both loved good stories and could tell them with style.

That shared amusement continued over the years. Professor Patricia Worthy, who was an associate in Branton's D.C. firm in the 1970s, recalled that office meetings were held on Wednesday afternoons. After the business was completed, the story telling would begin. Marshall sometimes showed up and participated. Once, she said, Branton and the other senior lawyers began telling jokes, each taking his turn in a friendly competition that lasted for hours. Branton, she believed, had hundreds of jokes in his memory.[15] Sterling Branton, Wiley's brother, shared jokes he heard with Wiley. And he knew that Wiley passed them on to Marshall, because Wiley would often telephone to let Sterling know when Thurgood really liked one.[16]

The men differed in a number of ways, also. Marshall liked parties and drinking, while Branton was a homebody. Most important, Branton lacked the ego that Marshall and many of the civil rights leaders carried with them. As Wiley's son Richard explained, his father knowingly played a "prime minister's" role in the movement, believing he could contribute more to the movement as a "facilitator," helping people work together, than as a final decision maker. "He didn't need to be the symbol of it."[17]

Soon after the Mound Bayou meeting, the NAACP was asked to become involved in the 1953 trial of a white truck driver accused of the sexual assault of a seven-year-old Negro girl.[18] At that time, few trials included Negro jurors and the prevailing climate when such victims were involved often meant there was a real chance that an accused would not be seriously punished. The local community sent a call to the national NAACP. Branton was asked to see what he could do. The trial was held in Ashley County, about seventy miles south of Pine Bluff, bordering the Louisiana state line. Branton was appointed a special prosecutor under state law and worked with the local white prosecutor at trial.[19] They were successful. The defendant was convicted and the conviction was affirmed on appeal to the state supreme court.

Many years later, Branton noted that the *Watt* case "was considered … the first known conviction of a white man anywhere in the South for the sexual molestation of a African American female, except in instances of homicide or great physical injury."[20] The Arkansas NAACP State Conference, an umbrella organization of local NAACP chapters, had funded Branton's work, and received the national NAACP's Thalheimer Award at its 1954 annual convention.[21] Thurgood Marshall was "very generous in his praise," reported Branton, and was excited to learn that "a local lawyer in Arkansas could handle a matter of that type without the personal involvement of NAACP's New York lawyers."[22]

Representing Negro parties against whites could be dangerous for a Negro attorney. On one occasion, when Branton represented a farmer in a dispute with a white man over the ownership of land, he was warned anonymously that if he appeared in the Star City (AR) Chancery Court on the matter, he would be killed. Star City is located in Lincoln County, about twenty-five miles south of Pine Bluff. In response, Wiley took advantage of a state law that allowed the wearing of a gun, "as long as it is in full view and was the type normally used in the military and naval forces." He strapped on his army .45 and invited one of his uncles to accompany him. The uncle was a hunter and a good shot. He carried his rifle openly, which was within the law. Arriving at the courthouse, they left the rifle in the car but Wiley kept the pistol at his waist. No one bothered him, or commented on his appearance.[23]

The year 1954 proved to be a busy one for Branton. It also would be pivotal for his career. Personally, there were many changes in Branton's family life. When the family returned to Pine Bluff from Fayetteville in 1953, Wiley and Lucille had four children. A fifth child was expected. At that time, Negro women in Pine Bluff bore their children in the city hospital's only delivery room. After delivery, however, mother and child were moved to a segregated ward located across an alley, requiring mother and child to be taken into the open air when moved. Since his child was to be born in mid-January, Wiley was determined that neither mother nor child would suffer from the elements. He arranged for a home delivery. The doctor was on call but, when the baby arrived on January 7, Wiley was the only adult present and performed the delivery himself.[24]

With his family outgrowing the Watson Boulevard home, Wiley chose to purchase a lot next to his parents' home from his mother in late 1953. He was still managing the taxicab business, and income from it must have come in handy, as it had at other times. His mother may have been able to give him a discounted price, as well. The brick home he was able to build in 1954 held his growing family more comfortably. Even more important than extra space was the proximity of his mother and uncles, who could provide his children with the close family ties he had had growing up and that he wanted for his children.

Branton's children benefited from that decision. They learned of the family's history and its prominence in the community and they were sheltered somewhat from the effects of segregation, as Branton himself had been. This extra support allowed Wiley to follow his interest in civil rights activism more easily. Despite his travel for clients, his relationship with his children was a close one, and it seemed to them that he was almost always home for breakfast. Where it was possible, Branton took one or more of the children with him when he had appearances in nearby courts, so they could share the ride together. While he was in court, the children would remain in the car.[25]

Returning to Pine Bluff made it easy for Branton to resume aspects of the life he had known in his youth. Some of his earliest memories were of accompanying his grandmother to the meetings and events sponsored by organizations that made up her life outside the family. Branton saw membership in organizations as a normal part of life in any community and as a civic responsibility. Most of the groups Branton joined included some component of social action among their activities. Before he went to law school, he had been a member of the Negro Businessmen's League and the NAACP. He also was a member of the Prince Hall Masons, contributing so much time and energy to that organization that, in 1956, he was elected deputy grand master of the Prince Hall Grand Lodge of Arkansas, Free and Accepted Masons.[26] He remained in that post until he left Arkansas in 1962.

The Brantons were members of the St. Paul Baptist Church, the Pine Bluff church that had been founded by Wiley's great-great-uncle, George Robinson. Branton had been a churchgoer even as a youngster, despite teasing from his brothers. As an adult, he was not a passive member of a church, but undertook lay roles within it and otherwise contributed to its mission. He remained interested in the welfare of a church he had joined. In 1972, over ten years after he left Pine Bluff and St. Paul Baptist Church, Branton wrote to the pastor informing him that notice of a real property sale had appeared in the *Pine Bluff Commercial*. He believed the property lay immediately behind the church and suggested that the church might want to purchase it for future development.[27]

In a 1979 letter responding to a direct request about his "relationship with God," Branton said that he "believe[d] in God but" supposed he had adopted "an ecumenical belief in a savior and in religions."[28] At the time he wrote the letter, Branton was dean at Howard University School of Law and had not found a compatible church to attend since he left Atlanta fourteen years earlier. Noting that, he continued, "Even so, I don't think one has to have a big church or a lot of activity to have a fellowship or to be able to communicate with God." Rather, Branton believed in the church as the heart of a community and relished the historic leadership role in civil rights it had played since Emancipation. Branton thanked the young man for causing him to "concentrate on my views concerning religion." The exchange must have galvanized him in this regard. By the end of the year, he and Lucille had joined the Nineteenth Street Baptist Church in Washington, D.C.,[29] where he became a leader of the men's usher group and was involved in bringing many of his civil rights friends to speak before the congregation.

During this period, Branton began the custom of making what he termed "pop-calls" around the town. On Sunday afternoons, he and Lucille, sometimes with one or more of the children, would drive around the area "popping in" on clients and friends for a few minutes at a time. Calls were made both to current and former clients and showed his interest in them and their lives. That demonstration of "caring" was an excellent tool for getting business, but since the visits included the elderly and others who were not likely sources of legal work, they were not entirely orchestrated toward business. Branton loved talking with and learning about people.

In 1954, Wiley was invited to join the Little Rock chapter of the Sigma Pi Phi fraternity.[30] Known as the Boulé, it is a postgraduate society comprised of Negro professional men who are considered prominent in their communities. Sigma Pi Phi was created in 1904 when Negro men were excluded from similar white fraternal organizations. The Boulé was a mutual aid and networking organization that tried "by concerted action [to] bring about those things that seem best for all that cannot be accomplished by the individual effort."[31] One did not join the Boulé; one was invited to join. Branton's invitation signified that his work was recognized favorably by the Negro elite of Arkansas. Branton's attendance at the Boulé's annual meetings helped him create friends and acquaintances among the "best and brightest" Negroes across the country. At the time he joined the Boulé, it was primarily a social organization. As he worked his way through its ranks, Branton would be instrumental in modifying that focus to include action on civil rights issues.

The most important of Branton's organization memberships probably was the NAACP. Before law school, Branton was a hard worker in its Pine Bluff chapter. His devotion to the cause had led to his arrest and conviction in 1948, and to his lifelong willingness to respond immediately to its requests for help in matters of interest to the group. In 1954, Branton was president of the Pine Bluff NAACP chapter and also was an officer in the State Conference of Branches.

Branton's law practice also was going well. Although his files and correspondence from this period of his career have disappeared, some of his legal work can be traced through published court opinions. His 1953 work in the *Watt* case brought him new clients. He was hired in another civil rights case that helped to hone the advocacy skills he would demonstrate throughout his life. Samuel Alford, a Negro, had been convicted of the rape of a white woman and sentenced to death. As in the *Watt* case, local citizens who felt the sentence was unjust hired Branton. On appeal, Branton argued that the trial had not been fair because the judge had improperly allowed evidence of a similar prior crime into evidence and had failed to inform the jury that it could sentence Alford to a lesser sentence than death. These arguments convinced the state supreme court to grant Alford a new trial in March 1954.[32] Alford's life was saved, for the moment. A second trial was set for June 1, but never took place. The court issued an order committing Alford to the state hospital on May 22, 1954, and the criminal charges were dismissed four years later, on June 11, 1958.[33] It is clear that some kind of "deal" was made, but the record does not indicate precisely what it was.

The fact that Branton was called upon to help in two serious cases within two years of his admission to practice law demonstrates the dearth of lawyers available to Negro citizens. That he acquitted himself well in both matters proves he developed good legal skills in a very short period of time. It is unusual for a new attorney to handle matters of such importance with such success.

Not all of Branton's advocacy involved the courtroom. He preferred a nonconfrontational approach when it was available. In 1954, he was asked to help get the son of a local woman out of jail in Alachua, Florida. Intending to learn more about the charges and then to find a local lawyer to handle the matter, Branton drove down to Florida. In addition to being very light-skinned, Branton spoke with a southern accent that was not recognizably Negro. When he arrived at the jail, the sheriff thought Branton was white and invited Branton to his home for lunch. Branton declined the invitation and, after some discussion with the county attorney, realized that no one actually thought the man was guilty of anything. Branton paid a fine, just to allow the authorities to save face, and was ready to take custody of the young man.

While the man's release was processed, Branton was invited to, and did, attend a meeting of the county bar association, where he made "a few remarks" to the group. At that time, membership in the group was undoubtedly off-limits to Negro lawyers. Under the circumstances, Branton could not refuse the invitation without being impolite or making someone suspicious. He probably did not want to refuse it, either. Branton surely enjoyed the irony and the danger of the situation.

Once he had his young client out of jail, Branton learned the man had lost his job when he was arrested. Branton decided to talk with the employer and see if he could change the man's mind. Branton telephoned the employer, explained that he was an attorney and that the man had been released because he was not guilty. Branton then asked if the employer would rehire the man. Assuming Branton was a white man, the employer granted the request.[34]

In 1970, speaking to an audience of African American professionals in Florida, Branton told the story about the sheriff, then concluded, "that man should never have been in jail and, ... even if he had been put in jail, he should have been accorded all of his civil liberties and civil rights like anybody else, and it is a tragedy ... that that man stayed in jail solely because of his color. It is a tragedy that I got him out just like that, only because they thought I was white. It is a tragedy that he got his job back because they thought it was one southern white man doing a favor to another southern white man."[35]

This appears to be the first time Wiley deliberately used his personality, color, and accent to aid a client. It would not be the last. For a significant part of his career, the fact that Branton was not "obviously" Negro would be a boon to clients in sticky and dangerous circumstances. When he agreed to represent a client, Branton did what was best for his clients. The Florida episode is one example. Branton could not have anticipated that his youthful pranks in "passing" would become useful in more dangerous situations.

After *Watt* and *Alford,* more civil rights cases came to Branton. Some came through the NAACP and others because of his growing reputation as a successful lawyer. Two other civil rights cases are worth a brief mention here. The first was *Brooks v. Burgess,*[36] in which Branton was able to save an elderly widow from foreclosure of her farm for unpaid mortgage loans. Arguing that the interest provision on the loans was usurious, Branton persuaded the state supreme court to reverse the foreclosure action. Branton later noted that "[t]his case became a landmark case in Arkansas in determining interest on loans to farmers for 'furnishing' loans."[37]

In 1955, Branton undertook the case of Rubye Johnson, a public schoolteacher who had been fired by the Wabbaseka School District just two weeks before the school year began. This case also went to the state supreme court which, in 1956, affirmed the trial court's finding that the school district had failed to follow the law in firing Miss Johnson.[38] Branton was proud of this case because it was part of a long line of cases challenging discriminatory treatment of Negro schoolteachers. He included it on a list of his civil rights cases and mentioned the case numerous times in speeches.

On May 17, 1954, the United States Supreme Court published its decision in *Brown v. Board of Education*.[39] The Court held that laws providing for segregated education were unconstitutional. This was a great victory for America's Negro citizens and was the culmination of the decades-long legal effort by the NAACP and its legal arm, the Legal Defense and Education Fund, Inc. That effort began with cases involving segregated graduate school education in the 1930s, some of which were discussed earlier. In a series of favorable decisions, the NAACP established that segregated education could not provide an education of equal "quality" for Negro graduate students.

The five cases that were consolidated in the *Brown* decision extended that reasoning to students in the lower grades. In its opinion, the U.S. Supreme Court stated, "[t]o separate them from others of similar age and qualifications solely because of their race generates a feeling of inferiority as to their status in the community that may affect their hearts and minds in a way unlikely ever to be undone." Unfortunately, the *Brown* Court did not, as the NAACP had hoped, require immediate desegregation of all schools across the country. Instead, the Court recognized that different communities might have different problems in modifying their school systems to accommodate desegregation. It asked the lawyers in the consolidated cases to file briefs suggesting what would be an appropriate decree with regard to implementation of desegregation, promising a second opinion that would include more specific direction on how the states were to proceed.[40]

The day after headlines announcing the *Brown* decision appeared, Arkansas governor Francis Cherry stated, "Arkansas will obey the law. It always has."[41] Some school districts decided not to wait for the U.S. Supreme Court's follow-up decision. On May 23, the Fayetteville, Arkansas, school board (home of the university) voted to desegregate its high school in September.[42] A few other small school districts followed suit, though all were in areas with small Negro populations and economic considerations may have been a factor. The Little Rock School Board announced: "It is our responsibility to comply with federal constitutional requirements and we intend to do so when the Supreme Court outlines the method to be followed."[43] While not a wholehearted response, the Little Rock board's announcement did not imply any resistance. Since Little Rock housed the largest school district in the state, its statement made Arkansas's Negro population hopeful that school integration would be established swiftly and smoothly.

Within a few days of the *Brown* ruling, local NAACP chapters in Arkansas organized meetings to acquaint their communities with the details of the opinion. As president of the Pine Bluff chapter, Branton and his former law school classmate, George Howard Jr., scheduled a meeting at the St. John's African Methodist Episcopal Church in Pine Bluff. In 1989, Howard said that Negroes received news of the *Brown* decision as a new Emancipation Proclamation, "the opening of the door to African Americans for the enjoyment of first-class citizenship in America." He described Wiley Branton as "ebullient" about the decision.[44] Similar meetings were taking place across the country.[45]

Wiley Branton, as chair of the Legal Redress Committee, and Mrs. Daisy Bates, as President of Arkansas State Conference, held a meeting on August 6 at the Little Rock YWCA to convey information to Little Rock NAACP chapter members. Mildred Bond, field representative for the national NAACP, spoke with the group on how to petition school boards for implementation of integration where they did not voluntarily integrate their schools.[46]

The Arkansas State Conference began the process of obtaining parent signatures to petitions that requested admission of their children to white schools. As Redress Committee chair, Branton signed and mailed the letters and petitions to school districts across the state. One letter, dated August 21, was sent to Dr. William G. Cooper, president of the Little Rock School Board.[47] Branton's letter encouraged the board to act aggressively in desegregating, rather than waiting for the additional guidance promised by the Court, stating that the NAACP did not intend to sue where school boards began compliance in good faith. Eighteen parents with children in the public schools had signed the Little Rock petition, asking that "immediate steps" be taken to "reorganize the public schools" and citing the Court's May 17 decision. They also asked for a hearing before the board and offered their assistance in planning for integration.

Little Rock school superintendent Virgil T. Blossom scheduled a meeting with the school board on September 9.[48] At the meeting, Mr. Fay Dunn, the board's chairman; Mr. P. W. Dupree Jr., its president; Mr.

Tom Downie, its legal counsel; and four other board members were present. Attorneys Wiley Branton, Jackie Shropshire, and Thaddeus Williams spoke for the petitioners.[49] A transcript of the meeting was made and does not indicate that any of the parents were present.

Branton made the main presentation to the board. He said that the question of "whether" integration would occur had been answered by the *Brown* decision and suggested there was no need to wait for any other statement from the Court or for a lawsuit. His preference was "to work with you now in planning to bring about integration." Attorney Downie's response could not have been reassuring. Downie noted that while Arkansas's school segregation laws were now unconstitutional, there was no order requiring the board to act immediately, although the board would accept help or services "from anyone" on how to resolve the problem.

Frustrated, Branton asked whether the board intended to honestly work out a program toward integration. The board president, P. W. Dupree, stated that a public statement would be issued in due time. When pressed on a date for the statement, Dupree refused to give one. Finally, Branton reminded the board that, while the NAACP was willing to support any school board that "will work honestly and sincerely to bring integration about without a law suit," it was prepared to sue if necessary.[50]

Superintendent Blossom apparently had a separate meeting with Branton and Williams where he attempted to mollify the Negro lawyers. He reminded Branton that the board's May 22 statement had called for "studies" and said those would take thirty to sixty days to complete.[51] Little Rock was a big district and Blossom argued that it would be irresponsible to rush matters. Unimpressed, Branton replied that the cities of St. Louis and Baltimore had larger populations and more complicated school systems than Little Rock, yet they had been "told to put it [integration] into effect in their public schools." Branton must have been angry when he left that meeting. The board had promised nothing. It would not promise to do anything before the Supreme Court's next statement. In the meantime, Blossom would spend his time performing statistical studies.

After the September 9, 1954, meeting, the situation began deteriorating. Arkansas's commissioner of education, Arch W. Ford, advised school districts to wait until the Court's second decision before desegregating.[52]

The State Conference responded on October 24 with a resolution "deploring" the state's position.[53] The State Conference decided to adopt the national NAACP's policy of working with school boards until September 1955. On that date, it would take legal action against districts where no plan to desegregate had been established.[54]

Outside the education arena, opposition to school integration began to organize. On February 3, 1955, a group calling itself "White America, Inc." filed incorporation papers stating the group's objective was "Segregation."[55] In April, the Capital Citizens' Council was organized.[56] Several segregation measures were proposed in the state house of representatives. State senator and segregationist Jim Johnson managed to obtain enough signatures to put a proposed amendment to the state constitution requiring continued segregation on the November 1956 ballot.[57]

Little Rock's plan for school integration, known as the Phase Plan, was published on May 24, 1955. It proposed 1957 as the time for any school integration and limited the amount of integration that would occur. Little Rock would integrate only one high school, Central, and only with a few Negro students who survived a screening process. The city's junior high schools would open, again only to a limited number of Negro students, by 1960. No date was given for integrating grade schools, although 1963 was in consideration.[58]

Blossom had generated the Phase Plan on his own. Needless to say, he made no effort to work with the NAACP or others representing the Negro community. Blossom spoke before over 150 white groups during the summer of 1955,[59] repeatedly emphasizing that the Phase Plan was the "absolute minimum of what the law required."[60] His efforts seemed appreciated. Readers of the *Arkansas Democrat* newspaper voted Blossom "Man of the Year" in 1955.[61]

The Supreme Court's second *Brown* opinion (*Brown II*) was issued a week later, on May 31.[62] In it, the Court delegated responsibility for implementing desegregation to the individual U.S. District Courts in each state. This was not what the national NAACP and the NAACP Legal Defense and Education Fund, Inc., had wanted. They had hoped the Court would set a specific date or a timetable for integration. Instead, the Court mandated only that integration proceed with "all deliberate speed." Although the Court said it would not allow constitutional principles to yield "simply because of disagreement with them,"[63] the effect was to require litigation wherever a school district did not desegregate voluntarily.

Wiley Branton attended a meeting of civil rights lawyers convened by Thurgood Marshall in Atlanta, Georgia, shortly after *Brown II* was announced. At that meeting, Branton was designated the principal cooperating attorney to the NAACP for Arkansas and most of Mississippi.[64] This meant that the national office would refer to him any complaints and inquiries about school desegregation from people in the two states. The designation did not make Branton an employee of the NAACP, but it gave him access to the advice and help of the NAACP's attorneys. After the Atlanta meeting, the Arkansas State Conference filed updated petitions with school boards in Arkansas. It planned to file suit if it received a negative response from any district, or where it received no response at all.

At a public meeting in late July 1955, the Little Rock NAACP chapter protested the "gradualism" of the Phase Plan, especially the fact that it limited integration to only one high school and did not state when the lower grades would be included.[65] Despite the objections, the Phase Plan was adopted by the Little Rock School Board. Thoroughly discouraged by the board's actions, the chapter asked advice of the national NAACP's regional counsel, U. Simpson Tate. After some consideration, a majority of the Little Rock NAACP chapter members decided that they could not rely on the school board plan and voted to file suit in a December 1955 meeting.[66]

The decision to sue was not unanimous. A significant number of the chapter's members believed the school board should be given more time to prepare for integration. This internal disagreement over tactics would continue until September 1957, when it became clear that the school district and the state of Arkansas intended to minimize and delay any significant school integration. At that point, internal differences were swamped by the common goal of getting and keeping nine Negro students in Central High School.

Branton's time during 1954 and 1955 was not entirely given up to events surrounding *Brown*. Keeping his practice and the taxicab company going was more than a full-time job, and the NAACP work was voluntary. His growing relationship with Thurgood Marshall was pivotal in a case that began in late 1955, involving a nineteen-year-old

Negro man charged with the first-degree murder of his white employer. This case, *Payne v. Arkansas,*[67] provides us with examples of Branton's character and maturing advocacy style.

As character goes, Branton believed in "taking care of business." If he took your case, he would see it through to the end. That attitude kept Branton fighting for Frank Andrew Payne through three trials, two appeals to the Arkansas Supreme Court, and one appearance before the U.S. Supreme Court, over the course of five years. It is not known what Branton was paid for this work. However, since Payne had a fifth-grade education and worked for a lumber company, it is unlikely that he or his family could afford to pay what this effort was worth.

Payne was convicted of murder and sentenced to death by electrocution at trial on January 11, 1956. Branton appealed the conviction to the Arkansas Supreme Court, arguing that the jury selection process had discriminated against Negro citizens and that Payne's "confession" had been coerced from him.[68] Foresight prompted Wiley to ask his brother Leo to sponsor Wiley's admission to practice before the U.S. Supreme Court,[69] and he was admitted on October 8, 1956. When the Arkansas Supreme Court rejected both his arguments and affirmed the trial court verdict, Branton was prepared. He immediately asked the U.S. Supreme Court to hear the case. Permission was granted on April 8, 1957.[70]

Since this would be his first argument in the U.S. Supreme Court, Branton turned to Thurgood Marshall for "pointers on oral argument." Marshall invited Branton and his family to New York over a long weekend, during which the Branton family stayed in the Marshall home and the two men discussed Branton's proposed argument.[71] The matter would be heard almost a year later, on March 3, 1958.[72] When the time came, Marshall "detailed his deputy, Jack Greenberg, to go down to Washington and sit at the counsel table with me."[73]

When he appeared before the Supreme Court on the *Payne* case, Branton had arrived at the pinnacle of achievement for trial lawyers. He had been in practice only six years, and one might have expected that he would be awed by his surroundings and rigid in his presentation. In fact, the recording of his presentation and responses to questioning by various justices exhibits a high degree of comfort. He was so comfortable that when one of the justices inquired closely into one of the facts behind the confession, Branton was able to produce a quip that had the courtroom laughing.

The fact that piqued the justice's attention was Payne's transport from Pine Bluff to Little Rock without his shoes. The justice, who was not identified in the recording, asked when this had occurred. Branton replied that it was October and "people would put shoes back on by that time in Arkansas." The justice then asked whether people often went barefoot in Arkansas. Branton responded dryly, "Most of us don't go barefooted as late as October, your Honor."[74] The courtroom burst into laughter.

There were other aspects to the coercion argument. Payne had been held without formal charges, had not been given access to a lawyer, had been denied food for a sustained period of time, and had been threatened with a possible mob action against him. Branton's appeal was successful. The Court reversed the state court decision and returned the case to the state for a new trial.[75]

In a second trial, Payne again was convicted and sentenced to death. This time, Branton's appeal to the Arkansas Supreme Court was successful. The Court reversed the trial verdict, holding that a "re-enactment of the crime" that followed the now-discredited confession was tainted by the coerced confession and should not have been admitted into evidence. The case was returned for a third trial.[76] The third trial again resulted in Payne's conviction. This time, however, he was sentenced to life imprisonment. There was no third appeal. Although Branton believed there were errors at trial, Payne and his family were worn out and decided to accept the sentence.[77] Branton had, at least, saved Payne's life.

Much of Branton's work in the *Payne* case took place during the first phase of the suit against the Little Rock School Board. As *Payne* ended, the second phase of the Little Rock case was continuing. Little Rock tested Branton's abilities and commitment to civil rights. He would prove to be more than capable.

CHAPTER 6

The Little Rock "Crisis"

AFTER ITS DECEMBER vote, the Little Rock chapter notified the national NAACP of its decision to sue the Little Rock School Board. On February 8, 1956, Branton filed a complaint on behalf of thirty-three Negro students who were barred from registering at white schools. It was titled *Aaron v. Cooper*.[1] Since Branton was often described as an NAACP lawyer, and school board lawyers would claim that the suit was instigated and controlled by the national NAACP office, it is important to identify the different entities and clarify their connections. The relationship between the Little Rock chapter, the Arkansas State Conference, and the national NAACP was, in 1954, a combination of both independence and interdependence.

The national NAACP was composed of two legally separate entities: the NAACP proper, created in 1909, and the NAACP Legal Defense and Education Fund, Inc. (LDEF), created in 1939.[2] The two entities had shared the same board of directors until 1941 and the same New York office space until 1952. The LDEF acted as the national NAACP's legal counsel and also as its education arm in pursuing the organization's long-range civil rights goals.

The Arkansas State Conference, for which Branton was Redress Committee chair, was an umbrella organization made up of NAACP chapters within the state. The State Conference provided support and coordination for efforts of local chapters. Local chapters existed where a Negro population was sufficient in number to organize and where they were able to do so without hindrance by the white power structure. Each chapter paid dues to the national NAACP. In return, they received news and information about civil rights activities occurring across the country and ideas for improving conditions in their own communities.

Neither the national NAACP nor the LDEF could dictate action to a State Conference or to a local chapter, although both provided aid and consultation if desired. For example, Wiley Branton's involvement in the *Watts* case came through a referral from the national NAACP after it had received a request for help from a local NAACP chapter. If Branton was paid for his work on *Watt,* it might be either by the chapter, the national, or in part by both. Over the course of his professional life, Branton performed work for local chapters, the national NAACP, and the LDEF. Some of this work was purely voluntary (*pro bono);* some of it was on a contract fee basis. Generally, he received more of the paid work in his early practice years, when he needed the money, and performed more voluntary work in his later years, but there was no real pattern. He was always a private lawyer, retained for specific cases, and never part of the staff in any entity.

Since the Little Rock case was a consequence of the *Brown v. Board of Education* decision, the national NAACP and the LDEF wanted to keep tabs on its progress. Even if Branton had not been hired directly by the Little Rock chapter, the matter might have been referred to him in his designated role as principal cooperating attorney to the NAACP if the chapter had asked the national office for help.

Over the years, as it pursued the goal of integrated education, the national NAACP had had to develop a cooperative relationship with local Negro lawyers. Its own legal staff was small, including a few lawyers who worked at the New York headquarters and a few who acted as regional counsel in different parts of the country. But these attorneys could not handle every legal need in each state and seldom knew the situation in local communities. They needed the help and knowledge of local lawyers, who could recognize a good case and handle it properly at the trial level.

Local chapters had been asked to notify the national office in New York of any intent to begin legal proceedings concerning education.[3] When such a notice was received, a model complaint form created by lawyers at the national NAACP was sent to the local chapter for its use. The national office would review other court documents on request. A local attorney could receive advice on how to proceed based on the

NAACP's experience in other suits. In effect, the national NAACP lawyers were a resource for lawyers hired by the local branches. The process allowed the national office to coordinate issues throughout the country, while leaving the basic legal work to a local lawyer.

For local lawyers, who were usually sole practitioners like Branton, the structure gave them critical support on sophisticated issues. In return for that support, local lawyers agreed that the national NAACP lawyers would be listed on court documents and, when cases were ready for trial or appeal, would have authority to assume control of the legal presentations if the national organization felt it was necessary. Thus, the national NAACP's small legal department was able to multiply the effect of its work across the country. This procedure was used in the Little Rock case.

At first, however, the national NAACP and LDEF lawyers did not expect the case in Little Rock to be very important. They had decided to focus their attention on eight other states where total resistance to *Brown* was expected.[4] Arkansas was considered "moderate" in race relations. Little Rock citizens had relaxed strict segregation practices in many areas of the capitol in the years during and following World War II.[5] This had improved life in Little Rock for Negroes in a number of areas, and there was little obvious tension between the races. When they learned of the Little Rock NAACP's decision to sue the school board, LDEF lawyers agreed to review any pleadings to be filed, but said that lawyers' fees would be the responsibility of the Little Rock branch. They would have been pleased to learn that Wiley Branton would be handling the case against the Little Rock School Board. His work and competence already were known both to NAACP executive director Roy Wilkins and to Thurgood Marshall.

When he agreed to file the suit, Branton did not think the Little Rock case would be difficult, either.[6] The major complaints his clients had with Little Rock's Phase Plan, its limited nature and lack of specific dates for full integration, might easily be remedied. Branton's opinion would change as events in Little Rock took their course and the issue became the larger one of a state's challenge to the supremacy of the federal government. As he put it in later years, "It became rather obvious to the NAACP that the Little Rock board really was not going to move forward unless they were forced to."[7]

The Little Rock case became Branton's most formative lesson in civil rights law. In *Watt, Alford,* and *Wabbeseka* he had dealt with small-town lawyers and the issue of applying existing law fairly to Negroes. Little Rock thrust him into a more sophisticated level of practice in an area that had no law but that in the *Brown* opinion. Branton would be required to help create the law that carried out the Supreme Court decision. Little did he know that his commitment to the case would take a heavy toll on his life, and that of his family, but also would set him on a career path much different from the one he expected to have.

The complaint that Branton filed accused the defendants of violating the plaintiffs' rights by using unconstitutional state laws or regulations to keep the plaintiffs from attending the public schools closest to their homes and otherwise treating them differently from others on the basis of their race or color.[8] The complaint did not specifically refer to Little Rock's Phase Plan. Branton understood that the more-experienced NAACP regional counsel, U. Simpson Tate, would be the senior attorney in presenting the plaintiffs' case at trial and assumed that his responsibility as the local attorney would be secondary.

The school district's usual attorney, A. F. House, of the Rose, Meek, House, Barron & Nash firm, was augmented by four other attorneys, all from prominent firms in Little Rock.[9] They argued that the school board's plan was a good faith and reasonable effort to comply with *Brown* and charged that the national NAACP, rather than dissatisfied local parents, had been fomenting the litigation. To find evidence supporting its second theory, the school board's attorneys scheduled depositions of two local NAACP officials: Daisy Bates, president of the Arkansas State Conference, and the Reverend J. C. Crenchaw, president of the Little Rock chapter.[10]

At the depositions, Branton expected attorney Tate to take the lead. In fact, Tate did not even appear on May 4, 1956, and Branton, just three years out of law school, was obliged to protect both Bates and Crenchaw on his own. He faced Messrs. A. F. House, Frank E. Chowning, Henry E. Spitzberg, and Leon B. Catlett, a virtual "Who's Who" of Little Rock lawyers, representing the school board. These might have been Branton's first depositions, as even his most important previous cases were unlikely to have had the financial resources to support this expensive legal process. Both Bates and Crenchaw denied that they were puppets of the national NAACP when questioned by Leon B. Catlett, one of the board's attorneys. In his questioning of Mrs. Bates, Catlett made several references to "niggers" and called her by her first name throughout. When she objected, he petulantly said he wouldn't call her anything.[11] For the rest of the session, he did not use her name. Branton, who had not scheduled any depositions, probably because the plaintiffs' could not afford the cost, asked if he might direct some questions to Superintendent Blossom, who was present. The board's lawyers were playing hardball and that courtesy was denied.

Attorney Tate did appear for the trial on August 15, but failed to coordinate plans with Branton beforehand. At trial, rather than focusing on aspects of the Little Rock integration plan that the plaintiffs believed to be discriminatory and wanted modified, Tate argued that the entire Phase Plan should be abolished. Branton was taken by surprise. His clients really just wanted the Phase Plan to apply to more Negro children and to be more definite as to when full integration would take place. Although Branton followed Tate's lead at this point, he would take a more leading role in future court appearances.

In a decision on August 28, 1956, the Honorable John E. Miller, judge of the U.S. District Court in Fort Smith, rejected Tate's arguments, finding the school board's Phase Plan a reasonable response to *Brown's* requirements. The judge's assumption that the plan would begin operation in fall 1957 was the only bright spot for the plaintiffs in his decision.[12] Branton and his clients decided to appeal to the Eighth Circuit Court of Appeals, hoping to get the decision reversed. The Court of Appeals set arguments for March 11, 1957.

Events outside the courtroom began to affect the issue of school desegregation. Arkansas governor Orval Faubus was running for reelection in November 1956. During his campaign, Faubus began making statements against integration. He won reelection overwhelmingly.[13] The election also revealed other evidence of increasing support for segregation. State senator Jim Johnson, who had been Faubus's opponent in the Democratic primary election, proposed an amendment to the state's constitution forbidding school integration, which appeared on the November 1956 ballot. A second proposed amendment purported to nullify the *Brown* decision within Arkansas. Both measures were adopted by a majority of voters.

More was to come. During its spring 1957 session, the Arkansas

Legislature passed four segregationist measures. First, it created a state sovereignty commission. Second, it enacted a statute that exempted students from compulsory attendance laws if they attended an integrated school. Third, it authorized school boards to hire lawyers to defend against integration suits. Fourth, it passed a law requiring all groups favoring integration to register with the state and to reveal the names of their members. The goal was to throw as many roadblocks as possible against the NAACP, causing as much disruption in time, money, and fear as possible, in hopes of delaying integration.

By the time the Court of Appeals heard *Aaron v. Cooper* in March 1957, the national NAACP had recognized the importance of the Little Rock case. NAACP attorney Robert Carter, who was Thurgood Marshall's chief deputy, appeared with Branton before the Court in St. Louis, Missouri. This time, Branton made the arguments his clients wanted. Despite their efforts, however, the Court of Appeals agreed that the school board's plan was not unreasonable and, on April 26, affirmed Judge Miller's decision.

After extensive discussion between Branton, his clients, and the various levels of the NAACP, they decided not to appeal the case to the U.S. Supreme Court. The national NAACP was concerned that the board's Phase Plan might become a model for the nation if it also were upheld by the high court. A more practical reason, as far as Branton's clients were concerned, was the fact that the district court's decision ordered the school board to begin implementing its plan in August 1957, just over four months away.[14] Any further appeal might encourage additional delay by school officials. At this point, it appeared that *Aaron v. Cooper* was concluded. Had the Phase Plan been implemented in a reasonably fair manner, without interference, possibly nothing more would have occurred.

On the other side of the case, however, the matter was far from settled. There was increasing public pressure to delay or stop integration. In a March 1957 election, two members of the Little Rock School Board had been challenged by segregationists and barely managed to retain their seats.[15] The published rhetoric of the segregationists became increasingly militant. While it was worried about the situation, the board and its lawyers were determined to avoid any suspicion that its members favored integration and refused to ask the district court for help.[16]

Superintendent Blossom began implementing the Phase Plan during the summer. Two new high schools had been constructed, one in a predominantly white area and the other in a predominantly Negro area of the city. Central would be the only high school to have Negro students, and the existence of a brand-new school close to home dissuaded many Negro students from applying to Central. Blossom also began using a new Pupil Assignment law passed by the legislature. He created a questionnaire that, while explicitly stating it did not use race as a criteria, was drafted so as to disqualify most of the Negro students living in the Central High School district.

In the Negro community, Daisy Bates organized an effort to encourage students to apply for admission to Central High School. Ozell Sutton, an NAACP member, recalled "[e]very day when I got off work we would go and we would talk to parents about trying to send their kids to Central High School." NAACP members, and especially Daisy Bates, began working with the students who had requested admission to prepare them, both academically and mentally, for the challenges ahead. Sonny Walker, who taught in the Negro schools, was later quoted as saying they put a special emphasis on "getting our very best kids ready to go into an integrated setting." The community wanted to demonstrate "a very positive side of those African American students."[17]

It soon became clear to Branton and the plaintiffs that Blossom was using the student selection process to further "limit the number of Negroes" attending Central that fall. More than two hundred students were eligible by residence to attend Central High School. This number was whittled down to seventeen, not one of whom was among the plaintiffs in *Aaron v. Cooper*.[18] Branton and other NAACP state officials were considering a request to the district court for a contempt order against the school board when other events intervened to focus their energies on getting even those few students into school.[19]

Georgia's segregationist governor, Marvin Griffin, delivered a speech to a Little Rock audience on August 22, touting his own state's complete defiance to *Brown* and sparking more tension.[20] On August 27, Mrs. Clyde A. Thomason, secretary of the segregationist Mothers' League of Central High School, filed suit in the state chancery court against the school board and asked for a temporary injunction barring the board from continuing its efforts to integrate. During the hearing on her request, Governor Faubus testified that violence would occur if the integration plan were continued.[21] Branton attended the hearing, although his clients were not involved and he had no role to play. When the state court judge granted the injunction, the school board immediately applied to federal court for nullification of the state court injunction.

A new federal judge presided over the August 30 hearing on the state court injunction. Judge John Miller, who originally approved the Phase Plan, had requested removal from the case. The Honorable Ronald N. Davies, from Fargo, North Dakota, was temporarily assigned to preside. The school board asked the Court either to quash the state injunction or modify its previous Order and allow them to delay integration. This was the first time that the idea of postponing all school integration was raised formally. Branton supported the board's request to quash the state court injunction. The district court obliged and the chancery court's order was quashed.

As of September 1, then, everything was set for Central High's integration when school began on September 3. No one expected trouble after the district court's ruling. Daisy Bates recalled, "It had been thoroughly thrashed out in court and we felt that the community had been pretty much prepared for this day."[22] To everyone's surprise, Faubus appeared on television on September 2, announcing that the Arkansas National Guard would be stationed outside Central High School the next day to "preserve order" by preventing entry by the Negro students. Branton later said he was "floored" by this action.[23] On September 3, the school board asked the district court for "instructions." Judge Davies held a hearing at 7:30 that evening, at which he ordered that the original plan of integration should proceed. Branton attended that hearing, but was not involved.

Only nine of the seventeen Negro students attempted to enter the school on September 4. Although this activity might have proved dangerous for the students, it was necessary to challenge Faubus's orders to the National Guard.[24] The students were turned away. Eight of the Negro students arrived in one group, but one of them, Elizabeth Eckford, arrived separately and was mobbed by white protestors when soldiers prevented her entrance to the school. Luckily, she was defended by a white woman named Grace Lorch, a member of the Little Rock NAACP, and remained physically unhurt.[25] The situation was captured in pictures by the news media and broadcast around the world.

On September 5, the school board made a second request for the

Court's permission to suspend its integration plan. Branton saw that matters were getting out of control. He knew that he could not handle all the legal ramifications on his own, and he made a formal request for Thurgood Marshall's assistance. By this time, Marshall had established complete separation of the LDEF from the national NAACP. From September 1957, the national NAACP office was not involved directly in the *Aaron v. Cooper* case, although it continued to provide support to the Little Rock NAACP and would be instrumental in numerous lawsuits erupting over the legislature's various anti-integration statutes. Thurgood Marshall arrived in Little Rock the next day.

Judge Davies denied the board's request for delay on September 7. Wiley Branton, Thurgood Marshall, and George Howard Jr. represented the Negro plaintiffs at the hearing. For the next two weeks, there was frenetic activity. The school board attempted to reason with the governor.[26] Thurgood Marshall urged U.S. attorney general Herbert Brownell to intervene, while one of Brownell's subordinates was urging Branton to withdraw the students from school for a year to provide for a "cooling off period."[27] Branton recalled that "[o]ther well-placed individuals in Little Rock suggested that my future in Arkansas would be far more promising if I would support a one year delay."[28]

At a hearing on September 20, the federal court considered whether Governor Faubus and the National Guard officers should be made defendants in the case. At the hearing, the governor's lawyers presented their position and then left the courtroom. The hearing continued, and Judge Davies issued an injunction against Faubus's interference the next day.[29] Later, speaking about the departure of the governor's lawyers before the hearing ended, Marshall said, "Now, I've seen everything."

Governor Faubus withdrew the National Guard from its position around the high school over the weekend and left the state. School was re-scheduled to open on Monday, September 23. The nine Negro students finally were able to enter Central High. However, the Little Rock Police Department was quickly overwhelmed by a growing mob, and the students were withdrawn after threats and disturbances made school officials fear for their safety. The mayor of Little Rock, in the governor's absence, then made a formal request for federal help. President Dwight Eisenhower federalized the National Guard and sent units of the 101st Airborne Division to reestablish order on September 24.[30]

Branton later recalled that his reaction to the news, which he heard on his car radio, was, "Wow! What have I started." He continued, "I had never felt so proud of my country, . . . as I did on the day when troops moved into Little Rock to protect the right of nine African American children to go to Central High School."[31] Many years later, Branton would accuse Faubus of deliberately withdrawing the troops after the hearing, even though the Court's order did not require it, leaving the Negro students open to potential violence. If President Eisenhower had not used the troops, Branton said, "we would have had utter chaos, and you would have had 'states' rights' occupying a position of supremacy over federal laws."[32] The Negro students returned to Central, where they attended school under military guard for the rest of the school year.

Again, one might have expected that the beginning of the school year, the district court's decision, and the presence of soldiers would have been the end of it, and that matters would settle down thereafter. Branton was optimistic that, once the white students were used to the presence of Negroes in their classrooms, attitudes within the school would calm down. He knew that any kind of change breeds resistance. He knew that the virulent segregationists were small in number and he counted on the common sense of the "silent majority" of whites to prevail. His expectation was disappointed. Despite protection of the troops, the students endured "relentless harassment" throughout the year. Thirty years later, Melba Pattillo Beals, one of those students, recalled, "Every morning we got up, we polished our saddle shoes and went to war."[33]

At the same time, other suits filed in both the federal and state courts were ongoing.[34] Branton was involved in only one of them. When Arkansas attorney general Bennett filed suit against both the NAACP State Conference and the LDEF under the February 1957 registration statute, Thurgood Marshall and Branton represented the defendants. Bennett wanted lists of all NAACP chapters and of the members in each chapter. Marshall and Branton were willing to give the locations of NAACP chapters, but refused to turn over membership lists, believing that NAACP members would be put at risk if their names were circulated. Branton, in his role as Legal Redress chair of the state NAACP, recalled pressure put on him to reveal client information he considered confidential.[35] A chancery court judge refused to order disclosure of the information and Bennett appealed.[36] In a 1980 commencement address at the University of Arkansas at Little Rock School of Law, Branton commented bitterly, "There was no protest from the organized bar. I don't recall many individual lawyers speaking out."[37] The profession he loved and revered had failed him.

For Branton, the period between mid-August and the end of September 1957 was difficult, both professionally and personally. Although he was not involved with ferrying the nine students back and forth to school, or with their personal protection, Branton's time was consumed by the legal aspects of the case. He recalled, "We were either in court or in conference with people from the Justice Department and others for 30 some odd consecutive days, and meeting on all kinds of legal situations, from the state court to the federal court."[38]

Although Branton usually "drove back and forth between Pine Bluff and Little Rock (a distance of 45 miles) . . . during the height of that crisis," he and Marshall also spent a number of nights in Daisy and L. C. Bates's Little Rock guestroom. There, they jostled in a macabre manner over who would sleep in the bed next to the window that had been blown out by shotgun blasts. Using metal nameplates with his and Marshall's names on them, Branton would put the one with his name on the bed away from the window, "only to find that, in the wee hours when he and Marshall got a chance to go to bed, Marshall somehow had had the signs changed so that Branton was sleeping next to the window in the greatest point of peril."[39]

Branton's work on *Aaron v. Cooper* had ramifications at home in Pine Bluff, as well. For Lucille Branton, the effort at maintaining a sense of normality for the children, while worrying about the danger to her husband, was extremely stressful.[40] Their youngest child, Debra, was born prematurely on September 15, 1957, when the Little Rock struggle was at its peak. During Lucille Branton's first night home from the hospital, a cross was burned on their lawn. She said, many years later, that she called Wiley in Little Rock when she found the cross and was told to contact his father for help as he could not leave Little Rock.[41] Living next door to extended family members had been a good idea. Another cross was burned at the family's plot in the local cemetery during that period.

There were numerous telephone calls from anonymous cursing racists to contend with, as well. This led to some bizarre conversations when the Branton children, well trained in manners, might respond to the verbal abuse by saying, "I'm sorry, sir, he's not here, but I'll give him your message."[42] After the cross burnings, friends and neighbors of the family—of both races—joined older family members in guarding Branton's wife and children.[43] Branton began carrying a gun in his car and there were guns at home and at the office.[44] He also began regularly to change his route to and from the office, rarely staying in the same house twice when he traveled overnight, and always leaving messages as to his whereabouts with his wife, habits he continued for the rest of his life.[45]

Wiley Branton Jr. says that while he knew at the time that his father was working to improve race issues, his parents managed to keep most of the negative aspects of that involvement from the children. Their father's work seemed normal to them, even though they now realize it was not. Branton's older son, Richard, agrees, recalling that the entire family was bundled off to stay with relatives in Memphis, Tennessee, at one point.[46]

In the midst of this chaos, on October 19, 1957, Branton received the record of the Arkansas Supreme Court's decision in the *Payne* case. He filed his brief to the U.S. Supreme Court on December 3, 1957. Arguments before the Court were set for March 3, 1958. The Little Rock case was ended and he could get on with work for other clients, or so it seemed.

CHAPTER 7

Little Rock Continued

To Branton's surprise, *Aaron v. Cooper* was reactivated on January 20,
1958, halfway through the school year. The school board asked the district
court for permission to suspend operation of its Phase Plan and to delay
school integration for an indefinite period.[1] Judge Davies had returned to
North Dakota and the petition requesting postponement was assigned to
yet another judge, the Honorable Harry T. Lemley.[2] As justification for its
request, the board cited a litany of harassment against the Negro students
that had occurred within Central High School over the period since
school began and argued that these events reduced the quality of education it could provide to all students to an unacceptable level.

The list of hostile actions by white students against the nine students
is truly appalling. Even a generalized summary in a court opinion clearly
demonstrates that the Little Rock Nine went through a species of hell
during their first semester at Central High School. While teachers kept
the classrooms under control, "there were a number of incidents in the
halls, corridors, cafeteria and rest rooms, consisting mainly of 'slugging,
pushing, tripping, catcalls, abusive language, destruction of lockers, and uri-
nating on radiators.'"[3] Some of the Negro girls were held "under scald-
ing water in the showers and had their clothing 'fouled,'" while the boys
were hit "with wet towels in locker rooms."[4] There were other assaults, as
well. The school dealt with forty-three bomb threats, "numerous small
fires," destruction of school property, and the like.[5] The nine Negro students did not instigate any of these actions. They were victims. One author,
who was a student at the school during that year, recalled the "exemplary
conduct" of the Negro students, despite lack of a support system within
the school and against "organized harassment" by white students.[6]

It seems odd that the school board would use the actions of white students against the nine Negroes as the basis for an argument that the education it could provide was substandard. The trouble was known to be limited to a small determined group, about fifty in a school of over two thousand students. The board's January claims that the quality of education was substandard are even more suspect when juxtaposed with statements by both Blossom and Jess W. Matthews, principal of Central High School, two months later. Superintendent Blossom wrote a four-page letter to Dr. Ed McCuistion, Arkansas Department of Education, in March citing a general improvement in grades and higher scores on the national Scholastic Aptitude Tests given in January 1958 compared with the prior year.[7] He noted the senior class had produced nineteen National Merit Scholarship finalists and concluded by saying that most students "seem[] to have gone about their usual school work and teen-age activities without too much concern." On March 22, Principal Matthews spoke at a conference in Grafton, Illinois, repeating many of the accomplishments cited in Blossom's letter and stating, "We're doing our best, we're misunderstood, but we're doing a good job."[8]

Branton filed an opposition to the board's request, and arguments were heard on June 3. After presentations by both parties, the judge granted the board a two-and-a-half-year delay. Lemley apparently was not impressed with the plaintiffs' main argument—that constitutional rights should not give way to those who disagreed with them. The judge, when speaking with newspaper reporters afterward, refused to blame the white students for their actions. Instead, Lemley said that "the course of the trouble was the deep-seated popular opposition . . . to the principle of integration which . . . runs counter to the pattern of Southern life."[9] One newspaper editorial declared that Lemley's decision put him in "the absurd position of saying that the public interest demands the denial of the constitutional rights of citizens."[10]

The judge refused to "stay" his Order, withholding its effect until the plaintiffs could appeal. Without some kind of intervention, the timing of Lemley's decision meant that students would be back in segregated schools before the appellate courts could make a final decision. Responding to questions, the judge reportedly said that the plaintiffs had two months to get his Order overturned. When Branton was asked about his next move, he quipped, "Have motion—will travel."[11] And travel he did.

Over the next seven days, Branton, Thurgood Marshall, and two LDEF attorneys (Constance Baker Motley and Jack Greenberg) appealed Lemley's decision to the Eighth Circuit Court of Appeals[12] and to the U.S. Supreme Court,[13] hoping the higher court would be sufficiently affronted by Lemley's decision to bypass the appellate court. They were disappointed. On June 30, the U.S. Supreme Court held that the matter was properly in the court of appeals and declined to act.[14] In denying plaintiffs' request, however, the Supreme Court said it was sure the court of appeals "will recognize the vital importance of the time element in this litigation."[15]

In later years, Branton told the story of his scurrying around to get the correct Orders and records in the correct appellate court at the right time. His considerable personal charm achieved several miracles during that period. Normally, the record of a district court decision is sent to the court of appeals and, if further appealed, to the U.S. Supreme Court. At the time, however, the Eighth Circuit Court of Appeals would not receive district court records unless the appellate judges first had requested them. When the district court clerk refused to give him a copy of the transcript because there was no request from the court of appeals, Branton "got on the phone and called Judge Lemley." After telling Lemley of the problem, the judge spoke to the clerk, saying, "Listen, give Wiley that transcript. I trust him quicker than I would the United States mail and if they don't want to take it up there at the Eighth Circuit, he'll just bring it back to you all. Fine."[16] Branton obtained his transcript, but it was not a certified copy since the appellate court had not requested it.

After taking the transcript to the court of appeals in St. Louis, Missouri, and "showing" it to the clerk, who would not accept it, he took a plane to Washington, D.C., where the Supreme Court clerk refused to accept it without a formal certification from one of the two lower courts. There was no time for Branton to fly back to Little Rock and obtain a certification from the district court in time to be assured that the Supreme Court would see the documents before the offices closed for the court's annual recess. Over the phone, Branton was able to persuade the clerk of the district court in Little Rock to file-stamp another copy of the trial record, take it to the airport, and personally pay the charges for shipping it to Washington, D.C.[17]

While the courtroom battle about suspending the Phase Plan was going on, Ernest Green, the only one of the nine Negro students to enter Central High School as a senior, graduated. Although local authorities were geared up for major disruption from segregationists, and the now-federalized National Guard was clearly evident throughout the day, the graduation ceremony itself went smoothly, and there were no demonstrations when Green walked across the stage to receive his diploma. Sitting next to Green's mother in the audience was the Reverend Martin Luther King Jr., who had come to salute Green's (and the other eight students') achievement.[18] The only incident to mar that ceremony was that a white boy spat on a Negro girl in the audience. The boy was arrested, but when he appeared before a state court judge, the judge dismissed the charges, saying, "This boy just gave way to an emotion he couldn't control."[19]

The national NAACP decided to award its highest award, the Spingarn Medal, to the "Little Rock Nine," as they came to be known, at its July 1958 annual meeting.[20] Although Mrs. Bates's name initially was not included, the students refused to accept the honor without her.[21] Branton's efforts and the intense legal activity that kept the students in Central had been distanced enough from the parents and students that they did not think to urge his inclusion in the award. Branton was saddened by his omission from that award. Many years later, after he had received numerous other awards for his civil rights work, Branton would say that the Spingarn Medal was the one he would have appreciated most.[22]

The court of appeals responded to the high Court's June 30 hint. Oral argument on the appeal took place on August 4 before the full court of seven justices.[23] The hearing was held in the largest air-conditioned room in the courthouse, as the temperatures outside were in the high eighties that day. Many people were interested in the case and the 150 seats in the audience were filled quickly. Fifty additional people were standing in the courtroom, while another 200 were standing in the outside corridor.[24]

For the plaintiffs, Thurgood Marshall focused on the larger picture, arguing that Lemley's decision supported mob rule, where victims were punished to keep lawbreakers from temptation. In his opinion, the school board was responsible for integrating and should do what was required to keep the educational program operating. The school board attorney, A. H. House, said the school board was made up of ordinary men, serving without compensation, and it was unfair to expect them to "get into unending, vicious turmoil with all their neighbors." House concluded, "You can't expect them to enforce integration."

Wiley Branton presented more of the local details to the court, noting that Central High's administrators had failed to discipline student ringleaders and had allowed quick reinstatement of the few who were suspended. He suggested that the delay "would continue indefinitely if segregationists were permitted to drag one new state law after another through the various courts of appeal." Branton rejected the board's charge that, without Marshall and other LDEF lawyers, the plaintiffs would disappear, stating, "This will be carried on whether Marshall or anybody else comes in." A newspaper reporter noted that Negroes in the audience could be heard to murmur, "That's right."[25]

The court of appeals issued its decision two weeks later, reversing Judge Lemley's decision with one dissenting vote. The appellate court chided the district court judge for viewing the situation as caused by the presence of the Negro students rather than as a result of opposition to their presence. While noting that the school board had responsibility for a somewhat thankless task, the court of appeals clearly had seen the board's complaints as evasive.[26] It stated that "the time has not yet come in these United States when an order of a federal court must be whittled away, watered down, or shamefully withdrawn in the face of violent and unlawful acts of individual citizens in opposition thereto."[27]

Despite the strong words, however, the chief judge (who had been the only dissenter) refused to allow the court of appeals' decision to replace Lemley's until the school board could appeal to the Supreme Court. This meant that the original order granting suspension of the Plan was still in place. With the fall semester scheduled to begin in just a few weeks, the school board could take its time with the appeal and assure that the new school year did not begin on an integrated basis.[28] To its credit, the board did not delay. Although the Supreme Court was in its summer recess, it agreed to hear the appeal on an expedited basis so that a decision might be made before the school year began. Oral arguments would be heard on September 11, 1958.[29]

Between the August 4 court of appeals hearing and September 11, Governor Faubus, anticipating reversal of Judge Lemley's Order, scheduled a special session of the Arkansas Legislature. Faubus proposed a number of laws to prevent continued integration should the Supreme

Court agree with the court of appeals. One measure would give the governor authority to close the public schools. Another would allow him to lease school buildings to private groups that would provide segregated education. All his proposals were adopted by the legislature, and the governor waited to see if he would need to use them. The school board, surprisingly, delayed the opening of school until September 15, after the Supreme Court hearing.

On September 11, the Court asked hard questions of Richard C. Butler, who represented the school board. Butler's main presentation repeated the argument that the situation was unfair. It was preferable, he said, "to defer certain intangible constitutional rights of a few than to destroy the full educational opportunities of [the many]." Butler admitted that the board had made no plans to use the delay to change community attitudes, nor had the board any ideas for what to do if those attitudes had not changed in two and a half years.

Thurgood Marshall, speaking for the plaintiffs, repeated his concern about the long-range consequences of a delay at this point. He was worried about the white children who were being taught that "the way to get your rights is to violate the law."[30] He also worried about what would happen to other Supreme Court decisions if the segregationists were allowed to prevail over *Brown*. The next day, the Court made a brief announcement of its unanimous decision in favor of the plaintiffs, and ordered the school board to continue its Phase Plan. A written opinion would follow.

Many years later, Branton would admit that he was not happy about giving way to Thurgood Marshall in the Supreme Court arguments.[31] However, Branton was a realist. Marshall had decades of experience before the high Court and when Branton brought the LDEF into the case, he understood the terms. In exchange for its help, LDEF would decide what lawyer would make any appellate arguments.[32] And, after all, Branton had, with Marshall's help, argued his first case before the U.S. Supreme Court just a few months earlier. The struggles Branton and Marshall shared during the Little Rock case strengthened their friendship and they would remain fast friends for the rest of their lives.

The Little Rock case had reached another decisive point. Faubus could have turned up his hands, bowing to the Supreme Court's final pronouncement. Instead, immediately after learning of the Supreme Court's decision, Governor Faubus closed the public high schools in Little Rock. He also scheduled a special election on September 27, when voters would be asked whether or not they favored integration. He promised that if the voters rejected integration, he would assure a continuing educational program by leasing school buildings and funneling state education funds to a corporation that would operate private, segregated schools.[33] Faubus knew he could not prevail in the end, but was beyond the point of reason by now. The delay would carry him past his November 1958 reelection bid.

The school board refused to turn school buildings over to the governor when its lawyers expressed "grave doubts as to the legality of such a segregated private school system" and suggested the board ask the district court for instruction, which it did on September 23.[34] Faubus excoriated the board's caution and charged that the board was in league with Thurgood Marshall, Mrs. Bates, and Superintendent Blossom to thwart the will of the people.[35]

Thus began a third period of intense activity for Branton and Marshall. They asked the district court for an order preventing the transfer of school buildings. The case had been reassigned yet again, back to the original judge, the Honorable John E. Miller. When Miller refused to act, the school board was left out on a limb once again. If the board were to do what the Supreme Court required, it would have to directly oppose Faubus. When the public voted against integration almost 2–1, the board surrendered and began negotiating with the Little Rock Private School Corporation.[36]

Branton and Marshall went to the court of appeals on September 29. At a district court hearing that same day, the school board had revealed that it had signed a lease with the Private School Corporation earlier that day. The plaintiffs were asking the court of appeals for an order prohibiting the lease from taking effect. On the same day, the Supreme Court's written opinion in *Cooper v. Aaron* was released in Washington, D.C. That unanimous opinion contained forceful language, including the bald statement that "law and order are not here to be preserved by depriving the Negro children of their constitutional rights."[37] Every argument of the school board was denied and, although the decision was satisfying to the plaintiffs, it did not end the battle.

On learning of the Supreme Court's opinion, the court of appeals was willing to issue a temporary restraining order forbidding any property transfer by the board. However, to obtain the order, plaintiffs were required to provide a surety bond of $1,000. No bond company in Omaha, Nebraska, where the hearing was held, would issue the bond. Branton saved the day by telephoning his father, who contacted a local insurer and put up his personal property to guarantee the bond.[38] The court's order did not change the overall situation. A state trooper prevented personal service on Governor Faubus and the schools remained closed.

There were additional hearings in the court of appeals on October 6 and 15. The board argued it was "in a position of neutrality" and the Court should be going after Governor Faubus.[39] In a November 10 opinion, the court of appeals held that the school board was under specific order of the Supreme Court to proceed with its integration plan and could not hide behind the actions of third parties. The board had violated the Court orders by "yielding to local desire or clamor and to the importuning of the Governor."[40] The court of appeals ordered Judge Miller to require the board to "take such affirmative steps" as were needed to accomplish integration.[41] The problem for Branton and Marshall was that the court of appeals could not force the school board to act properly. Only the district court could hold the board in contempt of court and assess fines or order the board's incarceration. But Judge Miller was not in favor of integration and found ways to avoid any action that might advance that cause. In fact, he did not respond to the order until January 9, 1959, at which time he gave the board another thirty days to inform him of what it had done or intended to do to comply with the order to integrate.

What the board had done after the November court of appeals decision was to pay Superintendent Blossom for the remainder of his employment contract and to resign *en masse*.[42] By the January 9 hearing, a new school board comprised of three moderates and three segregationists had been elected. The board also was represented by a new lawyer, Herschel Friday of Mehaffy, Smith & Williams.

The U.S. attorney asked that the board be held in contempt for refusing to proceed. Ignoring that request, the judge noted that the court of appeals had not required him to order the board to reopen the schools. He interpreted the court of appeals mandate as requiring "that when and if the high schools are opened, they must be operated as a non-segregated system."[43] Matters were at a standstill. Not two weeks later, the board reported that it had no plans to advance integration and asked for permission to reopen the four public high schools on a segregated basis. It was as if nothing had happened since the schools were closed. Judge Miller denied the board's request.[44]

Branton and Marshall had to come up with some way to get things moving again, or all of their work for the past three years would be destroyed. They filed a Supplemental Complaint that added new defendants and directly challenged Acts 4 and 5, the state laws on which Faubus relied to close the high schools and to divert public money, as unconstitutional.[45] Two earlier suits attacking Acts 4 and 5 were wending their way through the state court system, and on May 4, 1959, the state supreme court released opinions in both earlier cases, finding both laws were constitutional.[46] The federal court disagreed with the state court, and its decision was affirmed by the U.S. Supreme Court on December 14, 1959.[47]

By the time of the U.S. Supreme Court decision, the situation had changed in Little Rock. Faubus's decision to close the Little Rock high schools affected white families across Little Rock, not just those in the Central High district. Approximately four thousand students were affected by the closing.[48] Most went to schools elsewhere in Arkansas or in other states, living with relatives or friends. Others had no such alternatives and never completed their high school education. While an effort was made to provide high school classes within the Negro community, it was not very effective.[49]

Several groups began agitating for reopening of the high schools soon after they were closed by the governor. First was the Women's Emergency Committee to Open Our Schools.[50] They began an unsuccessful campaign to defeat Faubus's "segregation" election in September 1958 by educating Little Rock citizens, using newspaper advertisements, a newsletter, and telephone calls. A group of sixty-three Little Rock lawyers also published "a full page statement pleading for our public school system."[51] After segregationist members of the school board illegally fired forty-four schoolteachers in May 1959, the Little Rock business community became aroused, urging the reopening of schools "on a controlled minimum plan of integration acceptable to the Federal Courts."[52] They forced a special school board election in May that ousted the adamant segregationists.[53] The new board began working on opening the high schools for the 1959 fall semester. This was not the dawn of a new day, however.

The white groups working to open the schools were not joined in common cause with the Negro community. The Women's Emergency Committee believed "[i]f we accepted or tolerated a single hint of favoring integration, we were a lost cause."[54] As the new school board worked to reopen the high schools in fall 1960, it ignored suggestions that it sponsor educational programs for the white parents, teachers, and students on how to prepare for integration, and that it work with the Negro community.[55] Instead, the board used pupil placement statutes to manipulate the location and amount of integration in the high schools, just as Blossom had done in 1957.

When the school board announced that only five Negro students would be assigned to Hall High School and five at Central High, Wiley Branton went back to court. Under the school board's machinations, two of the Little Rock Nine, Thelma Mothershed and Melba Pattillo, had not been allowed to return to Central High and fifty-one other Negro students were forbidden to register at the white schools. Judge Miller ruled against the plaintiffs, finding that the school board had no obligation to assign students to any particular school and "[t]here is no evidence that the defendants have used the [law] as an instrument for maintaining or effecting a system of racial segregation."[56]

Judge Miller's decision was reversed by the court of appeals, which noted that this current board had prefaced its actions in reopening the schools by declaring its preference for segregation and making "an earnest[] request" to Governor Faubus for any ideas he might have for avoiding integration.[57] The Negro students were treated differently from white students in the assignment process, and had been subject to factors "not ordinarily deemed relevant to normal school criteria ... applied by defendants for the purpose of impeding, thwarting and frustrating integration."[58] The district court was ordered to assure that the board did its work. By this time, however, the case had lost its intensity. Although more Negro students were eventually admitted to schools at all grade levels, full integration in Little Rock was never achieved. "White flight" and private white schools emptied Little Rock public shools of many students. Litigation continued, but there was no final resolution.

It was a frustrating experience for Branton. The successes in the federal appellate courts were never enough to overcome reluctance at the district court level and recalcitrance of the school board and the community. Integration required constant vigilance of the lawyers. In early 1962, Branton transferred primary responsibility for the school integration work to his protégé, Little Rock attorney John W. Walker, when he accepted the position of executive director of the Voter Education Project in Atlanta, Georgia. However, except for two years during which he worked for the federal government, Branton never really left the case. He acted as a consultant in subsequent legal actions and usually was listed as one of the attorneys on the filed briefs. And he never lost his hope for a truly equal society in America. Later in life, he expressed his sorrow over the slowness of desegregation efforts and acknowledged that "[w]e have had to give up some things" like neighborhood schools and Negro teachers who were role models.[59] Still, Branton maintained, "I am an ardent advocate of school desegregation."[60]

The Little Rock school case made Branton a national figure. It also exhibited character traits that would make him loved and respected throughout his life. He was a man of principle. When it most counted, he stood up for doing the "right" thing, when many others failed the test. He was a man of courage and refused to give in to threats of personal physical harm. He was independent and could not be swayed from his path by hints of future rewards. His dogged determination and devotion to his clients' cause impressed many. Branton also demonstrated generosity and an ability to subdue his own interests in a common cause.

In late 1958, Thurgood Marshall wrote that "too many people . . . get the mistaken notion that Wiley is not actually the general counsel in the Little Rock case . . . we must not only give due credit to Wiley for his legal strategy, etc. in these cases but also his willingness to take the press coverage which features Thurgood Marshall."[61] In his 1978 speech delivered at Branton's investiture as dean of Howard University School of Law, Marshall said, "I got the credit mostly. But I would go to those places, and [then] I would get out on the fastest damn thing that moved. . . . [Wiley] stayed there. He didn't go. . . . He stayed there, and made them take it and like it."[62]

While the Little Rock school desegregation case was keeping him pretty busy during the period 1959 to 1962, Branton was also handling other civil rights matters. When the first "Freedom Riders" sent by the Congress on Racial Equality (CORE) to test the desegregation of interstate transportation facilities were arrested in Jackson, Mississippi, in May

1961, Thurgood Marshall asked Wiley Branton to go to Jackson and help with their defense. By that time, Branton had had more civil rights litigation experience than local Negro lawyers in Mississippi, and Marshall knew he could handle the situation.

Branton spent two days in Jackson, which was about 250 miles from Pine Bluff, participating in a massive municipal court trial. One of those Freedom Riders, John Lewis, a Negro, recalled that Branton was the first lawyer to arrive, a "shepherd and defender" from the forces of violence.[63] The Freedom Riders were convicted and sentenced to jail. Branton always believed that the judge had decided the case before hearing the evidence because the judge read his decision from a typewritten page without taking any break for contemplation after hearing the testimony. Tensions in the town were so high that Branton was compulsive about checking his car for wires that might indicate explosives and again carried a gun for his personal protection.[64]

Despite his concern for personal safety, Branton did not flinch from doing what was necessary to represent his clients. When the Mississippi court physically separated black and white Freedom Riders according to the segregation law, Branton protested and was successful in having the proceedings integrated—at least to the point of having all defendants seated together. Later, he accused the state of "'entrapment,' having 'deliberately brought these defendants from the state line to Jackson to arrest them.'" In his closing argument, Branton "reminded the judge that he and other Mississippi officials had taken an oath to uphold the United States Constitution."[65] His remonstrations had no noticeable effect on the sentences imposed.

Marshall called on Branton's aid in this manner on numerous occasions, and Branton always responded. He participated in a number of Louisiana sit-in cases where protestors were charged with criminal anarchy and in other challenges to school desegregation in Dallas and New Orleans.[66]

When he left Arkansas in 1962, Branton expected to be gone only for a limited period of time. And, though he never again resided in the state, Branton never left Arkansas entirely. He continued to run the taxicab company until September 1962, when it became clear that the Voter Education Project would take all his energy. He continued to vote in Arkansas until 1970.[67] He owned property in Pine Bluff for the rest of his life.

He subscribed to Pine Bluff's daily newspaper, the *Commercial*, and contributed his comments on events in his hometown until his death. One example, which his papers indicate was not unique, is his letter to a retired AM&N College librarian. Branton had been reading the list of real estate tax delinquencies in the paper and noticed her name. He wrote, saying, "I understand that you have been ill and perhaps you over-looked paying your taxes as you usually do, and I thought I would bring it to your attention."[68] For the newspaper, Branton wrote a twenty-three-page memoir on "Post-War Relations in Pine Bluff" in 1985. Despite the harshness of the racism it recalled, the essay is a letter of love for his home town, closing with a statement of regret that the times prevented him from having a normal relationship with all its citizens.[69]

Branton also returned occasionally to handle special cases in Arkansas. He could not say "no" when the subject of the case was civil rights. For example, in 1962, Branton represented Little Rock's Council on Community Affairs (COCA) in working out the desegregation of public facilities, including parks, other recreational areas, and the main performance auditorium.[70]

Public swimming pools were deliberately left off the list, Branton's clients being sure that the inclusion of pools would result in hysteria among the white community.[71] A year later, Branton described this omission as a "gentlemen's agreement" where city officials agreed to move swiftly to integrate the other facilities. Otherwise, he said, "the lawsuit still might be tied up in court." Branton continued, "A lot of my personal feelings and attitudes went into this agreement. . . . When people are willing to work things out in a friendly spirit, it's much better for all concerned."[72]

In 1963, Branton was part of the team that represented George Whitfield in a suit against the University of Arkansas for discrimination in campus housing.[73] A second matter in 1963 involved the family of his law school classmate George Howard Jr., whose daughter was one of the first Negro students to integrate Pine Bluff's Dollarway High School. When William M. Howard, George's brother, was charged with stabbing a white high school student who was harassing his niece, Branton was on the defense team.[74] Two years later, when George Howard Jr.'s daughter had graduated successfully from the high school, Branton sent her a letter, commending her courage.[75]

In 1964, Branton and local attorney L. M. Mahon successfully defended a Negro named Paul Louis Beckwith from first-degree murder charges following the "brutal beating death of a very prominent young housewife and mother in her home in Brinkley, Arkansas." The editorial headline in the local newspaper read "Justice Is Done at Clarendon, Arkansas."[76] In 1970, Branton joined with attorney John Walker in Little Rock to represent six Negro youths charged with the rape of two young white women. This representation continued through three trials before a settlement was reached and the men were released.[77]

In spring 1962, Wiley Branton left Arkansas to become director of the Voter Education Project. Created under the umbrella of the Southern Regional Council, it was intended to educate southern Negroes about their voting rights and encourage them to register and vote. It turned out to be much more than that.

CHAPTER 8

The Voter Education Project

ONE OF THE civil rights organizations that Branton joined during his Arkansas practice years was the Southern Regional Council. It is head-quartered in Atlanta, Georgia, and was created in 1919 to collect and high-light statistics on various forms of racial discrimination, including those preventing Negroes from exercising their voting rights. Branton probably learned of the organization and joined it soon after World War II, when he became heavily involved in voter registration. When the idea of a mas-sive southern voter registration drive funded by private foundations was raised in 1961, the Southern Regional Council was asked to be its sponsor.

The Voter Education Project, as it was named, was the first effort to reach all classes of Negroes in the South. A valuable addition to the civil rights movement, the VEP had politics behind it. John F. Kennedy had become president by a narrow margin in 1960 and analyses showed his election could be attributed to Negro voters.[1] Reelection might be more certain if more Negro voters were registered, particularly in the south-ern states where registration was low.

The idea of the VEP apparently began in conversations between Louis Martin, Harris Wofford (both advisors to President Kennedy), and Burke Marshall, assistant attorney general for civil rights in the Justice Department.[2] Harold Fleming, director of the SRC, was convinced to sponsor the program and the Ford, Field, and Taconic foundations agreed to provide $870,371 over a two-and-a-half-year period. The group then lured the larger civil rights organizations to support the VEP in exchange for potential grant money for voter registration drives. After overcom-ing a number of objections from all parties to this kind of cooperative venture, the VEP became a reality.[3] But it needed someone to run it.

When the search for an executive director for the VEP began, a number of people suggested that Branton take the position. He was not interested initially and, instead, solicited a number of other people he thought would do a good job. He was unsuccessful in convincing anyone but himself that this would be a good career move and challenge. Branton agreed to take the job in early 1962.[4]

In later years, it was reported that each of the major civil rights leaders —Roy Wilkins of the NAACP; Martin Luther King Jr. of the Southern Christian Leadership Conference (SCLC); James Farmer of the Congress of Racial Equality; Whitney Young Jr. of the National Urban League (NUL); and representatives of the Student Nonviolent Coordinating Committee (SNCC)—had to approve Branton's appointment.[5] They readily agreed to Branton's hiring. By 1962, he was a seasoned attorney, nationally known for his work in the Little Rock case. His personality and frequent attendance and participation in conferences and conventions concerning civil rights had made him personally known to almost everyone in the civil rights movement. He would be included in *Life* magazine's 1962 list of one hundred "most important" young Negro men and women in the United States later in the year.[6]

Since the VEP was a unique concept, Branton started from scratch to build its structure. He was given almost full control over what that would be. In addition to hiring a small staff to help solicit and review grant applications, he created a reporting structure that would fit within the Southern Regional Council's charter. After gauging the workload his new job would impose, Branton decided he had to sell the family taxicab business. This must have been a hard decision, but he could not maintain oversight of its operations from Atlanta. He sold the business in September 1962 to Daniel Jones Jr., one of the drivers, for $7,000.[7]

Both the available time and the amount of funding for the VEP were limited. To conserve funds and avoid duplicative efforts, Branton encouraged the civil rights groups to cooperate in locating registration drives. The groups, however, were very competitive and, with one exception, Branton was forced to designate specific "territories" for each.[8] The exception was Mississippi, where the NAACP, Southern Christian Leadership Conference, and Congress on Racial Equality all had chapters. Robert Moses of the Student Non-violent Coordinating Committee, Tom Gaither of the Congress on Racial Equality, and Aaron Henry and Medgar Evers of the NAACP, proposed to work through the Council of Federated Organizations (COFO), which they had created in 1961.[9] When Evers consulted Branton about the idea, Branton was pleased.[10] He suggested that Evers convene a meeting of local activist groups to discuss this and he agreed to attend. At a meeting in Clarksdale, Mississippi, Branton recalled being asked to preside over the election of officers. He was considered a neutral party and could assure that the procedure was fair.[11]

Otherwise, the division of territory for VEP purposes was fairly straightforward. The NAACP and Urban League worked in states where they already had active branches that were making efforts much like those Branton helped pursue for the NAACP in Arkansas. The branches tended to be located in larger cities and in states that were not totally resistant to Negro political organization. While the task of expanding voter registration was never easy, this preexisting presence allowed the NAACP and Urban League to register more voters once they could educate the people and overcome the inertia and fear.[12]

The younger organizations, CORE, SNCC, and SCLC, on the other hand, began new efforts in states that were very resistant to the idea of Negro voting. In rural Georgia, for example, they faced hundreds of "church burnings, jailings, physical attacks, and economic reprisals."[13] Much of their effort was put to convincing people they could make "decisions solely on the basis of their personal opinion," rather than what the local white people would think.[14] Fear kept many people from daring to think of change.

The worst of these resisting states, however, was Mississippi, where COFO was located. Branton was able, through the Voter Education Project, to provide grant funds for its work. Not quite a year after beginning operation, in March 1963, the VEP reported "64 acts of violence and intimidation against Negroes in Mississippi since 1961," most of them in reaction to registration efforts.[15] One of those incidents occurred when shots were fired at a car transporting three workers, including Branton's assistant Randolph Blackwell, in February 1963 near Greenwood, Mississippi. The driver, SNCC worker James Travis, was seriously injured.[16]

A year of frustration about Mississippi impelled Branton and the civil rights groups to announce an all-out push for voters in Greenwood.[17] Branton announced a "saturation campaign."[18] He also sent a telegram to Attorney General Robert Kennedy announcing the decision and stating, "You must anticipate that this campaign will be met by violence and other harassment. We are notifying you in advance so that you can provide the necessary federal protection to prevent violence and other forms of intimidation against registration workers and applicants."[19] Branton and the civil rights leaders were under the impression that the Kennedy administration had promised to provide protection for the voter registration workers.[20]

Predictably, racist reaction to VEP pronouncements increased in Greenwood. "'In the state of Mississippi,' [Sam Block, SNCC worker] said publicly, 'every animal has a season but the Negro; you can shoot him anytime.'"[21] Police dogs were used to intimidate those attending meetings and to inhibit marches to the courthouse to register.[22] Toward the end of March, Bob Moses, one of COFO's leaders, James Forman of SNCC, and six others who were working on registration efforts, were arrested.[23]

Wiley Branton flew in to counsel and represent the jailed workers.[24] Accused of being an "outside agitator," Branton responded at an evening mass meeting that he was no outsider, "his great-grandfather was Greenwood Leflore, a person of some historical importance to the area!"[25] Charles M. Payne reports that Branton's words "brought the house down," despite much "oratorical competition."[26] In response, some white Greenwood residents "are said to have responded, '[That nigger] ought not to be talking about things like that.'"[27]

Moses, Forman, and the others were convicted summarily and given a four-month jail sentence, which they decided to serve rather than appeal, believing this would pressure the federal government to act.[28] The Justice Department requested an injunction in federal court against local officials who were preventing Negro voter registration, and Branton must have been jubilant on hearing about it. This was the first time the Justice Department had acted directly to protect the right to vote.

Branton was to be disappointed, however. The Justice Department quickly reached a compromise with Greenwood officials, agreeing to drop its request for an injunction if local officials would release the convicted civil rights workers until they were given a full trial. Others in the community who had been arrested at the same time were not included in the deal and there was no promise by Mississippi officials to stop the violence against civil rights workers. Under the compromise, Greenwood also agreed to resume federal government food distribution programs to the poor, "but only after the government agreed to pay for the cost."[29]

The Justice Department's failure to pursue a full settlement of the civil wrongs occurring in Greenwood shocked many. There was public discussion on whether the government should bring troops into Mississippi to maintain order. This was the point when some civil rights workers began to believe that the federal government was part of the "enemy," and where the Justice Department's legal approach was furthest from being understood by civil rights workers.[30] Wiley Branton was among those who blamed the government for failing to protect voting rights.[31]

Kennedy's Justice Department was in a bind. By 1963, the Justice Department had filed fifty-eight suits in federal court under the 1957 and 1960 Civil Rights Acts.[32] It had lost most of them in the district courts and been required to appeal. Even its successes in the appellate courts had not resulted in much change in the South. Unless the government was prepared to use force, as it had done in Little Rock, white resistance would be successful. And the effects of force were limited.

Although Branton had been thrilled when President Eisenhower sent troops into Little Rock to protect the Little Rock Nine during the 1957–58 school year, white resistance openly revived once the troops left. As noted earlier, Little Rock schools had been closed the following year despite the Supreme Court's 1958 opinion in *Cooper v. Aaron*. When the schools reopened, the Little Rock School District's grudging movement prevented any significant desegregation for years. In Mississippi, unless the government declared martial law, there was little it could do when people refused to obey court orders. Eisenhower had been soundly criticized in the South for his action in Little Rock and Kennedy was not ready to repeat it.

By the end of 1963, registration results in Mississippi were minimal, despite all the effort and suffering. Continued financial support of COFO by the VEP could not be justified. After spending $51,345 in Mississippi, only 3,228 new voters were registered. A similar amount ($52,958) spent in Georgia during the same time period created 46,347 new voters there. Making a difficult decision, Branton was forced to give up on Mississippi in October 1963. He had rarely failed in anything and he was not a "quitter," but he had to keep the larger picture in mind.

Mississippi was only one state among many. He would receive some solace from the creation of a new organization, the Council for United Civil Rights Leadership (CUCRL), through which the Mississippi activists would continue to fight.

CUCRL was the idea of white philanthropist Stephen Currier of the Taconic Foundation, one of the entities that had given money for the VEP.[33] Cheered by the level of cooperation between civil rights groups and the VEP achieved by Branton, Currier aimed higher, hoping to eliminate the competition for donations between civil rights groups by creating a single vehicle that would receive money for various civil rights causes. The new money would not be limited in how it might be spent, as was that given to the VEP.[34] Contributions would be divided among the constituent groups in proportion to their individual memberships. The groups involved in CUCRL were the NAACP, National Urban League, NAACP LDEF, the National Council of Negro Women, SCLC, CORE, and SNCC.[35]

CUCRL began in June 1963 with a breakfast at which Currier and a number of his wealthy friends pledged more than $500,000 to the cause. A short time later, another $300,000 was donated to CUCRL. It was to CUCRL that Dr. Martin Luther King Jr. donated $17,000 of the $54,000 awarded him with the 1964 Nobel Peace Prize, to be divided among the other members.[36] To avoid tax complications, CUCRL was divided into two entities. The second was the Committee for Welfare, Education and Legal Defense (WELD), which would be allowed to fund advocacy efforts.

Branton had impressed the civil rights leaders with his fairness in distributing VEP funds and they asked him to direct CUCRL/WELD. When he was appointed, the *New York Times* said that Branton was "known for his directness, energy and ability to convince people to accept compromises."[37] The effort was an easy fit with his VEP work, and the Southern Research Council approved, assigning a young Vernon Jordan Jr. to assist Branton with VEP business.[38] Branton would become, first, Jordan's mentor, and last, his good friend.[39]

The two jobs were quite compatible. In fact, CUCRL enabled Branton to promote and participate in direct action efforts that were forbidden to the VEP, with its focus on voter registration. From CUCRL, Branton was able to, for example, provide grants to COFO for a "mock election" gubernatorial campaign and election in October 1963, and for planning 1964's "Freedom Summer," when thousands of college students went to Mississippi from across the country to register voters.[40] Some of the money helped create the Mississippi Democratic Freedom Party, which challenged the regular Mississippi electors at the National Democratic Convention in August 1964.

Through CUCRL, civil rights leaders became active in lobbying for passage of the 1964 Civil Rights Act.[41] It also acted in other areas. For example, it contributed funds to support a "Leadership Conference for Civil Rights" in Washington, D.C.,[42] supported the holding of hearings on southern brutality,[43] and lobbied to influence appointments to the Commission on Civil Rights.[44] The minutes of CUCRL meetings reveal Branton's efforts to focus the group on action in numerous areas and it is clear that the ideas for most of CUCRL's effort began in the brain of Wiley Branton.[45]

The CUCRL, like the VEP, was a unique organization that performed a significant service during an important time for civil rights. A young John Lewis gave it credit for unifying the civil rights groups at a critical time in the movement.[46] CUCRL never became an established power, however. An initial goal to raise $1.5 million failed and, when donations subsided, CUCRL could not keep the interest of its members. Meetings gradually became less productive. Branton moved on to positions in the Johnson administration in early 1965. The CUCRL survived until January 1967, two years later.

Between VEP and CUCRL/WELD, Branton had moved into a higher echelon of civil rights work. He was among those who met with President Kennedy on June 21, 1963, when Kennedy tried to convince black leaders to slow down their protest activities, especially a planned March on Washington in August.[47] Kennedy was worried that the protests would have a negative effect on his pending civil rights bill.[48] Kennedy was wrong. The March took place and "gave voice to the growing public support for Kennedy's civil rights program."[49]

Branton was not present at the March on Washington, although his name appears on a list of those who had priority seating on the stage. His papers do not indicate why he was absent, but it would have been out of character for Branton to miss such an event without good reason. His sons remember watching the march on television in a hotel room.[50] Richard, who had wanted very badly to attend, says his father told him there had been a decision among the civil rights leaders to keep someone who had intimate knowledge of the movement tucked away and safe in the event of violence at the march. While no corroboration of this decision has been found, the idea is not fantastical. Kennedy and others in his administration feared violence and were on alert for it, with troops readied just outside the city, if needed.

Although he had been hired as an administrator of the VEP and not its lawyer, circumstances did not allow Branton to remain in his Atlanta office. After Thurgood Marshall, he was one of the best-known Negro lawyers in the country. His office was often the first place called when civil rights workers funded by the VEP faced trouble, and there were few alternatives for legal representation. Even where there were volunteer attorneys available, Branton often was the only one who knew how the law in rural communities operated. He also had a couple of qualifications not shared by the few other Negro lawyers around. The light skin color and accent that allowed him easily to be mistaken for white would prove useful on numerous occasions.[51] Only a few instances of his legal work for the VEP have been memorialized and are included here.

Branton often appeared in court to represent civil rights workers. On two occasions, Branton was called to represent James Forman, later head of SNCC, against charges brought by Mississippi authorities. The first, in late August 1962, involved charges of loitering after Forman left a Clarksdale, Mississippi, COFO meeting. Wiley Branton was required to argue that one could not loiter in a moving car.[52] Of that case, Branton commented, "I had practiced law for about eleven years, . . . and I must admit I never heard of [that]." The second occurred on March 29, 1963, after Forman had been arrested with seven others for refusing to disperse during a march to the courthouse in Greenwood, Mississippi.[53] On another occasion, Branton successfully obtained the release of David Dennis, a CORE worker arrested in Clarksdale, Mississippi, [in 1962 or 1963] for refusing to say "sir" to a policeman who had stopped him for questioning and called him "nigger."[54]

Branton described his experience in representing a number of civil rights workers accused of various misfeasance in Indianola, Mississippi (precise date unknown), to the U.S. Civil Rights Commission in 1965. On that occasion, without hindrance from the chief of police or remonstrance from the judge, a white man sprayed Branton and his clients in the face with an insecticide, stating loudly, "I have got to de-niggarize this."[55]

Several of Branton's well-known "saves" occurred over the telephone with officials who were strangers to him. Andrew Young of SCLC called Branton "one of the most important and effective black civil rights attorneys during the Southern movement."[56] On one occasion, Young had been sent to obtain the release of COFO workers Fannie Lou Hamer, Annelle Ponder, Rosemary Freeman, Elvester Morris, and June Johnson, who had been arrested and beaten in Winona, Mississippi. While he was in the sheriff's office working up his courage to broach the subject, Wiley Branton telephoned and was able to cajole the sheriff into releasing the prisoners on bail into Young's care.[57]

In another case, two young voter registration workers, one white and one black, were jailed in one of the plantation counties of south Georgia. Branton called the sheriff, put on his best drawl and "good-old-boy" informality, and greeted him like an old friend. After quickly convincing the sheriff they knew each other, Branton was able to arrange bail for the workers.[58] In later years, Branton would tell this story, stating that it was the only time he was willing to devalue the life of a black man as compared with a white one, because it meant paying a lesser fine.

Branton was always available to others needing advice about conditions in the South. In June 1963, Jack Pratt, a lawyer for the Commission on Religion and Race of the National Council of Churches, needed Branton's help to work his way through the maze of the state's criminal justice system in an effort to obtain the release of Mississippi movement people.[59]

In April 1964, John Due, a VEP fieldworker, was arrested while gathering affidavits throughout Mississippi for submission to the U.S. Commission on Civil Rights. When the affidavits and his other identification were confiscated, Due paid a bond and was released, but was ordered to return for trial. He contacted Branton and followed Branton's advice to "ask [a representative of the U.S. Commission on Civil Rights] to be a witness or ascertain whether a member of the FBI would be present."[60]

President Kennedy's assassination in Dallas on November 22 provided a catalyst for the civil rights movement. President Lyndon B. Johnson used it to push a strong civil rights bill through Congress.[61] Johnson was careful to include civil rights leaders in his planning and the Civil Rights Act of 1964 was signed into law on July 2, 1964. At a private meeting immediately after the signing ceremony, Johnson met with Negro leaders at the White House, hoping to obtain their cooperation with implementation of the Act.[62] Wiley Branton did not attend the private meeting, and his calendar indicates he was in New York to attend a CUCRL meeting. Since that meeting was cancelled at the last minute to allow the civil rights leaders to attend the signing ceremony, it is not clear whether or not Branton also was present.[63]

As President Johnson's initiatives were beginning, Branton was winding up VEP operations. The VEP's original period of operation ended in fall 1964.[64] Branton had used all his skills during the thirty-month period. His legal ability and courage were required to travel into hostile territory and oppose illegal acts by local officials. His knowledge of the South, nurtured by his grandmother and strengthened by his law practice in Arkansas, had been instrumental in deciding what registration programs should be funded. His business skills allowed him to create a structure that complied with the documentation requirements of funding and to adjust that structure constantly as the needs of the workers and communities required.

Branton's "people" skills had been needed to keep civil rights leaders and workers focused on registration efforts. His ability to handle stress, developed primarily during the Little Rock crisis, was tested by the circumstances surrounding the VEP. His sense of humor must have been tickled by the absurdities involved. One example occurred soon after he rallied the Greenwood community to a concentrated registration effort after the shooting of James Travis in February 1963. Within a couple of months, he was exchanging letters with the rental company, arguing about whose responsibility it was to pay for damage to the car caused by the bullets.[65]

The VEP was a success, having registered or supported groups that registered 688,000 new Negro voters in eleven southern states. While that total was only just over 40 percent of those eligible, it was more than half the number registered in the South over the preceding twenty years. This was accomplished despite intense resistance by some state officials and with little support from the federal government. In testimony before the United States Commission on Civil Rights in February 1965,

Branton suggested that Negro civil rights would be respected only if the President forced the issue, to the extent of imposing martial law on the states if need be.[66]

On a personal level, the VEP brought Branton into contact with a wider audience that recognized his skills and ability to get things accomplished. CUCRL had kept Branton in constant communication with civil rights leaders during the 1963–1965 period, and it helped him to cement personal relationships with them.[67] Through CUCRL/WELD and the VEP, he was on a first-name basis with every Negro leader of importance in the country. His direct involvement with individual VEP registration efforts received substantial publicity, so ordinary Negro citizens across the country knew of him, as well.

Although he had expected to return to his Pine Bluff law practice at the end of his commitment to the VEP, the successful group effort he supervised had been a heady experience. It placed him at the center of a whirlwind and expanded his vision of what might be accomplished in civil rights. The 1964 Civil Rights Act promised equal rights, but he knew from experience that a "paper" right is insufficient without implementation and enforcement. The idea of handling individual cases that came to him haphazardly and one at a time must have seemed slow and unwieldy by comparison. He began looking for new challenges. They were not long in coming.

Branton's family had settled into life in Atlanta during Branton's time with the VEP. Richard, the oldest, was attending Georgia Tech University. Daughter Toni would soon begin college at Fisk University. Wylene was in high school, and Wiley Jr. was leaving home to attend a boarding high school called Millbrook School. The two youngest were in grade school. The family had found a church, the Union Baptist, where they were staunch members.

Branton was being considered favorably for the post of southeast regional director of the Office of Economic Opportunity, which would keep him in Atlanta, when he received a request from Vice President Hubert H. Humphrey to come to Washington, D.C. Humphrey had convinced President Lyndon B. Johnson to create a President's Council on Equal Opportunity, to be chaired by the vice president, that would coordinate implementation of the 1964 Civil Rights Act by government agencies and departments. Humphrey wanted Branton to help him achieve this. Branton accepted the offer.

In a farewell talk to the church congregation as they were leaving Atlanta in 1965, his children saw Branton cry for the first time.[68] In that talk, Branton noted that his life was changing significantly. His family was dispersing and they were leaving the church that had become part of their family.[69] While he expressed those regrets, Branton must have been excited about working with Vice President Hubert H. Humphrey on the government's approach to assuring civil rights. Branton had been critical of government action in Little Rock and in connection with the VEP. Now, he might be in a position to influence the government's response to the denial of civil rights. The move to Washington, D.C., would be a revelation to Branton.

Effa Stuart Wiley, maternal grandmother and role model–mentor to a young Wiley A. Branton. She demonstrated the importance of incorporating civil rights activism in one's life. *With permission of the Branton family.*

James A. Wiley, maternal grandfather, whose hard work and business sense helped to mold the characteristics that would make Wiley Branton so valuable to civil rights leaders. *With permission of the Branton family.*

The Wiley's family home at 1301 Alabama Street, Pine Bluff. Having his grandparents and uncles living next door gave young Wiley and his siblings the security of a close, extended family. *With permission of the Branton family.*

Leo A. Branton Sr. (*right*), and Joseph Wiley (Wiley's uncle, *left*) in front of what is thought to be one of the first cabs of the Branton Cab Company, about 1920. *With permission of the Branton family.*

Leo Branton and Pauline Wiley Branton about the time of their marriage in 1921. *With permission of the Branton family.*

Wiley A. Branton, anticipating his future. *With permission of the Branton family.*

Wiley A. Branton, about the time of his graduation from high school in 1941. *With permission of the Branton family.*

Wiley A. Branton, serving his country in the U.S. Army during World War II. *With permission of the Branton family.*

The Branton family, Christmas 1947, all safe home from the war. Leo Sr. and Pauline in front, *rear:* Leo Jr., Paul, Julia, Wiley, Sterling. *With permission of the Branton family.*

Wiley and Lucille Branton in the early 1950s. *With permission of the Branton family.*

Preparing petitions to Arkansas school districts following *Brown v. Board of Education* in summer 1955. *Left to right:* the Reverend J. C. Crenchaw (president, Little Rock NAACP), Wiley A. Branton (chair, NAACP State Conference, Legal Redress Committee), Mrs. Daisy Bates (president, Arkansas State Conference, NAACP), Mildred Bond (Roxborough) (NAACP fieldworker). *With permission of Janis F. Kearney, owner-publisher,* State Press News, *Pine Bluff, Arkansas.*

Wiley A. Branton holding photo of cross that was burned at the Wiley and Branton family plot, Bellwood Cemetery, Pine Bluff, during the 1957 Little Rock Central High Crisis. Another cross was burned on the lawn of his home. *With permission of the Branton family.*

Wiley A. Branton and Thurgood Marshall, director-general, NAACP Legal
Defense & Education Fund, Inc., outside the clerk's office, Eighth Circuit
Court of Appeals, St. Louis, August 4, 1958. *With permission of the* St. Louis
Post-Dispatch.

Wiley A. Branton, speaking before an audience in the late 1950s. *With permission of the Branton family.*

Wiley A. Branton and the Reverend Martin Luther King Jr. exhibiting a phonograph record of the 1963 March on Washington program that included King's "I have a Dream" speech. The recording was offered for sale by the Council of United Civil Rights Leaders to raise money for civil rights groups. *From the Wiley A. Branton Papers.*

Wiley A. Branton and Vice President Hubert H. Humphrey, date unknown,
worked together in 1965 for the President's Council on Equal Opportunity.
From the Wiley A. Branton Papers.

Wiley A. Branton and President Lyndon B. Johnson in a meeting at which the president requested Branton to become his "point person" on civil rights as a special assistant within the Civil Rights Division of the U.S. Department of Justice, September 24, 1965. *From the archives of the LBJ Library, image by Yoichi Okamoto.*

Wiley A. Branton, in the procession to his investiture as dean, Howard University School of Law, November 18, 1978. *From the Wiley A. Branton Papers.*

Wiley A. Branton family on the occasion of his investiture as dean, Howard University School of Law. *Left to right:* Wylene, Toni, Beverly, Wiley, Lucille, Debra, Richard, Wiley Jr. *With permission of the Branton family.*

Branton siblings in Pine Bluff, Homecoming Celebration, Arkansas Agricultural, Mechanical & Normal College, 1983. *Left to right:* Leo Jr., Sterling, Julia, Wiley, and Paul. *With permission of the Branton family.*

Wiley and Lucille Branton, about 1987. *With permission of the Branton family.*

Wiley A. Branton, with Senator Ted Kennedy on the left and Vernon E. Jordan Jr. on the right. Branton was being honored with the Whitney North Seymour Award by the National Lawyers Committee for Civil Rights Under Law and the Washington Lawyers' Committee for his dedication to civil rights and his contributions to the work of the Lawyers' Committee. *From the Wiley A. Branton Papers.*

Supreme Court Justice Thurgood Marshall and Wiley A. Branton, at the 115th Annual Banquet of the Bar Association of the District of Columbia, when Branton was named "Lawyer of the Year," 1986. *From the Wiley A. Branton Papers.*

Wiley A. Branton, partner, Sidley & Austin, Washington, D.C. This was Branton's final portrait. *From the Wiley A. Branton Papers.*

CHAPTER 9

Burrowing from Within
Working in the Johnson Administration

WILEY BRANTON BEGAN working with Vice President Hubert H. Humphrey for the President's Council on Equal Opportunity in April 1965, moving his family to Washington, D.C., shortly thereafter.[1] President Lyndon B. Johnson had asked Humphrey to review the federal government's implementation of the 1964 Civil Rights Act and to suggest improvements. Humphrey found more than eleven different government entities that had specific responsibilities under the Act and other government offices that had similar responsibilities.[2] This meant that assignments were unclear and officials could unintentionally duplicate the efforts of others or avoid acting altogether. Coordination clearly was needed.

The council, as proposed by Humphrey, would have no operational responsibilities. Instead, it would "perform planning, evaluative, advisory, and coordinating functions."[3] Humphrey's plan gave the council authority to require regular reports from all agencies on how they were working to implement the Civil Rights Act. Council members would review the reports, focus on specific problems, and move resources and personnel where needed to assure the swift pace of government action. President Johnson approved Humphrey's plan in Executive Order 11197 on February 5, 1965.[4]

Humphrey was chair of the council, and its members were cabinet officers and agency heads. Since Humphrey could not personally supervise committee activities, however, an executive director was required. Branton's experience, reputation, and credibility within the Negro community made him ideal for the position. He had created, from scratch, the mechanism that made the Voter Education Project a success. He could be expected to do the same with the President's Council. In fact, there were probably very few people in the country who could match his qualifications.

Use of a special council to focus on particular presidential initiatives was not a new idea. President Harry Truman had appointed a Presidential Committee on Civil Rights in 1946 to investigate and recommend steps "to secure racial justice in the [southern] region."[5] The committee's report led Truman to propose "the first civil rights legislative package . . . to Congress since Reconstruction."[6] President Dwight D. Eisenhower had created the President's Committee on Equal Employment Opportunity, which required federal contractors to "search aggressively for qualified minority applicants" in an effort to increase the hiring of minorities.[7]

Humphrey was most interested in the 1964 Civil Rights Act's application to equal employment and education, and he wanted the council to establish a process that would receive and handle complaints from across the country. As executive director of the council, Branton would be the staff conduit that channeled citizen complaints to appropriate agencies. He would work with civil rights groups to assure their involvement in changes created by the Act. Given his existing close ties with these groups and his broad knowledge of the situation in the South, Branton also could advise Humphrey and the administration on local community concerns.

In an address to the Fifty-sixth Annual NAACP Convention on June 30, 1965, Branton described the council as "a clearing house for ideas—ideas that can be put into action to facilitate and improve the national effort to remove the ominous threads of discrimination from the fabric of society."[8] Soon after his appointment, Branton began weekly reporting to Humphrey on the activities of council staff, its various subcommittees, and council members.[9] Portions of these memos were sent virtually unchanged by the vice president to the president.[10]

It may have been during this period, when Branton's exposure to new groups and individuals expanded exponentially, that he developed his habit of keeping a list of names at the back of his pocket calendar. When he was scheduled for a meeting or had to give a speech, he would review that list in advance to remind himself of whom he might encounter. This made it easier to connect a name with a face.[11] His daughter, Beverly, also mentioned that the children were trained to introduce themselves whenever they traveled with their father, so that Branton could hear the person's response and be able to greet them by name himself.[12]

Securing Branton's services for the council was considered a major coup, particularly in the Negro community. *Jet* magazine called Branton "the new 'wonder man' in the LBJ Administration in Washington, [assigned] 'to put flesh on the skeleton' [of the Civil Rights Act]." It predicted that Branton "not only will become a major advisor to Vice President Humphrey but the President will look to him for immediate action on coordination of a huge government program which touches school integration, housing, the anti-poverty set-up and the employment programs."[13] Dr. Martin Luther King Jr. sent a congratulatory telegram to Branton, stating, "It goes without saying that this is a most significant appointment and I can think of no one who could do the job more competently and superbly as you. Your unswerving devition [*sic*] to the cause of civil rights, your tremendous effective ability to work with all civil rights groups and your great talents uniquely equip you to do this job. We are all very proud of you."[14]

Branton's files indicate that he took his charge seriously. He scheduled speaking engagements across the country to explain what the council and the federal government were doing to promote civil rights. His exhortation to those attending the NAACP annual conference that year is typical. He said, "We have torn down barriers; now we must do what is even harder—we must build. We must educate the illiterate, train the unemployed, invigorate the ghettos, and bring new hope to the forgotten. It is a job of grand dimensions and great demands. It requires the acceptance of distinct responsibility. But the civil rights struggle has no relevance for the child in the inferior school, the family in the slum, or the man in the relief line until it helps them obtain a better education, better home, better job, and better medical care."[15]

Branton received all complaints of discrimination sent to the council, reviewed them, and forwarded those having merit to the appropriate government office. He maintained contact with that office until a resolution was developed. If he determined there was no basis or evidence for a complaint, he dealt with the complainant directly.[16] For many Negroes with complaints about discrimination, Branton WAS the federal government. In a 1969 interview, he recalled that the council was "going great guns" a few months after its creation, with "agencies really jumping and moving trying to do something about civil rights."[17]

Although President Johnson had intended to let the 1964 Civil Rights Act carry the burden of his civil rights agenda and to switch his focus to poverty programs in 1965, reports on voting patterns from his 1964 election led him to add voting rights legislation to his 1965 agenda. Like Kennedy, he recognized the value of additional Negro voters.[18]

The proposed bill moved quickly through Congress after Alabama state troopers used "clubs, with horses, with whips, and with tear gas" to subdue a voting rights march led by Dr. Martin Luther King Jr. in Selma, Alabama, on March 7.[19] Shock at the violence exhibited on television news programs brought support for the bill from the public and representatives of both political parties. President Johnson signed the Voting Rights Act of 1965 on August 6, and Branton was invited to attend the ceremony.[20]

According to his calendar, Branton did not attend the ceremony. Instead, he was on the job, holding meetings with several people. This seems surprising, given his intense involvement in the fight for voting rights. But Branton was a practical man. The ceremony would be crowded and there was no special reason to be there. It was better to continue his current work than to be one of hundreds milling around in the audience. His files contain a memorandum dated August 6 to Vice President Humphrey detailing various issues with which the council was active.

The Voting Rights Act gave federal officials authority to act against the intimidation and illegal restrictions that kept Negroes from the polls in the South. It was the kind of protection Branton had wanted during the VEP, and his experience and expertise suddenly became even more valuable to the Johnson administration.

He was consulted by John W. Macy Jr., chair of the U.S. Civil Service Commission, which had been investigating voting rights abuse and now had the power to act.[21] William L. Taylor, of the U.S. Commission on Civil Rights, even suggested to President Johnson that the council was the appropriate agency to coordinate and implement programs to disseminate voting information and provide voter education as an aid to implementing the Act.[22] If the recommendation had been accepted, Branton again would be in the middle of voting rights action at the highest levels. It was not to be.

Six weeks later, on September 22, President Johnson surprised Vice President Humphrey by abolishing the President's Council on Equal Opportunity, returning responsibility for civil rights implementation to the Department of Justice and the various government agencies.[23] In other words, things were back where they had been at the beginning of the year.

The whole story behind Johnson's action never was made clear. Some speculated that he was concerned Humphrey might receive too much credit for the administration's civil rights work.[24] Others believed Johnson was reacting to Humphrey's disagreement with him about the Vietnam War.[25] As early as May 14, Johnson had complained to his staff about "leaks" to the press for which he blamed Humphrey, and he told his aides that Humphrey was not to do anything without White House instructions.[26] Humphrey himself put blame on Joseph Califano, of the president's staff, who "was smart and able, liked power, and did not want to share it."[27]

On September 24, President Johnson announced the changes. Reaction was negative. Humphrey had long been known for innovative civil rights activism, while Attorney General Nicholas deB. Katzenbach, who led the Department of Justice, was thought to be too wedded to a "methodical [and] legalistic approach."[28] Newspapers reported that civil rights groups were concerned that the changes would lessen the government's involvement in civil rights.[29]

The president's action might have left Branton stranded, particularly given the outcome of a September 21 dinner cruise meeting between Humphrey and several of the civil rights leaders. The event was arranged by Branton and was intended to provide an opportunity for "off the record" discussions concerning civil rights. Those attending included the vice president; Branton and other staff from the council; the Reverend Martin Luther King Jr. and Andrew Young (SCLC); Jack Greenberg (NAACP Legal Education and Defense Fund); Clarence Mitchell (NAACP's D.C. office); Whitney Young Jr. (National Urban League); Stephen Currier (Taconic Foundation); the Reverend Walter Fauntroy and Floyd McKissick (SNCC); Louis Martin (National Democratic Committee); and Lloyd Garrison (civil rights attorney).[30]

The "frank" discussion became heated and Branton became involved in an exchange with Clarence Mitchell, the NAACP's Washington, D.C., point man. Branton later was accused in print of having said that

"Negroes should be thankful and grateful for the extraordinary gains of the Johnson administration . . . [and] should take stock of the advances and solidify them rather than continue agitation."[31] The accusation generated a letter clarifying Branton's remarks from Whitney M. Young Jr., Jack Greenberg, Floyd B. McKissick, Martin Luther King Jr., and Stephen R. Currier to John H. Johnson, editor and publisher of *Jet* magazine.[32] Mitchell and the NAACP's John Morsell did not sign.

Branton did not publicly deny or affirm the incident. In a note to a friend, however, Branton denied the statements attributed to him, and called it an "attempt to discredit [him]."[33] Branton's files contain many similar letters written during this period. He was hurt by the accusation and took every opportunity to "clear his name" privately with those persons whose opinion he valued. Many years later, Branton spoke with author Taylor Branch, stating that the argument grew out of matters that occurred during his VEP years when, he believed, the NAACP had inflated its voter registration figures in order to "boost its share of available [VEP] funds."[34]

The fallout of the September 21 meeting did not affect Branton's prospects with the administration. President Johnson's awareness of Branton's prestige kept Branton from being summarily fired when the council was abolished. Attorney General Katzenbach had cautioned the president that his action in abolishing the council could cause "a political problem unless another important assignment is found for Wiley Branton."[35] His concern was heeded. On September 24, Johnson announced that Branton would become his personal representative on civil rights at the Department of Justice.[36]

Branton was ambivalent about the shift. Being the president's special assistant sounded pretty important, but he had no great admiration for the Justice Department. In a letter to a Pine Bluff friend, he said, "I have not physically moved to the Department of Justice yet, as I want to take a good, long, hard look at everything involved before making that move and this includes some serious consideration as to whether or not I want to return to the active practice of law which I am really beginning to miss."[37] His consideration of the job resulted in a statement in the *New York Times* saying he was "willing to try the Justice Department job and see if [I am] permitted to put some of [my] ideas into effect."[38] After supervising the closing down of council activities, helping its staff to find other jobs in the government, and working on a previously scheduled national conference on civil rights, Branton showed up for work at the Justice offices on November 19, 1965.

In his position with the President's Council, Branton had acted as a facilitator, conduit, and promoter for the Johnson administration. The credibility he had developed with Negroes throughout his career, and particularly with the VEP, gave luster to his statements about what the administration was doing with civil rights. Katzenbach's belief that firing Branton would be a bad move probably was accurate. Branton's name recognition and reputation remained strong with Negroes across the South.

Branton also had new skills to offer. In less than five months with the council, he had enhanced his knowledge in a new arena. The intermediary role he played within the council gave him an intimate understanding of the inner workings of government departments and introduced him to many of the people who performed the work.

President Johnson told the media that Branton would focus on voting rights, conducting a "'full and vigorous and swift' program of voter registration for Negroes in the South."[39] The day after the announcement of Branton's transfer to the Department of Justice, White House press secretary Bill D. Moyers was quoted as saying, "The President told Branton that he considered voter registration 'the paramount concern of the Federal Government at the present time.'"[40]

Despite these grandiose descriptions of his role, it was never made clear to Branton precisely what he was to do. When Branton asked Attorney General Katzenbach for guidance on what Katzenbach would expect him to do,[41] he received no response.

Ramsey Clark, who was assistant attorney general for civil rights at the time of Branton's appointment and later became attorney general, said that Branton did not "fit" in the hierarchy of the department. He was too experienced and knowledgeable to become one of the many assistant U.S. attorneys, yet all the higher-level positions for which he was appropriate were occupied by good men.[42]

As Branton put it, he "was technically *in* the Civil Rights Division, [but] was not *of* the Civil Rights Division."[43] This awkward situation was apparent to some outsiders. An article in the Washington *Post,* analyzing the state of the civil rights movement, noted that the council's "energetic Negro director, Wiley Branton, was ... dispatched to a quiet office in Justice, ... [where] telephone operators didn't have his extension for a while and ... he has been given little to do."[44]

Branton was somewhat of an entrepreneur, however. He "made" a job for himself, attempting to fit into the existing program in his own way. That path turned out to look very much like what he had been doing with the council. He funneled complaints to various agencies, acted as liaison between the federal government and civil rights groups, educated groups around the country about the government's efforts to implement the 1964 and 1965 Acts, and advised various department employees, including the attorney general, about special situations in local communities.[45]

One example of his informal advocacy within the administration occurred when he and Roger Wilkins met with an official in the Department of Agriculture to discuss the idea of the government's providing food stamps to low-income families and individuals. The two men made their suggestion, and the official responded that "we just couldn't do that, because people who made that little money were really not bright enough to handle food stamps. They weren't discriminating enough, they couldn't distinguish things, they couldn't see things clearly."

As Wilkins recalled it, Branton then "sat back" and told the story of how the prejudice and stupidity of a Florida county sheriff had allowed Branton to obtain the release of a young Negro man who had been jailed illegally. After completing his story, Wilkins said, Branton "just sits quietly and he looks at this guy. The guy looks back, and he said, 'I get your point. I get your point, Mr. Branton.' And the Agriculture Department signed off on the food stamps [program] because Wiley told the story about a very dumb white man."[46] Branton's point was obvious, that stupidity was not limited to the poor and was not a reason to deny federal benefits to them.

Conditions for a federal focus on civil rights were changing during this period. The Vietnam War was taking more and more of President Johnson's time and energy. Its cost was reducing the amount of money Congress was willing to devote to civil rights, particularly since black communities across the country were exploding with riots in protest against the government.[47] Attitudes toward the government and white society were changing, particularly among young blacks. No one seemed to know why. John Lewis thought the bad experiences of thousands of young men and women during the 1964 Freedom Summer in Mississippi were catalysts for "a crisis of spirit [and] faith in the fundamental promises and premises of the American system" that resulted in the Black Power movement and an increasing distrust of government.[48]

The author Charles M. Payne, in discussing the situation in Mississippi, saw the changes as resulting from the Civil Rights Movement's successes. In Payne's view, "It had become more difficult to say what the movement was trying to do."[49] For many black people, "The movement was about freedom, not just civil rights. At the very least, their conception of freedom would have included decent jobs, housing, and education." The programs established with government funding "departed from the SNCC-COFO-FDP [Freedom Democratic Party] tradition that the poor have to define their own self-interest," and moved erratically and too slowly for many.[50] Though Payne was speaking of Mississippi, his conclusions seem applicable to the situation in the rest of the country. Whatever the reason for the changes in attitude, riots began occurring in 1965 and became a constant concern for President Johnson.

Branton, too, was changing his mind about how much could be expected from the federal government on civil rights. His position in the Justice Department exposed him to the inner workings of government and the myriad considerations that impelled it to move cautiously in any area. At forty-three, Branton also was maturing in his own thinking about the division of responsibility between citizen and state and federal government, and understanding that the use of force might not provide the sort of positive change in society that he desired.[51]

Within the office, Branton "would raise hell about things, trying to prod people to make decisions or to send in examiners or observers, or this, that and the other. Sometimes I won my point; sometimes, I didn't."[52] But he also spent "most of his time traveling in the South, checking into motels, introducing himself to local Negro leaders and asking them what they [were] doing to interest Negroes in registering to vote."[53]

Branton's speech before the National Bar Association's annual convention on July 25, 1967, is representative. He celebrated the changes in American society that made "[t]he picture look unusually bright and challenging to Negro lawyers today." Black lawyers were critically needed, "especially in the South."

For those lawyers who were doing well, he had a special message. "Yes, some of us feel that we have escaped the problem, that we have achieved a victory, that we are now in the mainstream of all the fine things which America has to offer. But I can tell you today that it's a mighty polluted stream and while we can take pride in our many accomplishments and in our great progress toward freedom, the plain simple truth is that none of us are really free until all of us are free. . . . In fact, for those of us with responsibility, we must not live on past words and former positions of good intent. We must rather dedicate ourselves to the action which the times require and conscience demands. . . . I hope that we can see that our job is to make sure that the vast resources of government are mobilized for action, . . . which demands your commitment, too, as lawyers and judges and civic leaders."[54]

Nevertheless, Branton was finding his job frustrating. He could advise an official of a situation needing correction, but had to rely on that official's attention, understanding, and action for any change. He had access to power, but lacked any real authority of his own. Later, he would recall that he had "recommended time and again that action be taken" without any result.[55] Although he was able to cobble together activities that allowed him to feel useful and a part of civil rights progress, his role provided no concrete achievements.[56] After a year, when Katzenbach was named undersecretary of state, his departure offered Branton an opportunity to leave federal employment.[57]

Branton sent a note to Joseph Califano, the president's aide, indicating he believed he had served his purpose in the administration.[58] Califano informed the president that both Katzenbach and Ramsey Clark thought Branton had done a good job and might have continued usefulness to the administration. They suggested an appointment to the Equal Employment Opportunity Commission as a member or as its general counsel.[59] Califano told the president that Branton would leave without bitterness if no other position were forthcoming. Johnson suggested they try to find something else for Branton.[60]

Branton remained with the Justice Department for another year, working under Ramsey Clark when Clark became attorney general. There is no indication precisely how this occurred. Branton had more in common with Clark, who was more receptive to Branton's advice and ideas than was Katzenbach. For example, Clark was more willing to

use the Voting Rights Act assertively, for example, sending federal regis-
trars into an area rather than negotiating with the local white structure.[61]
Clark also appreciated what Branton was doing for the department,
believing Branton's greatest skills were his ability to get along and talk
with both established and new, younger black leaders.[62] Clark spoke with
Branton soon after Branton sent his memo to the president, and may
have urged that he remain.[63]

It also is possible that Vice President Humphrey, who wrote to
Branton on December 2, stating that there was still much to do in civil
rights, was the deciding factor.[64] In a memorandum to one of his aides,
Humphrey wrote, "Wiley is an important figure. We should not let him
leave Washington. There must be a place found for him worthy of his
talents. . . . I want to keep Wiley in our set-up."[65]

Although there was more respect shown him during that second year,
Branton's duties remained pretty much the same. In the end, Ramsey Clark
thought it was "hard for Wiley to be happy [at Justice], because he needed
to have more consistent, direct, responsibility than to be in what was more
of a consultant role."[66] Much later, Clark compared Branton favorably with
Dr. Martin Luther King Jr., saying, "Wiley was always serene in the sense
that—I never saw him lose his cool under all this tension and pressure, or
his judgment. He had a gentleness that was deceptive, because he was very
strong."[67]

On October 12, 1967, Branton wrote a letter to President Johnson,
stating that he had finished his assignments at the Justice Department,
and announcing he was leaving to become executive director of the
United Planning Organization, the anti-poverty effort for the District
of Columbia.[68] On October 18, the president invited him to the White
House "for a thank you for a job well done."[69]

Over the next four years, Branton would hold two positions that
demonstrated different aspects of the ebbing civil rights "movement" that
had carried him so far from his roots: the United Planning Organization
and the Alliance for Labor Action. First came the United Planning
Organization.

CHAPTER 10

Last Gasp at Direct Action
The United Planning Organization and the Alliance for Labor Action

IN MOVING TO the United Planning Organization (UPO), Branton was entering a different world, one that provided him with a kind of challenge he had not faced before. All his life, he had taken advantage of the opportunities presented to him, following his goal of changing circumstances for black citizens. Branton believed that the country's poor, if education and job training programs were made available to them, would respond in large numbers. They would use those programs to lift themselves and their families out of poverty. During the next sixteen months, he would learn that the mere availability of tools for advancement in society was not enough for many in need.

The United Planning Organization had had a long and troubled history. When Branton joined it, UPO had been without a leader for six months and was involved in internal dissention concerning its efforts to provide services to the community in a manner that involved members of the community. Branton recalled that "morale was at a very low ebb."[1] Branton initially had not been interested in leading the organization but, as he became more aware of its mission, he was intrigued. When he met with the search committee, he charmed and impressed people on both ends of the political spectrum.[2] Despite his belief that the job would involve a "thankless" role, he decided to accept the challenge.[3] Branton's appointment was announced on October 4, and he began work on October 16, 1967.[4]

Branton could not say he had not been warned about the difficulties he would face. In May 1967, well before his interview and appointment to the post, Branton received a copy of an article by William Raspberry, a columnist with the *Washington Post,* analyzing the situation at UPO and speculating about the demands that would be placed on its next director. Raspberry predicted that "the only man likely to [take over] would be one with enough brilliance to succeed in spite of nearly insurmountable problems, one who is willing to risk marring his record with failure to accomplish whatever good he can or one who in his optimistic naiveté believes that the war on poverty was meant to be won."[5] A personal note says, "Glad to be of service, Genius!" and is signed "Bill."

Conditions within the country had changed since the successful efforts of the VEP. The alienation of young blacks across the country had led to the rise of the "Black Power" movement and to riots in major cities. The National Advisory Commission on Civil Disorders, known as the Kerner Commission, reported in March 1967 that, despite burgeoning poverty programs, the country was "two societies, separate and unequal."[6]

No one seemed to have an answer for the times, neither the President of the United States nor the traditional civil rights leaders.[7] President Johnson announced that he would not run for a second term on March 31, 1968. Richard M. Nixon, who would be elected president in November, did not have the same commitment to ameliorating poverty and the problems it created.

Despite these disheartening conditions, the election of 1968 also demonstrated the effect of the decades-long voting rights efforts made by Branton and others. The number of elected black officials in the South increased from fewer than 100 to 385. By 1972, the number had increased to 873.[8] Although the right to vote did not magically change circumstances for many blacks, Branton would always feel proud of his role in establishing that right.

The United Planning Organization began as a private venture of the Ford and Meyer Foundations to coordinate and assist in meeting human services needs in the District of Columbia.[9] When Congress passed the Equal Opportunity Act of 1964, the Act provided funds for Community Action Programs that would involve community members in developing self-help programs tailored to the particular needs of that community.[10] The goal was to create opportunities and "produce social change through participatory democracy."[11] The United Planning Organization was selected as the Community Action Program for the District of Columbia.[12]

By the time Branton came into the UPO, three years after the Equal Opportunity Act was passed, problems with the Act's goals and operation had begun to surface. While the idea of involving the poor in their own uplifting was a fine one, it had unintended consequences. The Community Action Programs created a new social services bureaucracy headquartered in local communities. There were internal conflicts, as community members often disagreed with each other on what was needed by the community. The programs also competed with existing city and state agencies and private welfare groups for federal dollars. There was a perceived loss of "coherence" among black communities in their goals,[13] and this weakened traditional Negro political power and threatened social service agencies.[14]

In hindsight, this outcome was inevitable. One community's answers for bettering its lot were likely to differ from those of other communities, even in the same town. Many of the more militant civil rights groups that had performed successful grass-roots voter registration organizing work in small towns across the South turned their attention to the cities.[15] The tactics of protest they used were transferable, but the discipline and control demonstrated in the VEP activities and derived from hard experience were not. City poor with urban problems were a much different group from the rural poor.

Aside from these difficulties, there was decreasing support in Congress and from local government for the idea of handing over control of significant federal funds to local communities.[16] The inexperience of poverty groups with handling the documentation and paperwork required by granting authorities made it difficult for the government to keep track of how the federal grant money was being used across the country. These problems were multiplied in the District of Columbia by the fact that several different congressional committees directly authorized and supervised the D.C. budget.

When President Johnson's efforts to provide self-rule within the District of Columbia were successful, a new mayor and city council took over in August 1967.[17] Walter Washington, a black resident of the District and chair of New York mayor John Lindsay's City Housing Authority, was appointed as the new mayor. President Johnson also appointed black residents to five of nine council positions, giving the District a majority black governing body for the first time since Reconstruction.[18]

Although Branton was pleased about the governmental reorganization, which would give District residents more control over how their city was run, the new government ran into problems.[19] Mayor Washington found the civic leadership of the District splintered, which made it difficult to obtain coordination and unity in approaching issues. This, and the council's inexperience, led to a certain amount of chaos.

A number of newspaper articles conveyed the turmoil as it related to the UPO. For example, there was open warfare between an ad hoc Committee for Citizen Participation in Model Cities, created by some UPO staffers in their spare time, and representatives of the District's twenty Neighborhood Planning Councils, established by one of the District's former commissioners, over who would be involved in the District's participation in the federal Model Cities project.[20]

Neighborhood Planning Councils also were disputing with the Metropolitan Citizens Advisory Council, created by UPO with delegates from the city's impoverished areas, about how to use leftover "summer enrichment program" money awarded to the District by the Office of Equal Opportunity.[21] UPO's board chair was charging the Federal Housing Administration with being too rigid in its approval and funding of housing development proposals by the Housing Development Corporation (a UPO-sponsored entity).[22]

There was wrangling going on within the UPO, as well. For example, a lengthy news story disclosed struggles between the chair of the Community Improvement Corporation (CIC), a UPO-created citizens' group, and the director of the Near Northeast Poverty program (also established by UPO). Apparently, the director had been instrumental in fostering creation of the CIC, which then turned on him in a struggle for control over the $279,058 in funding involved.[23]

Branton called his new job "the most challenging thing I have undertaken."[24] His talent for working with disparate groups and personalities to coordinate efforts in a common cause would be put to the test. His government experience and contacts might help reduce conflict between the District and the federal agencies that supplied much of UPO's funding. Whether he could reduce the UPO's internal power struggles was in question, since his reputation tied him to the more traditional leaders and approaches to civil rights and he might be viewed with suspicion by younger blacks. Branton's job was made more difficult by the riots that occurred in cities like Detroit and Newark during the summer of 1967, which led some within the federal government to reconsider any support of anti-poverty programs.[25] Branton was walking into a hornets' nest just as the country was beginning to sour on the War on Poverty.

One of his first moves, he told reporters, would be to learn more about UPO. In late 1967, "most of the key personnel [at UPO] were white," which had been the case from UPO's inception, and Branton wanted to increase the proportion of black personnel at UPO, particularly at the higher levels of operation.[26] He was well aware of the growing concern about "black nationalists," but believed that their rhetoric frequently masked the "continuation of programs supported for years by other organizations, under different names." The "talk" he heard did not scare Branton. He was, Branton said, bringing to the job a "real commitment and severe concern for the problems of poor people," but he believed in changes that created "race pride" rather than separatism and violence.[27]

As he had shown in both the VEP and in his government work, Branton believed that the federal government had some responsibility for ridding the country of poverty and its consequences. However, he also believed that every individual shared in that responsibility, and it was his personal creed. To members of the Mt. Zion Methodist Church, he said, "I personally act as an optimist because I cannot act at all as a pessimist. One often feels helpless in the face of confusion of the times, of such a mass of apparently uncontrollable events and experiences to live through, to attempt to understand and, if at all possible, to give order to. But one must not withdraw from the task if one has some small thing to offer; if one does, one does so at the risk of diminishing humanity."[28]

UPO's basic framework was not so different from that of the Voter Education Project Branton had created in 1962. The organization received grant money, obtained or developed proposals for programs that would improve economic opportunities for District residents, and either implemented those programs deemed worthy or made grants to other entities for their implementation. There was, however, a huge difference. The VEP was a new entity that had an annual total budget of less than $300,000 over a thirty-month period. In directing UPO, Branton took over an existing agency that had an annual budget of almost $33 million, employed over two thousand people and supervised indirectly the activities of another two thousand who worked in entities funded by UPO.[29]

As Branton described it a year later, "You could get up at 8 on a weekday morning, start out in a car on a tour of our activities, and . . . go until the end of the day and still not see all of them."[30] The scope of UPO's operations meant that Branton, however much he might wish otherwise, had to rely on staff for much of his information. He had to deal with an existing structure that was used to a certain way of operating. He also had an active board of directors that had final authority over what was decided. This was very different from VEP, where the structure was his to create, his staff was small, and his authority virtually complete.

Branton's appointment was well received by the District's new mayor, although Branton was very quickly faced with an example of the conflict between UPO's interests and those of other D.C. agencies. In a December 14, 1967, letter to Mayor Washington, he questioned a proposed program that would create a public-private corporate venture within the District. In his opinion, the proposal duplicated some services offered by UPO and a similar program conducted by the Department of Labor. The new venture also did not appear to involve the local community in its decision making.[31]

Branton turned his attention to reorganization efforts that he hoped would make the management and oversight structure of UPO more efficient. In a January 19 interview, Branton announced a reorganization of UPO after three years of "trial and error" as part of the War on Poverty. He wanted to decentralize numerous specialized programs currently providing services from only one office of the District and, under a new Neighborhood Services Program, establish offices where a variety of services "from job placement to day care to health care" would be available in numerous locations. District residents would have to visit only one office to make use of a variety of social services. Branton was quick to say that there would be no decrease in available services or in staff to administer the program.[32] That assurance may not have allayed either a normal concern about change or the preexisting tensions among the staff, which would explode a few months later.

In addition to reorganizing UPO's operations, as top-level white personnel left, Branton used his contacts to fill their positions with skilled black individuals. This raised objections from some existing staff and UPO board members. When he hired a black deputy executive director, UPO's treasurer and a couple of board members resigned. Historically, a black man had held the top position at UPO but the chief deputy had been white. Even a supportive Executive Committee had its doubts.

However, Branton convinced them that it would be hard for UPO to motivate an almost entirely black poor population, if it did not see competent black people in charge.[33] Branton believed in providing role models for the community he served. He also knew there were many highly qualified blacks stuck in lower-level government jobs because the private sector provided them with no real alternatives. He believed that if he recruited these individuals for UPO, he might shake the complacency of government agencies by demonstrating that valuable employees had alternative employment opportunities.

President Johnson's January 1968 State of the Union address to Congress admitted that the Great Society could not be built in a day and indicated a major shift in the direction and budget of the War on Poverty. Funding to several UPO programs was reduced and monies reallocated.[34] The federal government began to "prepackage" specific initiatives that then were given to organizations like UPO to oversee, eliminating the original idea of allowing the communities to decide what was needed.

Branton was not happy with these changes. He believed they could result in loss of UPO's independence and would limit the ability of its staff and their service communities to pressure city government for necessary changes in the way public services were provided.[35] Branton was not the only critic of this aspect of congressional action. There was a general belief that local politicians were "unconcerned about the poor or fearful of their growing demands for better schools, jobs, housing and recreation."[36]

Branton and the UPO staff were working their way through these changes when, on Thursday, April 4, 1968, the Reverend Martin Luther King Jr. was assassinated in Memphis, Tennessee.[37] Riots broke out across the country. The District of Columbia, which had escaped the violence of the previous summer, was immediately caught up in it. Within an hour of the first news reports of King's assassination, crowds of young people were roaming the commercial center of the black community. Overnight, the "roaming" expanded to include the breaking of store windows, then to looting and some threats of physical violence. The next day, conditions were still unsettled and authorities had not asserted control over the situation.

At 4:02 P.M. on Friday, President Johnson signed a proclamation and an executive order that brought the military in to restore order. By 4:40 P.M., the first army troops were brought into the District.[38] At 5:20 P.M., Mayor Washington declared a curfew that exempted only "police, firemen, doctors, nurses, and sanitation workers." Over the next week, over fourteen thousand troops were used to quell the riot. On Tuesday, April 9, Branton was among those who attended King's funeral in Atlanta, Georgia. By Wednesday, the riots were over, although the curfew was lifted only gradually. It was finally dissolved on Friday, April 12. More than one hundred cities were, like Washington, engulfed with violence.[39]

Some of UPO's Neighborhood Development Programs were located in areas where the worst rioting occurred. On the third day of the riots, UPO's Neighborhood Development Program staff sent its youth directors out into the streets to help calm down the teenagers who had begun the demonstrations that led to the riot. As things calmed down and control was restored, UPO staff tackled the aftermath of trying to find food, shelter, and jobs for their client population that had been burned out during the riots.[40] Later analysis disclosed that about twenty thousand residents of the immediate area, one of every eight persons between the ages of ten and fifty-nine, had participated in the riot in some way.[41]

Less than a week later, on Thursday, April 18, 1968, the executive offices of UPO were the scene of a "work stoppage" demonstration by UPO employees.[42] It is not clear precisely what precipitated the protest, although the stresses created by Branton's organizational changes and the clean-up efforts following the riots earlier that month certainly would have played a part. It began while Branton was out of the office.

In an interview given shortly after his departure from UPO, Branton described the demonstration. He had returned to the office, he said, where he faced a crowd of about two hundred people. At first, Branton "stood and listened to several of the speeches." He decided that the complaints were vague and had little relevance to UPO, "except that every once in a while they would make the statement that the agency was not relevant to the problems of the African American community."[43]

A newspaper article stated that the leaders of the demonstration charged UPO with "not [being] responsive to the needs of Washington's low-income Negroes," a result of its taking a "bureaucratic" position. They cited the firing of a staff member who refused to accept reassignment to another office as evidence that the UPO was turning away from "planning with strong community participation."[44] A later memorandum from one staff member to Branton stated that some of the staff demonstrators believed the riots themselves were evidence that UPO had not been successful in changing conditions and attitudes among the poor.[45]

Branton recollected that when the lunch period ended and they were on company time, he asked to speak. His words were thoughtful. He had maintained control of his emotions during periods of greater stress, when his physical safety was at risk. Here, he had had time while listening to the speeches to decide how he would handle the situation. As his son stated in an interview long after that event, the people leading the demonstration had chosen the wrong approach to convince Branton of a need for change.[46] They could not intimidate Wiley Branton. His strength had been tempered by death threats during both the Little Rock case and his time with the Voter Education Project, and he would not stand for anarchy.

Branton listed the problems he saw facing UPO and some of the remedies he had put into place since his appointment to the job. He pointed out that none of those leading the demonstration and speaking about Black Power had "ever approached [him] about anything whatsoever," and went on to deliver his opinions about the methods and practices that were being used by Black Power adherents on the payroll.[47] While some in the audience left following Branton's comments, a few continued to urge action against UPO. Branton recalled that one man suggested burning down every UPO center and a woman speaker implied that anyone abandoning the demonstration would suffer personal violence and bodily harm.[48]

Branton did not indicate how the day's event finally ended, except to say that notices of immediate termination were delivered to nine people the next day. UPO had a reputation of never firing anyone, so his action was a surprise to many. Grievance hearing procedures were established and the terminations were upheld. Several suits were filed against Branton and UPO, but were "thrown out of court."[49]

Paul Pryde, an upper-level UPO staff person, later suggested that the demonstration resulted from an internal disagreement about program goals. Some believed UPO should have a primary focus on community organization for political purposes, while others believed in organizing communities in order to deliver better social services. King's death and the riots had worsened that division. Pryde hoped that Branton would talk with the different factions in an effort to resolve the differences.[50] Another staff person who resigned following the demonstration told Branton that it resulted from "staff concern, frustration and anxiety which long predate your leadership."[51]

Branton could not have been sanguine about the situation. Yet, in a lengthy statement on June 27, 1968, eight months after he began as director and two months after the work stoppage, he focused only on UPO's accomplishments. Branton noted the way in which UPO's Neighborhood Development Programs had led to independent community entities that were administering services to residents and had influenced the appointment of neighborhood representatives to city agency boards.[52]

He praised the Neighborhood Legal Services Project, the "first large-scale program of [its] type in the nation," which operated nine offices throughout the District as a "delegate agency of UPO." He described nine credit unions and a Consumer Action Program that were helping to educate the community in handling its money. He mentioned other programs that helped budding entrepreneurs, families and children, and the elderly with housing, child and health care, and youth programs. Branton was particularly proud of several employment programs that covered the gamut of training and recruitment, and other services, like child care, designed to aid workers in maintaining employment.[53] Another item for pride was a grant, over a period of years, of more than $18 million to establish and operate community schools.[54]

Finally, Branton listed additional goals for the organization: improving coordination with existing city and federal entities, expanding existing programs, and discussing new ways in which to match the unemployed with jobs. In his only reference to recent events, Branton said that "not nearly enough [had been accomplished], for the expressions of anger and frustration of our unemployed and underemployed let us know how awfully much remains to be done."[55]

The riots combined with other events to reduce congressional support for President Johnson's 1968 Civil Rights Bill and the funding of poverty programs.[56] Congressmen had reacted badly to having to make their way through the "smoke from burning buildings" in getting to their offices during the riots.[57]

In August, a Poor People's March on Washington, conceived by Dr. Martin Luther King Jr. and implemented after his death by the Reverend Ralph Abernathy, caused new concern about violence and led to a polarization of white and black Washington residents.[58] When, in the final speech of the program accompanying the Poor People's March, Abernathy accused the administration and the Congress of "five years of 'broken promises,'" President Johnson, who felt he had done much to improve the conditions of black citizens, became unwilling to reward such disloyalty.[59] Once Johnson reduced his involvement, there was little interest in Congress for continuing the poverty programs.[60]

The war in Vietnam and the protests against it, including riots and police overreaction at the Chicago Democratic Convention in August 1968, distracted almost everyone from what looked, to much of the country, like a losing battle on behalf of ungrateful recipients. Branton continued with the work of UPO, but there was less funding for existing programs and virtually no funding for new projects.

In January 1969, while Branton was still fighting for UPO funding, White House records reveal there was an investigation of criminal activities within UPO's Manpower Program. The Federal Bureau of Narcotics alleged that some UPO employees were involved in narcotics, prostitution, and gambling and were using the UPO office as a front for their activities. The agents believed Branton to be unaware of the situation.[61] President Johnson's aide, Joseph A. Califano Jr., reported that information to Johnson, who ordered an immediate investigation.[62] Nothing in Branton's personal papers indicates that he was told about the Justice Department investigation, but the decreasing resources and increasing criticism of and demand on poverty program efforts had worn him down. Branton, like President Johnson, had had enough.

Although he had sounded a positive and energetic note in an interview with a reporter for the *Pine Bluff Commercial* in September 1968, Branton had given a clue to his plans when he said, "When I took this job, I more or less committed myself to staying with it for at least a year and a half or so, but I think that I would be receptive to a new, challenging job."[63]

He announced his resignation in mid-May, to become effective on June 13, 1969. On May 26, Branton warned that the "separatist power" rhetoric was growing and would gain adherents if a "real commitment to the poverty war" was not forthcoming.[64] On July 10, he expressed concern about the Nixon administration's "conservatism."[65] A newspaper story reporting on his resignation stated that "[w]ithin UPO [Branton] has earned a reputation as a strong and stern administrator."[66]

When Branton announced his resignation as executive director of UPO in May 1969, he intended to return to private practice with the firm of Thompson, Evans and Dolphin in Washington, D.C.[67] In fact, his name was already on the law office doors when he received a call from Whitney Young Jr. of the National Urban League. Young asked Branton whether he was acquainted with Walter Reuther, president of the United Auto Workers (UAW) and former vice president of the American Federation of Labor and Congress of Industrial Organizations (AFL-CIO). When Branton answered in the negative, Young invited him to a dinner meeting where he introduced the two.[68]

Walter Reuther was a longtime labor activist and supporter of civil rights for workers and for minorities. He was also a strong believer in the need for societal change. At college, Reuther had organized the Social Problems Club, which prevented the creation of a campus ROTC unit and was able to desegregate the school's swimming pool.[69] Like the young Wiley Branton, Reuther appreciated the Socialist stance giving equal treatment to all races, an appreciation that was crushed when Reuther spent some time working in Soviet Russia in the 1930s.

Returning from his travels in 1935, Reuther found a job in the auto industry and became active in the union movement.[70] He joined the United Auto Workers and worked his way up the ladder until he was elected president of the UAW in 1946. He immediately created a department of Fair Practices and Anti-Discrimination within the UAW, which worked for inclusion of black workers in the union.[71]

As he became more well known, Reuther became a leader in the Democratic Party and counselor to every president from Roosevelt to Johnson. He pushed presidents and politicians to take a larger role in the creation of social programs and the preservation of civil rights. He was a supporter of Dr. Martin Luther King Jr. and the Southern Christian Leadership Conference. His union helped to finance the King's Freedom

Marches in Detroit and Washington, D.C., and Reuther marched with civil rights leaders in Mississippi, Alabama, and D.C.[72]

Aaron Henry called him "one of the oldest friends of the civil rights movement."[73] Reuther was one of the few white men invited to speak on the program of the 1963 March on Washington. He became a consultant for President Lyndon Johnson in planning for the War on Poverty,[74] and he created the "Citizens Crusade Against Poverty" in 1964 to involve labor unions in that war.[75]

When the AFL-CIO resisted his ideas for expanding the reach of labor unions through social action programs, Reuther withdrew the United Auto Workers from the organization in 1968. He then teamed with his friend, Frank Fitzsimmons, acting president of the Teamsters' Union, to create the Alliance for Labor Action.[76] The Alliance was intended to combine innovative efforts to unionize workers, especially in the South, with creative ideas for social programs to support the poor. Contributions of ten dollars per month from each member of the allied unions funded the activities.

In February 1969, the Alliance created two committees. The first, headed by Fitzsimmons, was the Committee on Organizing and Collective Bargaining. The second, headed by Reuther, was the Committee on Community and Social Action. Although the unionizing effort headed by Fitzsimmons, initiated in Atlanta, Georgia, is an interesting story in its own right, it is the second of these committees that brought Wiley Branton into Reuther's plans.

The Committee on Community and Social Action intended to create "community unions," composed of "welfare recipients, the working poor, the unemployed, and the underemployed," that would "cooperate with established community groups in supporting socially oriented activities and legislation on local, state, and national levels." Branton must have been enchanted with the idea. One of the basic needs of the poor was employment. At the UPO, he had watched the diminution of the federal government's interest in eradicating poverty. The momentum of Johnson's War on Poverty had been stalled by wave after wave of funding cuts to poverty programs.

Here was a labor leader who had established a track record in civil rights, and who was determined to provide jobs and organization for the poor. Reuther intended to give the underclass a voice on other issues, as well. As Branton put it, "Walter wanted me, at urging from Whitney [Young], to take over the job heading up the community and social action [division]. Now they wanted somebody who knew something about organized labor. But they didn't want anybody who came out of either one of the *participating* unions because there's a lot of jealousy at the various unions."[77] Branton was being offered another chance to help make a difference on a national scale. He could not resist.

In July 1969, Reuther announced that Wiley Branton would become director of social action for the Alliance.[78] Branton agreed to join the Alliance for two years, telling the D.C. firm that he would return to private practice in 1971.[79] This venture appealed to Branton in several ways. In addition to allowing continuation of his work against poverty, the position seemed to provide an autonomy similar to that he had had with the VEP and that had been lacking at UPO. Although Reuther was chair of the committee, as president of the UAW and in his fight with the AFL-CIO, he was a busy man.[80] Branton would create the reality from Reuther's vision, working with established community groups and helping to create new ones where they did not exist. He and Reuther shared a belief in the value of community and cooperation.

Branton would work directly with the poor and disadvantaged to sponsor education and training projects, meet housing needs, provide health care and other essential social services, and furnish legal aid and consumer protection programs. Once people had been aided by Alliance's social programs to improve their lives and obtain jobs, they would be interested in union membership, where they could continue to help themselves. Unlike the UPO, program funding was not dependent on fickle government agencies or on Congress, but on members of unions who saw the Alliance as ultimately benefiting their own lives and increasing union power.[81] To Branton, the Alliance was a "bright spot" in the area of social action, where the federal government was in retreat.[82]

Personally, this was another impressive appointment for Branton. With its national scope, the Alliance provided challenges and exposure that were potentially greater than either the VEP or the UPO. Branton's work also would expand to include all minorities, not just blacks. Arkansas's senator William J. Fulbright entered the news release of Branton's appointment into the Congressional Record of August 5, 1969. The release contained praise of the appointment from such prominent leaders as Roy Wilkins of the NAACP, the Reverend Ralph Abernathy of the Southern Christian Leadership Conference, Whitney Young Jr. of the National Urban League, Mayor Richard Hatcher of Gary, Indiana, and Mayor Carl Stokes of Cleveland, Ohio.[83] All these men knew Branton personally, as well as through his record of achievement in civil rights.

Branton first had to create a mechanism by which individuals and communities could apply to the Alliance for funding and other organizing help. After the structure was in place, the programs for which Branton recommended Alliance funding were varied in scope. Recipients included the Watts Labor Community Action Committee (to purchase a chain of grocery stores within that Los Angeles community); the East Los Angeles Community Union (to promote economic development for Mexican Americans); and the Transportation Opportunity Program (to train a culturally diverse group of truck drivers and mechanics).[84] Some other examples are a housing program in St. Louis, Missouri, economic support of striking workers in Daytona Beach (Florida), and a poverty group in Scottsdale (Pennsylvania). In one year, the Alliance made grants totaling almost one million dollars, and Branton was spending much of his time in travel across the country.[85]

Walter Reuther died unexpectedly in an airplane accident on May 9, 1970. Branton recalled that he "really wanted to leave right at the time [of Reuther's death]," but decided that there was still a lot of money in the Alliance treasury that could be put to good use in local programs with whom he had developed communications.[86] Rather than leaving those programs in the lurch, he determined he would remain for his full two-year commitment.

Even before Reuther's death, however, Branton had begun to feel some frustration over his role in the Alliance. Although he had heavy responsibilities, he was unable to execute them in a timely manner. His recommendations had to be approved by the Alliance's executive board, so he did not have the autonomy he had anticipated. The infrequent meetings of the board meant that decision making moved slowly. In addition, a bitter and expensive union organizing effort by the Alliance in Atlanta (Georgia) distracted the organization's focus away from community social action. Even Reuther had been preoccupied before his death by difficulties within the union.

On May 28, 1970, Branton made an effort to realign executive decision making. He sent a confidential memo to the new chair of the Alliance's Committee on Community and Social Action, Leonard Woodcock. In it, Branton stated that the Alliance needed an executive director who could make day-to-day administrative decisions for the committee, including the discretion to award small grants without full board approval. He believed that smaller, less-organized, community groups with good ideas and energy to implement them often were unable to cope with the "red-tape" and delay required by the existing system. Branton offered to provide the needed administration, in addition to his other duties.[87] Woodcock apparently did not respond.

In August 1971, when Branton's two-year commitment ended, he resigned. Leonard Woodcock acknowledged the resignation in a memorandum that thanked Branton for his work and expressed "regret" that the union's finances had left the Alliance in a bad situation.[88] It was clear to Branton that, without Reuther, the Alliance's social programs work were a secondary goal for the organization. When funding decisions were required, the "organization of factory workers" was critical to the Alliance's survival, while the community action programs were not. Branton later told a friend that the Alliance was Reuther's dream and when he died, "the idea of the Alliance pretty much went with him."[89] To an interviewer in 1984, he said Walter Reuther "was a man who was 50 years ahead of his time" in thinking about alleviating poverty.[90]

Branton's departure from the Alliance was the end of his direct involvement in providing social services to the poor. It would not be the end of his contributions toward the goal of ending poverty. He would spend the next several years practicing law to support his family. He would handle the civil rights cases that came his way and would work through existing organizations of which he was a member to improve society.

CHAPTER 11

Private Practice Again
A Respite

BRANTON LEFT THE ALA in August 1971. During the two years he was
working with Reuther, however, the firm with which he had made a
connection in 1969 had seen significant changes. One of the senior
lawyers had been appointed to the bench. Another partner had died.
Branton joined with the remaining attorneys to create a new firm—
Dolphin, Branton, Stafford & Webber.[1] Before Branton's arrival, the firm
had a general practice, with an emphasis on personal injury defense matters from its representation of a large local cab company.[2]

Branton expanded the firm's practice, bringing in clients who knew
of his national reputation. Branton spent the next six years performing
legal services for individuals and business entities, much as he had in
Arkansas. The significant difference between his D.C. and Arkansas practices was the breadth of his activities. His D.C. clients included some
larger corporate entities and high-profile individual clients although, as
was true with his Arkansas practice, they were primarily black.

As Branton described it, his practice "range[d] from the hourly
worker who is seeking the return of a $125.00 security deposit on her
apartment to a major university filing suit against a federal agency seeking more than one million dollars under a contract for funding, . . . to
persons charged with felony murder, kidnap or rape . . . ; in other words,
my clients are almost as varied as the subject areas of law."[3] A look at
some specific cases provides examples of the variety. In September 1971,
he defended a police officer on appeal from charges of negligent homicide.[4] In March 1973, he argued an appeal for a client who alleged

receiving injuries when jars, cans, and other packages fell on her from a grocery store balcony.[5] Branton also registered to handle a number of indigent criminal cases on referral from the D.C. courts.[6] The last published case in which Branton was involved during this period was *Flack v. Laster*, where he opposed efforts by attorneys for singing star Roberta Flack to overturn a trial judgment in his client's favor on a contract dispute.[7] He did not always win.

Branton also handled civil rights cases, primarily for the NAACP LDEF. In fact, only during his government service had Wiley Branton distanced himself from the LDEF. In 1973, Branton joined with other lawyers at the LDEF to intervene in two cases involving voting rights. The first was a New Orleans case that involved the city's effort to redefine the districts for election of city council members, which the LDEF believed to be discriminatory.[8] The second was a New York case opposing state officials' decision to exempt three counties from Voting Act requirements.[9]

In 1977, Branton was asked to represent the Southern Christian Leadership Conference in a suit against the FBI and the Estate of J. Edgar Hoover. The SCLC wanted to stop the FBI from distributing pictures, statements, and tapes it had accumulated during illegal surveillance of Dr. Martin Luther King Jr. in the 1950s and 1960s. The complaint also asked for money damages for the detriment to Dr. King's reputation by the FBI's actions.[10] The firm's associate, Patricia Worthy, performed most of the work under Branton's supervision.[11] In the midst of a large city full of lawyers who specialized in discrete areas of law, he was the traditional "general practitioner." Out-of-town lawyers whose clients had to file their claims in the District of Columbia courts knew of Branton's reputation and called on his services.[12]

Not all of Branton's work during this period was performed in the courtroom. In February 1972, Branton was chosen to handle distribution of the Voter Registration Fund. The fund involved almost $700,000 collected by the Democratic National Party in 1965 fund-raising efforts that became surrounded with controversy.[13] Until matters could be sorted out, the money had been deposited for safekeeping. Finally, a committee of the Democratic Party suggested it be distributed to tax-exempt organizations involved in nonpartisan voter registration efforts. Henry Hall Wilson, president of the Chicago Board of Trade and a former aide to President Lyndon Johnson, was selected to administer the fund.

Wilson hired Branton to direct the solicitation of proposals from appropriate organizations and to recommend grants to recipients that would exhaust the fund over a three-year period.[14] Proposed recipients had to be nonpartisan and also had to operate in five or more states. They had to be "grass-roots" organizations, not receiving more than 25 percent of their income from any single grantor. In addition to distributing the funds, Branton also offered technical assistance to the grantees.

Branton was in his element here. From his work with the VEP and in government, he had the experience and knowledge needed to perform the required tasks. His final report indicates that the money was distributed to eight entities between 1972 and 1976.[15] The recipients were the National Movement for the Student Vote; the A. Phillip Randolph Education Fund; the Voter Education Project, Inc.; the United States Youth Council; the NAACP Special Contribution Fund; the National Urban League; the League of Women Voters; and the Southwest Voter Registration/Education Project. Branton deposited his files on administration of the fund with the Moorland-Spingarn Research Center at Howard University in 1981.[16]

This period of his life saw Branton delve even more deeply into the operations of the various organizations to which he belonged. All his life, Branton had enjoyed the camaraderie and networking provided by membership groups. In 1974, he was a member of the NAACP, the NAACP LDEF, the National Bar Association, the Masons, the Sigma Pi Phi Fraternity, the American Civil Liberties Union, the Washington Urban League, the Travelers Aid Society, the Washington Center for Metropolitan Studies, the Health and Welfare Council, the Committee for Public Justice, the Earl Warren Legal Training Program, Inc., the Southeastern Economic Development Foundation, Inc., the Washington Home Rule Committee, the National Association of Inter-Group Relations Officials, and the Pigskin Club of Washington.[17] He was a member of the board for many of them.

Branton regularly attended meetings of these groups. Frequently, he was a featured speaker or a participant in panel discussions. When he spoke, he continually exhorted his audiences to do more for civil rights. Elaine Jones, former director-counsel of the NAACP LDEF, said that Branton often was the person asked to represent the organization on certain issues or for fund-raising. As she put it, if the issue was the Voting

Rights Act, "[y]ou'd want to send Wiley." If the audience was "not going to really listen to a lecture, but you want them to understand the issues, you'd want Wiley."[18] In 1971, Branton was vice chair of LDEF's board, and his humor, wit, and storytelling served to energize audiences.

He performed a similar role for the National Bar Association, speaking at conferences and responding to requests for advice. John Crump, the NBA's longtime director, says that Branton was one of the few people Crump could reach easily and quickly, without going through several secretaries.[19] Branton was Crump's favorite master of ceremonies. Branton also was an active member. Impatient with the organization's practice of holding elections for officers at the end of a week-long meeting, and feeling that the campaigning for office that occurred during the week caused people to miss out on the educational presentations, Branton was instrumental in effecting procedural changes that restricted the campaigning to the first few days of a meeting.[20]

Branton had nurtured his membership in the Sigma Pi Phi Fraternity (the Boulé), since his election to membership in 1954.[21] Once back in private practice, Branton became even more active. The Boulé was primarily a social organization providing the means by which black professionals met and interacted. One had to be invited to join, and one was not invited until he had made a "mark" in the world. Chapters of the group were located in major cities across the country and biennial meetings were held in different locations, allowing the professional elite to network. A younger member recalled that Branton was one of the "young Turks" of the group, pushing to make the Boulé "relevant" to the times.[22]

In 1970, while he was still with the Alliance, Branton participated in the Boulé's biennial meeting, held that year in Miami.[23] His speech was meant to stir the group to action toward civil rights. Beginning with a short review of the history of blacks in the United States since the Civil War, Branton compared the withdrawal of federal support in the post-Reconstruction 1870s with what was happening during the Nixon administration.[24] Two years after the riots following the assassination of Martin Luther King Jr., Branton argued that Boulé members had a responsibility to reach out to young blacks and to give them hope for the future. He said, "[W]e are really not going to begin to tackle these problems unless you and I in our respective communities throughout the length and breadth of this country become involved in a leadership role in trying to help solve the problems there."[25]

Branton's plea was quoted in a later history of the Boulé, where he was described as part of the "changing order" that pushed the group toward a more active role in the African American community.[26] A Social Action Program, likely an outcome of Branton's advocacy, was approved by the membership at its 1972 meeting. An annual tax of twenty-five dollars per member was established to create a fund, but nothing more was accomplished during that biennium.[27]

Branton was among those considered for the post of Grand Sire Archon-Elect, the Boulé's national president, in 1973, but he was not chosen. In 1974, at a meeting held in Cincinnati, Branton was a member of the Resolutions committee when the membership learned that the incoming Grand Sire Archon, Percy L. Julian of Chicago, was too ill to undertake the position.[28] An emergency election was held. Branton was among those nominated to replace Julian and, though he refused to "campaign" for the position, he won the election.

Branton quickly declared that he would focus on integrating the new Social Action Program into the Boulé's structure and on expanding the general membership to include younger men.[29] He appointed a committee to solicit and review suggestions for using the Social Action fund and to propose a plan for consideration at the 1976 meeting.[30] When some chapters failed to respond to the proposed program, Branton sent his own "Urgent!" memo asking for a decision.[31] His task was not easy, as there were some members who believed the Boulé was not designed or fit for this kind of direct action, particularly when its members all were active in their individual communities and elsewhere.

One Boulé member argued that voting on the Social Action Program had been affected by "the emotionalism of the times and the charisma of the social action proponents" and that the organization should stay with what it did well, "meeting a need for congenial interaction, intellectual stimulation and leadership consensus."[32] This disagreement mirrored the larger split between traditional civil rights leaders and the more activist next generation. Branton was a bridge between the two generations, not following the "black power" line but urging more forthright action than some people felt appropriate.

Branton also acted quickly regarding membership issues. During the two years of his term, Branton made thirty-three visits to twenty-eight individual chapters.[33] By comparison, his predecessor had visited seventeen chapters in the same period of time.[34] Branton also wrote to several other chapters urging them to expand their memberships.[35] To set an example, he worked very hard to reenergize the Pi Boulé in Little Rock, which had been reduced to three members. On July 9, 1975, Branton presided over the initiation of thirteen new members.[36] Branton's extensive files on the Boulé indicate his personal involvement in recruiting potential members and in pushing matters along.

When Branton's term ended, the new Grand Sire Archon was his friend Judge A. Leon Higginbotham, who appointed Branton chair of the Social Action Committee.[37] Branton also was a member of the Publications Committee that would oversee implementation of a part of the Social Action Program, the publication of several monographs on black leaders. These positions allowed Branton to continue his activist path within the organization. Branton also volunteered to continue working to "strengthen existing Boulés and to establish new subordinate Boulés."[38]

A younger member of the Boulé, Eddie Williams of the Joint Center for Political and Economic Studies in Washington, D.C., recalled Branton as a "good teacher" and "motivator." One simple example, Williams said, was the ritual pledge that begins Boulé meetings. Most people would read it from a paper or would mumble through it. Branton committed it to memory and would be "the loudest voice, and the early voice, helping others to recall the words."[39]

The riots and violence he had seen in the sixties and seventies were behind Branton's appeals to and exhortation of black organizations and communities to act. Although himself a product of the activist black church and a believer in the rule of law, he understood the frustration demonstrated in those destructive acts. In a speech at the Divinity School of Vanderbilt University, Branton said that "change can best be accomplished by the ballot, communication and nonviolent protest, but all within the structure of law." "Violence," he continued, "is division and . . . must be controlled or it will overthrow this nation." Ministers could contribute by "making people aware of their legal rights and . . . providing a forum for the airing of community and personal concerns."[40]

Branton's penchant for organizations and meetings was attributed by his law firm partner, Paul R. Webber III, to Branton's constant search for ways to help. Webber recalled riding home from work one day with Branton when they saw a sign announcing a meeting at a church. Neither of them had any connection with the church, but Branton asked if they might stop and visit. As it happened, the meeting was stymied with a question involving Robert's Rules of Order. Branton offered his help, which was accepted. He quickly straightened out the situation, allowing the meeting to continue.[41]

Toward the end of 1974, Branton was asked to submit an application to the Judicial Nomination Commission of D.C.[42] He was one of three persons, two men and a woman, recommended to fill a position on the D.C. Court of Appeals in 1975.[43] President Ford appointed the woman, who was acting general counsel of the Equal Employment Opportunity Commission.[44] Branton understood that he had received "number 1" ratings from the Justice Department and other groups,[45] although he "had mixed emotions about going on the bench and did absolutely nothing to try and obtain the position."[46]

It is probably best that Branton was not appointed to an appellate court. His extroverted personality would have been stifled in a job that imposes a lot of private time for reviewing case records. Branton probably would have made a good trial judge, where his quick wits, thorough knowledge of trial procedure, strong organization skills, and infectious sense of humor would have been distinct advantages.

Branton became a member of the Disciplinary board of the D.C. Bar Association, and eventually became its vice chair and chair.[47] During his time on the board, he participated in the deliberations over the nature of sanctions to be imposed on lawyers who had violated rules of professional conduct. Among the cases he was involved with were those of the lawyers connected with the Watergate scandal that led to President Richard M. Nixon's resignation in 1974.[48]

At the beginning of 1977, Branton began experiencing some medical problems. His papers contain a letter to one of his Boulé fraternity brothers asking whether his enclosed lab report required consultation with a specialist. In the letter, he mentioned that he was "back on" two medications—benemid and enduronyl (used to control high blood pressure).[49] Although Branton was concerned enough to inquire of his friend, he apparently made no mention of his concern to his family, as his son was not aware of any serious health problems until the mid-1980s.[50] The condition of his health did not seem to change his lifestyle, however, as he continued plunging into the vast variety of activities presented by career and avocation.

Branton's family continued to do well. By this time, five of his six children had graduated from college and his son Wiley Jr. was in law school. His youngest, Debra, was attending Spelman College in Atlanta, Georgia. When Debra was involved in a protest at the college, Branton indicated pride in her willingness to act for something she believed in but cautioned her about the "means" used in the protest, noting that locking the college trustees in a meeting room could have criminal law consequences.[51]

In 1977, there were momentous changes in Branton's work life. His law partner, Paul Webber III was named a judge of the D.C. Superior Court on May 31;[52] the firm's senior associate, Patricia Worthy, left to work for the Department of Housing and Urban Development;[53] and Branton himself was appointed Dean of Howard University School of Law on December 6, 1977.[54] Branton's arrangement with the school allowed him to "wind down" his practice, continuing to handle matters until he could extricate himself from it. As it happened, his son, Wiley A. Branton Jr., had just been admitted to practice in Georgia.[55] The younger Branton moved to D.C. and took over his father's practice.[56] Before he left private practice, however, Branton was honored with the Henry W. Edgarton Award from the D.C. chapter of the ACLU.[57]

CHAPTER 12

Dean at Howard Law School
Training Future Civil Rights Lawyers

HOWARD UNIVERSITY'S SCHOOL of Law had long occupied a place in Branton's heart. A student of history, particularly of African American history, he knew quite a bit about the school's past. Chartered by the federal government in 1869 to provide legal training for recently emancipated Negroes, it still received much of its funding from the government.[1] To Branton, Howard Law School was a monument to the civil rights movement of the twentieth century.

Branton knew about Charles Hamilton Houston, the school's dean from 1930 to 1935, who had been one of the primary strategists for the NAACP in planning the assault on racial inequality in the United States.[2] Houston, himself a graduate of Harvard Law School, had transformed a "mediocre night school" into "a respected institution."[3] Bringing high-powered lawyers to lecture at the school, he won its membership in the Association of American Law Schools (AALS) two years after he took the helm.[4] Thurgood Marshall, who would help lead the NAACP in executing the plan to destroy legalized segregation, had graduated from Howard in 1933.[5] Between 1934 and 1946, Houston and subsequent deans made the school available for planning sessions and Supreme Court argument "moots," at which proposed arguments were critiqued by faculty and private lawyers.

Sometime in the early 1970s, as the school suffered from several rapid changes in deans, Branton was approached about taking the job. At that time, he was not interested in a move, but he did spend some time talking with the search committee about the type of person they should be looking for.[6] In fall 1977, Branton began teaching in the school's trial advocacy program as an adjunct professor. This exposure to the school and its students, plus the fact that he knew many of its graduates both professionally and socially, brought Branton closer to the school. As he put it, "That exposure to young people and seeing their quest for knowledge and their reactions grew on me."[7]

When James Cheek, president of Howard University, again approached Branton during the fall of 1977 about becoming dean, Branton was in the running for a federal judgeship.[8] Branton was intrigued enough by the challenge to discuss the options with his family. The stated purpose of the meeting was for the family to help Branton weigh the pros and cons of the decision. However, his oldest son recalled that when Branton told them that, while it was his dream to be a judge, the law school was in trouble and he could help, they knew he would go to Howard.[9]

Branton told his family that Howard was threatened with losing its accreditation and, if he took the job, the American Bar Association (which has responsibility for accrediting law schools) would give him two years to "work things out." Taking the job would mean a reduction in his income, but Branton's law firm was going through major personnel changes and Wiley Jr., just admitted to practice, could take over the work of closing his father's practice. Having talked it through with his family, Branton decided to negotiate with the university administration.[10]

In the end, Branton decided he "could make a greater contribution to the legal profession as dean of the law school than as a judge."[11] The position would allow him to pull together many of his longtime interests: contributing to the future of African American youth, conveying the history of African Americans, transmitting his sense of honor and privilege concerning the practice of law, and creating younger lawyers who would pursue civil rights litigation. The position also would give him a pulpit from which to sound the need for continuing concern about civil rights.

Branton knew that accomplishing the job at Howard would require significant resources and a fairly free hand to make changes. After negotiating with the university's administration, although he did not obtain everything he wanted, Branton believed he had enough to make a difference at the school.

Branton brought distinction to the position. Although he was not an academic, he was respected for his civil rights work over the years and was known and well liked by many in Washington's power structure. His strength was in his practical approach to problems, both in administering the school and teaching the law. His rapport with some of the younger generation already was established. Branton was a mentor for a number of younger lawyers, such as Little Rock attorney John Walker Jr.; his successor at the VEP, Vernon Jordan Jr.; and attorney Weldon Rougeau.[12]

Branton wanted to expand Howard's clinical program, which provided students with supervised experience in the practice of law with actual clients, an idea that was just becoming popular in law schools across the country. And, although he felt that Howard's history required a "considerable emphasis on civil rights law," he believed it should come only after students had received a thorough grounding in basic legal education.

His appointment was announced on December 6, 1977.[13] Branton would be "the seventh dean at Howard law school in 17 years."[14] He was described as "trying to rescue the 108-year-old law school."[15] When Arkansas senator Dale Bumpers read the *Washington Post*'s article on Branton's appointment into the Congressional Record, he said, "It is a credit to [Branton] and to his spirit of public service that he has renounced this ambition [a judicial appointment] and decided to devote his considerable talents and energies to legal education."[16]

Howard's major problems, as described in a January 1978 article, were a low bar passage rate by graduates, internal disagreements among the faculty on what should be done to improve bar passage, and problems with its accreditation status.[17] Branton saw "morale" as the major issue behind these outward symptoms.[18] The faculty, staff, and students, he said, were not "clicking together on the same team."[19]

Branton began by making himself accessible, eating in the cafeteria and sitting in on classes to learn how the school worked.[20] His focus was on changing attitudes, expanding the curriculum, and helping students focus on their studies by reducing their need to work to support themselves.[21] Branton pushed for the creation of programs that would recognize academic problems early in a student's education and would provide appropriate remedial education.

On November 18, 1978, Branton was formally invested as dean. His good friend, Supreme Court justice Thurgood Marshall, gave the main address, stating that "'Wiley' stands for 'brain and guts.' I know both of them; I have seen him in action."[22] In January 1979, Branton needed both of these attributes as he began efforts to revitalize the school's civil rights activity. Between 1978 and 1980, matters appeared to move smoothly.

As part of his effort to make civil rights law "real" to Howard's students, and to revive great traditions within the school, Branton arranged for the "moot" (rehearsal) of a school desegregation case from Dallas in the school's courtroom in November 1979. Branton included faculty, local civil rights lawyers, and representatives from the NAACP on a panel that critiqued the plaintiff's attorney's proposed arguments. Branton himself sat with the presenting attorney and aided in the fine-tuning of his argument.[23] Branton wanted the students to feel in the midst of the action and to develop the habit of considering civil rights in everything they did, just as he did. His activities during his deanship, both within and without the school, were intended to provide students with a role model.

In May 1979, the law school hosted a conference reviewing the progress of racial equality since 1954. Branton was quoted as saying, "We are not as far as we thought we would be since *Brown*."[24] A few days later, Branton spoke at a dinner about the negative effect "perception" had played on national support for integration. After twenty-five years, Branton said, "the social injustices 'are perceived as wrongs,' but the social injustices still exist."[25]

At the end of his first full year with the law school, Branton gave an interview to the school's newspaper, saying the biggest problem he saw was the "lack of financial resources for students." In addition, many students did not seem "to be putting as much into their pursuit of a legal education as I think they should." Branton continued, "I don't see enough students in the library," or "doing what I regard as a minimum for adequate classroom preparation."[26] Despite his criticism, the 1980 graduating class presented Branton with a "certificate" of appreciation for his "juris-patience, res-ipsa-dedication, and more-than-arbitrary-and-capricious assistance in hatching the Class of 1980 LEGAL EAGLEs."[27]

Branton felt he was "receiving very good cooperation" from the Howard faculty, too, although "there is room for improvement." He had asked the faculty appointments committee to put an emphasis on hiring more women and faculty who "can communicate with the students," as well as produce scholarship. Branton himself recruited his former colleague, Patricia Worthy, to teach without pay.[28] He was in favor of a proposal for a comprehensive exam at the end of the second year, feeling it would give the students a sense of what the bar exam would require and would alert them to deficiencies in their knowledge in time to remedy them. In response to the interviewer's concern that such a practice would "hold [some students] back," Branton responded that they should not complain if it improved their ability to pass the bar exam in the end.

In a 1980 interview with a reporter from the *Pine Bluff Commercial,* Branton noted proudly that the school had a white student enrollment of about 20 percent. To him, it was a positive counterpoint to the school's preeminence "as it relates to black people." He saw Howard's historical "mission" as training lawyers, of any color, who were likely to return to practice in their communities.[29] The same article reiterated a statement he'd made at the twenty-fifth anniversary program for the *Brown* decision, that "[s]uccessful blacks have an obligation to take up the burden of their brothers and sisters who are crushed by inequality and injustice and make America listen to what they have to say."[30]

On May 29, 1980, Vernon Jordan Jr., now executive director of the National Urban League, was in Fort Wayne, Indiana, for meetings when he was shot in the back by a white racist. Jordan was near death and, many years later, recalled that when he woke up in the intensive care room, Wiley Branton was with him. Jordan valued Branton as "one of the few guys that I've known who would go the second mile with you." Five years later, when Jordan's first wife died, Branton again dropped everything to be at Jordan's side, helping him to deal with the situation. Noted Jordan, "There was this incredible compassionate side to him, that you never saw in the courtroom."[31]

Branton's new position made him a VIP in D.C. While he had long been active in civic affairs, most of it had been within the black community and the civil rights world. Suddenly, he was invited to speak and otherwise participate at more diverse events. He used the speaking invitations to press for further civil rights efforts for blacks, women, and other minorities. His presence on a board or committee meant there would be a strong voice for expanding opportunities for minorities.

For example, in March 1978 he was named to the board of Consolidated Rail Corporation (CONRAIL),[32] an entity created by Congress in 1976 to improve railroad services in the Northeast by reorganizing Pennsylvania Station (New York) and other bankrupt rail properties.[33]

One of CONRAIL's attractions for Branton was a provision for a minority contractors program that could help minority businessmen obtain contracts with the corporation.[34] He was active in putting "teeth" into the program. Branton remained on the board throughout the organization efforts and until the entity again was profitable. When CONRAIL became a public company without federal subsidies, he was elected a member of the new board. Branton was still on the board when he died.[35]

A public second forum for his work opened with an invitation to co-chair the Washington Lawyers' Committee, "one of 10 local affiliates of the National Lawyers' Committee for Civil Rights Under Law."[36] Originally founded in 1963 to recruit lawyers in private practice to handle legal work for civil rights workers involved in voter registration, in 1968 the Lawyers' Committee was focused on providing resources for "civil rights and poverty issues facing . . . major cities." Branton was important to the Committee both for his stature in the civil rights arena and for his new connection with Howard School of Law and its focus on training civil rights lawyers. In the two years that Branton served the committee in this capacity, he worked hard at expanding its activities and increasing both its funding and the number of attorneys who volunteered their time to its efforts.[37]

At least two of the programs initiated during his term on the Lawyers' Committee reflected his lifelong concerns with equal access to education. Branton is credited with developing a program that provided lawyers for parents' groups in the District of Columbia, helping them to better understand and oversee the way in which local school districts were operating.[38] He also was instrumental in creating a program in which lawyers would provide tutoring and mentoring to minority students about to enter law school.[39] A third area in which Branton was influential was the committee's expansion of support for the civil rights of other population groups, for example, immigrants, women, and those suffering from HIV/AIDS.

When his term as co-chair ended, Branton remained on the committee's board of trustees and as an outside advisor until his death. In 1987, the National Lawyers' Committee awarded him its highest honor, the Whitney North Seymour Award.[40] After his death, in 1989, it created the Wiley A. Branton Award, which is presented annually to "a member of the legal community whose lifetime efforts on behalf of civil rights advocacy exemplify [Branton's] deep commitment."[41]

These two organizations are only the most obvious of his civic activities during this period.[42] Branton used his public speaking engagements to spread his personal philosophy. In April 1979, he spoke to the University of Arkansas honors graduates about honor, ethics, and professionalism, noting he had been part of the D.C. board on professional responsibility that disciplined lawyers in President Nixon's administration who were involved in the Watergate scandal. He urged his audience to "help create an atmosphere of equal rights and equal respect" that would allow creativity and excellence to "flourish."[43]

In May 1980, Branton delivered the commencement address for the University of Arkansas at Little Rock School of Law, recalling that his application to the school's predecessor, the Arkansas Law School, had been denied in 1950, forcing him to attend the School of Law in Fayetteville. As he had the year before, Branton focused his remarks on the honor and integrity required of lawyers, particularly in speaking out against injustice. He used himself as an example, saying that his position during the Little Rock crisis had been a lonely one because other lawyers had failed to speak out.[44]

Branton's patriotism was evident at a naturalization ceremony on December 9, 1980, where he had an opportunity to speak plainly about his feelings for the United States. While the history of slavery and the treatment of Native Americans by the white immigrants did not "speak well" of American society, he said, "it is better than any other that I am aware of." He praised the peaceful transition of presidents that would occur in January, saying, "Americans know that political changes are the direct result of democracy in action, the effect of civilian control over the leadership of government."[45]

Wiley Branton tried to help anyone in need, even when no publicity or reward would be forthcoming. In early 1982, he did his best to sort out the legal affairs of a poor black woman whose church pastor called the law school after being unsuccessful at getting legal help for her from the University of Baltimore's School of Law. Luckily, the Reverend Herbert H. Eaton's telephone call was put through to Wiley Branton, who did not transfer it to anyone else.[46]

Branton's advice was always practical. Professor Patricia Worthy recalled venting to Branton her frustration about a judge's failure to rule on a motion she had made. His response was, "Well, file something." When she said there was nothing in the rules that allowed a filing, Branton said, "just make up a motion . . . and file it." Disbelieving, Worthy followed the advice, and the judge granted the "made-up" motion and resolved her original problem.[47] Branton knew that judges could "forget" an individual motion among their many cases. Bringing the case to the judge's attention through another motion could get the attorney over that problem without insulting the judge.

During this same period, Branton advised a group of D.C. private practitioners who handled court-appointed criminal cases for minimal fees. D.C. officials and the courts had rebuffed their request for a fee increase. Branton advised them to "do something dramatic," since they didn't have much political clout.[48] Although Branton may not have suggested the means by which they should dramatize their predicament, an attorney strike lasted just two weeks before the city conceded and raised their fees. Unfortunately, the Federal Trade Commission sued the lawyers for antitrust violations shortly thereafter. After six years of legal maneuvering, during which the case reached the U.S. Supreme Court, the FTC won its case amid much criticism.[49] One person who followed Branton's career said, "He had been in the trenches for so long that he learned to cut the wire and red tape without so much as batting an eye."[50]

Branton also began receiving formal recognition for his civil rights work during this period. In April 1978, the Washington Bar Association, a primarily black voluntary organization, conferred the Houston Medallion of Merit on him, as "exemplify[ing] the best in Houstonian jurisprudence," through his "commitment to the fight for economic and political equality."[51] The Honorable William Bryant, judge of the U.S. District Court in the District and a personal friend, presented the award, saying, "[g]ood judgment, high competence, resourcefulness, and sensitivity—all without even a trace of arrogance—have earned for Wiley Branton the high esteem of his fellow man."[52]

In May 1978, he received an honorary Doctor of Laws degree from the University of Arkansas at Pine Bluff.[53] In May 1980, he received a Distinguished Alumni Citation from the University of Arkansas. The other person receiving the award was poet Miller Williams, a longtime friend who had been one of the few white people to welcome Branton and the other early black students to the university.[54]

With the awards came more substantial recognition as Branton was sought out for his extensive knowledge of the 1950s and 1960s civil rights period. Branton had given a lengthy interview to Steven Lawson in 1970 for the Oral History Research Project of the Eisenhower Library at Columbia University. Additional lengthy interviews are lodged at Howard University's Spingarn-Moorland Research Library, and the University of Virginia's Civil Rights Lawyers Documentary Project. Other historians and authors also sought him out.[55]

Not everything during the Howard years was positive for Branton. In March 1979, longtime tensions between the NAACP (for which Branton was a frequent speaker, as well as a lifetime member) and the NAACP LDEF (for which Branton was vice president of the board) boiled over as the twenty-fifth anniversary of the *Brown* decision approached. An April newspaper column attributed the "rift" to plans by President Jimmy Carter to hold a White House reception "in honor of the 'heroes' of the school desegregation fight." that highlighted LDEF lawyers rather than the NAACP.[56]

The national NAACP believed that use of the "NAACP" initials by the LDEF harmed the national group by causing public confusion. In addition to its concern about who was getting credit for civil rights victories, the NAACP also believed that the LDEF was siphoning donations from people who thought they were giving to the parent group and that LDEF was interfering in its relationship with local NAACP chapters.

Branton had been actively involved in both organizations for over thirty years and must have been disturbed by the fact that two good organizations could not work in parallel. Subsequent exchanges of letters and two meetings of the principals failed to resolve the disagreement and on June 28, 1979, the NAACP board of directors formally revoked its permission, given in 1939, to allow the LDEF to use the initials "NAACP."[57] A letter was sent to William T. Coleman Jr., chair of the LDEF board of directors, requesting it to "cease and desist" from using the initials "NAACP."[58] A conciliatory reply from the LDEF in October refused to back down but offered to coordinate future efforts more closely with the NAACP.[59] The matter then simmered over the next several years.

The tensions between the NAACP and the NAACP LDEF again came to a boil on May 25, 1982, when the NAACP sued the LDEF for trademark infringement, asking that it be prevented from using the initials "NAACP."[60] Former U.S. senator Edward W. Brooke represented the NAACP and Vernon E. Jordan Jr. represented the LDEF.[61] The LDEF lost the case on a Motion for Summary Judgment,[62] but its appeal was successful. In January 1985, the D.C. Court of Appeals reversed the trial court decision.[63] The LDEF could continue to use the NAACP initials. Many prominent civil rights activists who had worked with both groups expressed sadness and regret at the suit.[64]

Branton's public response, however, was typical. He recalled that, after the U.S. Supreme Court's announcement of its opinion in *Cooper v. Aaron* in 1958, he (representing the Little Rock NAACP) and Thurgood Marshall (representing LDEF) caught a cab to their lodgings. The taxi driver "turned around to us and said, 'Wasn't that a great thing Dr. King did? He just got the Supreme Court to let those kids go to Central High School in Little Rock.'"[65] Dr. King, of course, had had nothing to do with the case. Rather, Branton was making the point that it was the results that were important, not the person the public thought deserved the credit. Yet Branton himself always was careful to give credit where it was due. In a letter to the *Pine Bluff Commercial* about the *Cooper v. Aaron* litigation, he clarified the fact that the local NAACP chapter had hired him initially and the national NAACP had supported him through the Eighth Circuit Court of Appeals decision in 1956. As of August 1957, and thereafter, he had worked solely with the NAACP LDEF, which financed the remaining litigation in that case.[66]

In March 1983, relations between Branton and the Howard University administration were outwardly quite good. His name and activities shed a good light on the School of Law and its reputation had improved. That same month, however, Howard University lost a suit charging it had discriminated against a white French language teacher. It appealed the result, arguing that while it could not exclude whites from employment, it was "not required to integrate the teaching staff in such fashion that teaching opportunities for blacks in the total work force would be diminished."[67] For Wiley Branton, who believed in equal rights and true integration, this position would have been anathema. It may even have been the reason for his meeting with President Cheek on April 8. Whatever the purpose, at some point during that meeting Branton apparently informed Cheek that he would be resigning as dean at the end of the school year.[68] One might guess that Branton attempted to convince Cheek that the legal arguments the university was making were inappropriate and harmful to the cause of civil rights, and that Cheek disagreed.

On July 1, President Cheek sent Branton a letter condemning a law faculty action that allowed a third-year Howard law student to complete her third year at Rutgers University School of Law and still receive her diploma from Howard. Cheek stated that the faculty did not have authority to grant such a request and the action violated university policies and bylaws. He called Branton's involvement in the decision "dishonest and irresponsible."[69] The issue on which the letter was based is a relatively common one, and many law schools allow such leeway in appropriate circumstances. It certainly did not call for such venom from Cheek, which lends support to the notion that the two had disagreed previously about some larger matter.

In a carefully worded letter on July 26, Branton formally resigned as dean of the School of Law. He would leave on September 2.[70] News reports indicate that both Branton and Cheek remained outwardly civil, with Cheek praising Branton for "a distinguished contribution to legal education and to the university." Herbert O. Reid, an influential senior faculty member said that Branton had helped them put "more emphasis on academic achievement . . . and impose . . . more rigorous standards."[71]

Branton disclosed that he had disagreed with the University's contention that it need not hire white teachers if a black teacher was available. As quoted, Branton said, "I just think that's wrong. You can't have your cake and eat it, too. I don't think a black school has any more right to discriminate in favor of black people than other schools have to discriminate in favor of whites."[72] He also noted that the law school had not been consulted about the case. The *Pine Bluff Commercial* praised Branton's stand, noting that "[t]o Wiley Branton, the protections of the 14th Amendment apply to all, regardless of color."[73] A July 30 newspaper article disclosed that four successful suits against Howard University in the past two years had resulted in judgments totaling $796,000, and other settlements amounting to $250,000.[74]

A column by Larry Still and Art Carter reported that "it had been rumored around Washington for more than a year that the dean [Branton] and the HU administration were not hitting it on all fours." They stated that "topflight" faculty candidates "are now shunning probable appointment [at Howard] because of uncertainty about tenure and peaceful operations."[75] Some believed Branton was frustrated by his inability to "restore the institution to its former prominence as a leading think tank for civil rights issues and a major training ground for top black lawyers . . . in the middle of nit-picking, 'incompetent,' insecure persons holding high places."[76] Certainly, the five years spent in academia were an eye-opener for Branton. He conveyed to a colleague his surprise that it took him so long to adjust to the new role.[77]

One of Branton's last acts as dean was to present the school's annual report to the university president.[78] The report listed several concerns, all relating to funding, and several successes, including a Plan of Action that provided for substantial curriculum revision intended to improve student skills tested on the bar exam.[79] The plan established a required grading curve and called for substantial revision and expansion of writing requirements. Other successes were an upgrade of the school's library to meet concerns of the ABA accreditation committee and plans to improve faculty reputation and output.[80] Branton had held the job longer than most of the recent deans, and his public activities had added luster to the school's name. Although he would never speak plainly about the difficulties he faced or his reasons for leaving, Branton remained proud of his time with Howard.

CHAPTER 13

Sidley & Austin

Elder Statesman

ON SEPTEMBER 1, 1983, after more than five years as dean of Howard Law School, Branton joined the D.C. office of Sidley & Austin, a large Chicago law firm, as "Of Counsel."[1] His recruitment was considered a "major coup" in a long legal news article analyzing the 435-lawyer firm.[2] His first contact with the firm had occurred while he was still at Howard, when the firm wanted the help of an experienced trial lawyer who was knowledgeable about D.C. juries and judges.[3] The Sidley firm represented AT&T at the time and was preparing for an important trial concerning antitrust allegations against the company.[4]

How Branton came to Sidley's attention is unknown. It may have been through one of the partners in the firm's D.C. office, Robert D. McLean, who had been a law clerk for Thurgood Marshall, or through lawyers he knew from the D.C. Lawyers' Committee for Civil Rights Under Law.[5] In any event, by late 1982, Branton was listed as an independent counsel for AT&T, separately from the Sidley lawyers.[6] Richard Branton recalled that AT&T was so impressed with Branton's work, it urged Sidley to hire him.[7]

George Jones, a Sidley partner, later said that he believed the "Of Counsel" status was Branton's idea.[8] As this would be Branton's first experience working within the structure of a very large firm, that speculation is probably correct. Branton was used to being his own boss. In a 1979 interview with the Howard School of Law's newspaper, he recommended solo practice for the new lawyer, saying that it improved legal skills, instilled motivation, and gave a feeling of independence and peace of mind. As he said, "You know that you are your own man or woman."[9]

Working within the D.C. city government at the UPO and within the union structure of the ALA had been frustrating for Branton. Some of his problems at Howard were due to conflicts arising between Branton and the president of the university in an intensely bureaucratic structure. It would not be surprising if he was cautious about joining Sidley. Despite any qualms, Branton would be named a full partner at Sidley less than two years later.[10]

Branton told his family that the firm would allow him to continue his volunteer work, to hire law clerks from Howard law school, and to generally have a free hand in what work he did.[11] In return, he would work with the firm's clients as needed. His reputation and knowledge about the D.C. court system and his ability to connect with people made him an asset in persuading clients that Sidley was the firm they ought to hire.[12]

Although his presence at the firm might bring minority and other business clients to Sidley, Branton also was a respected strategist and trial lawyer. William T. Coleman, now a partner with the equally prestigious firm of O'Melvany & Myers and formerly the secretary of transportation under President Gerald R. Ford, emphasized this when he said that most people would judge Branton by what he did "in terms of civil rights, . . . but he was a superb lawyer, and he [handled] many matters having nothing to do with race, and having nothing to do with civil rights." Continuing, Secretary Coleman said Branton "really understood the principles of the common law" and "knew how to capture a few phrases, what it takes to move a court" in his presentations. Branton also knew when to end an oral argument.[13]

In addition to the freedom it offered, the arrangement with Sidley & Austin meant a better income than Branton had had at any prior job. This was significant, since Branton was now sixty years old. Supporting and putting six children through college had not allowed the Brantons to build much of a retirement nest egg. Soon, they were able to move from a townhouse in southwest Washington to North Portal, a suburban-like neighborhood in the northwest section of the city that was racially mixed and home to a number of well-known D.C. residents.[14] It was not just the money, however, that attracted Branton to the firm. His children believe he also was intrigued by the challenge of working in a big firm because it would be a new experience.[15]

Sidley & Austin was not known for the kind of law practice and publicity that Branton would bring to it. Less than a month after he officially joined the firm, Branton again was asked to help the Southern Christian Leadership Conference and Mrs. Coretta Scott King, widow of Dr. Martin Luther King Jr., resist efforts by Senator Jesse Helms to gain access to the FBI tapes and transcripts that Branton's D.C. firm had successfully sealed in two 1977 cases.[16] The Congress was considering creation of a federal holiday in honor of Dr. King, and Helms argued that he needed the information to make an informed vote. Branton handled the matter without charge and invited the Lawyers' Committee for Civil Rights Under Law to participate in the case. They were successful in resisting Helms's efforts.[17] Branton performed a variety of legal work during his years with Sidley,[18] and he continued his involvement with the AT&T case.[19]

Branton's real value to the firm, however, may have been the example he set and his involvement in training younger lawyers. George Jones, a partner at the Sidley firm who worked with Branton as a very young lawyer, recalls an adoption case Branton was handling for free. As Jones stated, "From the beginning, Wiley's conception of the case was a lot broader than [the law]. . . . And it was a wonderful experience for me . . . [to see that zealous representation included spending the time to learn] what the client wanted and needed, [even in a case where no fee would be forthcoming]."[20]

Carter Phillips, another Sidley partner, recalled that "it was a delight to . . . watch him at an agency hearing." Branton would stand before a hearing panel that clearly was not favorable, tell a few great jokes that had everyone laughing, then convince the panel that his client's position was meritorious. "Those are unbelievable skills and they were the reason why Wiley was a fabulous civil rights lawyer and wonderful [human] being."[21] Robert D. McLean, the Sidley & Austin partner who hosted the firm's later lunches honoring Branton, said that Wiley was a "force who helped us, not only to define our values, but elaborate on those values."[22]

Over the next several years, Branton continued the pace of activity he set during his first few months with the firm. His public speaking events covered a wide range of organizations.[23] His most visible public service commitment began on February 1, when he was elected chair of the D.C. Judicial Nomination Commission, which vetted judicial candidates and made recommendations to Congress for appointments and on which he had served since 1982.[24] Branton's work with the Judicial Nomination Commission was high profile and took a great deal of his time. The commission was composed of members appointed by local officials, the private sector, the court and the president of the United States, and prided itself on its independence.[25] With that background, the commission was subject to pressure from all sides, its members could be intensely political, and its activities were thoroughly covered in the press.

Branton's calm nature and ability to engage with all types of people would prove critical in getting the task done, as his term was faced with particularly volatile matters. The commission usually reviewed and recommended candidates to fill vacancies left by deaths and retirements of judges. Soon after Branton took office, however, a pending application to Congress for funding of seven new positions on D.C.'s superior court was approved.[26] The commission was given thirty days to generate and recommend three candidates for each position. Additional pressure came from a split within the commission on the importance of race as a factor in appointments. That split reflected disagreement between local and federal officials on the same issue, and was tied into the larger issue of "home rule" for the District.[27] President Reagan had appointed fourteen of forty-four D.C. judges, of whom only three were minorities in a population that was 70 percent black.[28]

Branton had long been a proponent of "home rule" for the District and he was open about the fact that race would be included in his own decisions. However, he was careful not to let that issue overwhelm the operation of the commission. By May 21, he could say that background checks on one hundred applicants for the seven new positions were "pretty much over."

During his term as chair of the commission, Branton was frequently in the news. A political fight at the federal level delayed appointment of a court of appeals judge and almost led the commission to bypass the president and go directly to Congress for a decision in 1985.[29] In 1986, the Commission was responsible for nominating someone to replace the chief judge on the superior court.[30] In 1987, the commission submitted nine candidates for three superior court vacancies.[31] During this time, Branton fought to appoint more minorities, especially women, to the bench.[32]

As part of his work on the board of the Consolidated Rail Corporation, he fought for inclusion, in a contract for sale of the Norfolk

Southern Railroad Corporation, of a covenant that required continuing a minority vendor program. A letter from Congressman Parren J. Mitchell to Branton stated "few, if any minorities will know of the tremendous service you did them in forcing the inclusion of the covenant. I know of the yeoman work you did on this."[33]

The year 1986 was momentous for Wiley Branton, with extreme highs and lows. Over his lifetime, he had maintained a schedule that would have exhausted most people. His organization skills had always allowed him to squeeze more into a day than could anyone else. In early 1986, however, the stress caught up with him. In January and February, he was hospitalized for more than a month for treatment of a heart problem.[34] Tests were performed and Branton reported to a friend that "the prognosis looks good for me."[35] In a letter to the Honorable Gladys Kessler asking to reschedule court hearings, Branton stated the problem was "arrhythmia."[36]

On March 20, he sent a letter to the editor of the *Pine Bluff Commercial* expressing amazement at the number of Pine Bluff friends and acquaintances who had send cards or telephoned to learn about his condition, even though he had moved away almost twenty-five years earlier.[37] Among the well-wishers was Arkansas governor Bill Clinton, who also expressed congratulations on daughter Toni Branton's upcoming graduation from law school.[38]

In a confidential memorandum to Benjamin Heineman, another Sidley partner, on March 26, Branton stated that further examinations at Boston's Lown Cardiology Clinic indicated that his condition was "not nearly as serious" as D.C. doctors had thought. Medicine prescribed to treat his condition had caused "serious side effects" and he had been taken off the drug and had resumed a "full schedule."[39]

A very low point occurred on May 18, when Toni Branton Moore, the Brantons' oldest daughter, died suddenly in Chicago, Illinois, where she lived with her husband and children. A student at Loyola University School of Law, she had completed her final exams and expected to graduate in just a few weeks.[40] The cause was meningitis.[41] Wiley Branton immediately went to Chicago and handled all the necessary arrangements. His son said Wiley was like a "rock," but his eyes were red. After the funeral, Wiley returned to Washington, leaving Lucille to help their son-in-law with his family. Within a day or two, he called Lucille and asked her to "come home."[42] He needed her. Leaving her youngest daughter to help, she returned to the person who was her primary focus.

Toni was the acknowledged favorite of the family. Both Richard and Wylene, the two children closest to Toni in age, knew the "pivotal" role she played in the family dynamics.[43] Wylene recalled that "[Toni] was very *wise*, she was very, ah, *practical*, and she, too, was very straight forward, . . . Toni had the same quality that he [Wiley] had: she could make each one of us feel that we were the most special one to her. And so *her* loss was really almost like losing a mother, because she was a very nurturing person."[44] Branton never fully recovered from the loss. Wylene said that "a spark went out of Dad."[45] Work had always been his solace and he very quickly plunged into it again.

The awards, recognition, and interviews regarding his civil rights work began in earnest in 1986, perhaps because news of his ill health had spread. Branton was one of fifty-three African American Arkansans honored during the state's Sesquicentennial observances.[46] On December 6, the Bar Association of the District of Columbia awarded Branton its highest honor, "Lawyer of the Year," for his "public service and contributions to the local and national communities."[47] He received the National Lawyer's Committee's Whitney North Seymour Award at a program where Senator Edward Kennedy delivered the keynote address and Branton's friend Vernon Jordan Jr. presented the award.[48]

Branton's concern about historical accuracy led him to provide advice for Henry Hampton's video series, *Eyes on the Prize.* In June 1986, Branton flew to Boston to participate in "rough cut" reviews of one segment. When invited to comment, he said, "I guess I do get concerned from time to time about how history gets distorted. I'm a great believer in trying to document things as you go *along,* and there are some people who *I* recognize that perhaps some of you don't even know and had no *reason* to know, [but] who somehow or another ought to be identified, if not by name on the film, [then in the] book or something going along *with* it."[49] Henry Hampton, its producer, called Branton's comments "perceptive, provocative, and effective."[50] The series was first shown on the Public Broadcasting System in February 1987.[51]

Branton took another opportunity to set the record straight when *Ebony* magazine published an article titled "Civil Rights Lawyers Revisited" in a December 1986 issue that included Branton.[52] The article provided an "update" on the activities of those who became famous during the fifties and sixties. Although Branton was pleased to be included, he chastised the magazine for failing to mention other lawyers, including some who appeared in some of the pictures shown but were not identified, who had performed heroic acts but had never become national news.

In a letter to the magazine, he stated, "It is essential that we remember the black lawyers who sacrificed so much in leading our civil rights battles, and that we make an effort to have our children know of their contributions." He mentioned attorneys Donald L. Hollowell and Colonel A. T. Walden of Georgia, Arthur D. Shores of Alabama, Amos T. Hall of Oklahoma, W. J. Durham of Texas, A. P. Tureau of Louisiana, Scipio A. Jones of Arkansas, Z. Alexander Looby of Tennessee, and Jack H. Young of Mississippi. Branton concluded, "Many of these men gave me the inspiration and courage to become involved in civil rights and I personally feel a debt of gratitude to all of them."[53]

Branton's thinking about civil rights was not entirely retrospective. On August 20, Branton wrote to the two Arkansas senators, David Pryor and Dale Bumpers, urging them to vote against the elevation of U.S. Supreme Court justice William Rehnquist to be Chief Justice of the Court. He feared a Rehnquist Court, noting that only a belief that the system would ultimately provide justice to African Americans allowed him to continue urging others "to use [the system] . . . rather than . . . resort[ing] to other means in trying to protest or gain their rights."[54] He did not feel confident that Rehnquist could provide this. Branton was unsuccessful; both senators voted in favor of Rehnquist's elevation.[55]

On January 18, 1987, Branton heard author David J. Garrow say that Branton had informed Garrow of details about Dr. Martin Luther King Jr.'s alleged extramarital affairs. The remarks were made on a television program called *Tony Brown's Journal*. Branton immediately sent a letter to Brown demanding a public retraction. In a letter to Garrow, Branton denied making any statements on that subject and said he was "appalled" to hear the comment.[56] A letter to Coretta Scott King told her of his response to the comments and declared that he had not made such comments.[57] He asked that his letter be placed in appropriate files of the Martin Luther King Jr. Center so that future researchers would know of his response. Branton's papers do not include any response from Mrs. King, but a February 1988 *Jet* magazine article reported that Branton had filed a $6 million suit against Garrow and Brown.[58] His son, Wiley Jr., represented him in that suit and reached a compromise that required corrections in the book's next printing.[59]

On February 22, 1987, Branton suffered a second bout of heart problems, caused by "ventricular tachycardia"[60] (which describes a racing heart). Two weeks later, he was still in the hospital undergoing tests to determine what would stop the symptoms so that a defibrillator could be implanted to control the condition. His doctors told him he should not plan on performing any major work before May or June.[61] Branton was released after five weeks and, as of June 12, was still taking ten different medications.[62]

By the end of April, however, Branton was back to work on almost a full-time basis.[63] It was as if he felt that time was running out for him. His son, Wiley Jr., who was living in D.C. at the time, said that this hospitalization was the one that made him realize his father's condition was serious. The senior Branton never referred to any of his medical events as "heart attacks" within the family,[64] but Wylene Branton Wood recalls that her father told her he was afraid of having to live as an invalid.[65]

Life seemed to be back on track, however, with Branton making speeches and receiving awards.[66] In July 1987, Branton was interviewed by William A. Elwood, director of the Civil Rights Lawyers Documentary Project at the University of Virginia.[67] In September, Branton was leadoff speaker at a program at the University of Arkansas commemorating the thirtieth anniversary of the Little Rock school crisis. Branton's speech set the tone for the conference, but it was his rebuttal to the remarks of former Governor Faubus that highlighted his continuing passion about Little Rock and school integration.[68] It also demonstrated Branton's ability to separate the person from the position and to confer forgiveness.

Faubus was scheduled to speak the morning after Branton's talk, and Branton was in the audience. When Faubus had finished denying responsibility for the trouble, Branton asked if he might give a response to some of the statements made by Faubus. Before he proceeded to demolish Faubus's comments, he paused to shake hands and smilingly introduce himself by saying, "Governor, I'm Wiley Branton, and in all these years, I don't believe I've had the pleasure of meeting you."[69]

A similar instance had occurred in 1966 when Jim Johnson, the avid segregationist who had spearheaded enactment of numerous anti-integration articles into the Arkansas State Constitution in 1956, retired from the Arkansas Supreme Court. According to Johnson's son, on reading of Johnson's retirement, Wiley Branton telephoned Johnson, "thank[ing] him for his service and [saying] that he [Johnson] had truly been a colorblind judge, never allowing race or any other inappropriate factor to enter into his decisions."[70] The statement was probably true, according to Branton's view of Johnson's later career. Branton kept close tabs on civil rights issues in Arkansas throughout his lifetime, and there was no personal gain to be derived from that call.

In fact, Branton's papers are replete with instances of his going out of his way to congratulate or console. Usually, these notes were to people he had known at some point in his life, a grade school teacher or member of the church he had attended as a youngster. Frequently, however, they were made to perfect strangers who had performed some achievement the newspapers thought worthy of coverage. Branton believed in encouraging the performance of good deeds and accomplishments.

In January 1988, Branton participated in the fortieth anniversary program at the University of Arkansas commemorating enrollment of the school's first African American student, Silas Hunt. Branton was a featured speaker, describing the events that led to Hunt's enrollment.[71] Virtually all of his African American law school classmates also appeared and their recollections, always related in a joking manner, were inspiring. Later in the year, Branton would make a contribution to the Silas Hunt Scholarship Fund at the school.[72]

Branton's friendship with Thurgood Marshall had strengthened over the years, and they spoke with each other on a daily basis. As Marshall became more reclusive toward the end of his life, Branton was one of the few old friends who could get Marshall to attend a social function. Branton managed to produce Marshall for an eightieth birthday celebration on September 14, 1988, where the Justice was honored by the Congressional Black Caucus.[73] Branton had invited Atlanta civil rights attorney Donald L. Hollowell, who was Vernon Jordan's first employer, to the celebration. Hollowell wrote a few days later to thank Branton and noted that "Thurgood seemed most comfortable when you were close at hand."[74]

When Branton gave a talk for the NAACP LDEF at its *Pro Bono* Awards Luncheon in November, he did not appear in ill health.[75] Life was going on, and Branton was planning ahead. That month, Branton had committed himself to a number of serious responsibilities. He accepted the University of Arkansas's invitation to speak at its spring commencement on May 13, 1989.[76] He agreed to serve on the Affirmative Action Committee of the American Bar Association's Section of Legal Education and Admissions to the Bar;[77] and was named to the D.C. Public Education Committee, whose mandate was to evaluate the public school system and develop a long-term plan to improve it.[78]

On December 15, 1988, Wiley and Lucille had just returned from Philadelphia, where they had attended the Christmas party of the CONRAIL board. Wiley was not feeling well and thought he might be coming down with the flu, so they did not go out that night as planned. While they were sitting at the dinner table, Wiley Branton had a final and fatal heart attack. Daughter Wylene said, "I'm so grateful that, if he had to die, that he died in the manner that he did. He sort of died with his boots on, sitting with his favorite girl at the table."

Epilogue

WILEY BRANTON'S LIFE cannot be summed up easily. He was born with an interest in people. His grandmother's teachings would have fallen on deaf ears without that trait. He also must have been deeply empathetic, with an ability to truly listen to people, identifying with their feelings and experience. A responsibility to his community and his society was engrained in him. His own life was an easy one, yet he could not sit back and enjoy it. Instead, he chose to devote himself to work that would provide benefit to others. He was committed to that course of action, even at the risk of his own safety.

Oddly enough, Branton probably would rather have lived his life in an ordinary way. If segregation and discrimination against African Americans had not existed, he may have been well content as a businessman in Pine Bluff. He would always have been involved in civic concerns, but his efforts would have benefited the entire community. Toward the end of his life, looking back, he indicated regret that he and other African Americans were not accepted and treated with equality. He noted that such treatment deprived every community of the best contributions of all its citizens.

Branton was, despite his humor and penchant for storytelling, a relatively formal man. His children talked about the difficulty they had in getting him out of his suits and white shirts and into casual clothes. Even after they were both lawyers, and Wiley Jr. was taking over his father's law practice, their relationship remained that of father and son. They did not become colleagues. The children mentioned their surprise when their father cried before the church congregation in Atlanta, just before the family moved to Washington, D.C. Son Richard recalled his mother telling him that she had seen her husband cry over only three events—when he lost his first case, when they left Atlanta, and when their daughter Toni died.

Despite his bonhomie, and his many friends, Wiley Branton was a very private person. Supreme Court justice Thurgood Marshall, Vernon E. Jordan Jr., and Paul Webber III were his closest friends during the decade or two before his death. They spoke with each other almost daily, yet Jordan and Webber do not recall Branton ever revealing uncertainty or indecision about his next step. The children say that, if he talked with anyone about such things, it would have been their mother, Lucille. Lucille Branton died in 1998 and, if she heard them, she kept to herself any confidences Wiley shared with her.

Scores of people who knew Branton in different contexts tell stories about him, still exhibiting tears of regret at his loss. Thousands of pages have been devoted to histories of the decades during which he lived. Branton is mentioned frequently, and never in a negative way. The stories of his good humor, courage, and tenacity abound. Wiley Branton was a good man, who did his best to change our society for the better.

When he died suddenly in 1988, lengthy obituaries appeared in newspapers across the country, including the *Washington Post,* the *New York Times,* the *Chicago Tribune,* the *Arkansas Gazette,* and the *Pine Bluff Commercial.* Many were written by people who only knew of Wiley Branton. They spoke mainly about his work achievements, which were impressive. There were exceptions. Former Arkansas senator David Pryor said Wiley Branton would be remembered "as a hard-working, sincere man. Although a gifted attorney, he was quiet and unassuming. It is his humility and desire to always put the goals of the civil rights movement before self which probably accounts for the fact that [he] was not more famous than he was."[1] Fifteen years after his death, columnist Paul Greenberg wrote that Wiley Branton "lived fully aware . . . he fought—without malice . . . In the midst of the struggle, he always kept in his mind an idea of what peace would be like, and how he would make it."[2]

The columnist William Raspberry praised Branton's work, but said, "[his] special gift was his friendship . . . [his] kindness, his good fellowship and his incredible warmth."[3] Congressman John Lewis said Branton was "[w]arm, witty, diligent, exceedingly talented, genuine, and generous. Wiley was always there when we needed him."[4] Then-Arkansas-governor Bill Clinton said, "[Wiley] made it easier for blacks . . . and for white folks to be decent people."[5] Robert D. McLean, a Sidley & Austin partner, saw Branton as providing a moral compass. He said of Branton after his death, "so many of us have found that, though we can't ask him, we can ask ourselves, 'what would Wiley have done?'"[6] Thurgood Marshall, three years after Branton's death, said "virtually every day I miss his warmth, his wit, and most of all, his wisdom."[7]

It is fitting to end this chronicle with Wiley Branton's own words: "I am optimistic about the future and the basic good in mankind. Peace to all."[8]

NOTES

CHAPTER 1: Character-Building: The Early Years

1. The terminology of race changed over the years of Branton's life, and thereafter. This work will use the terms of the day, those that Branton would have used. "Colored" and "Negro" were used interchangeably until the 1960s, when the term "black" came into use. Later the term "African American" became preferred by some. Wiley Branton's brothers refuse to refer to themselves as African Americans. Quotes are left with the term used by the speaker.

2. 14th Census of the United States, Population 1920, Vol. III, Government Printing Office, 1922, Table 10, p. 98 (recording a population of 19,280, of which 6,403 were colored). Pine Bluff was located in Jefferson County, which is about forty-five miles south of the state capitol at Little Rock and had a total population of about 60,000, sixty-five percent of whom were African American.

3. Judith Kilpatrick, "(Extra)Ordinary Men: African American Lawyers and Civil Rights in Arkansas Before 1950," 53 *Ark. L. Rev.* 299 (2000) (hereinafter "Kilpatrick").

4. James W. Leslie, *Pine Bluff and Jefferson County, A Pictorial History* 165 (1981).

5. C. Calvin Smith, *Educating the Masses* 4 (2003) (listing Little Rock, Pine Bluff, Hot Springs, Helena, Fort Smith, and Texarkana) (hereinafter "Smith, *Educating the Masses*"). There were 160 white high schools in 1920. *Id.*

6. Michael B. Dougan, *Arkansas Odyssey, the Saga of Arkansas from Prehistoric Times to Present* 402 (1994) (hereinafter "Dougan").

7. Smith, *Educating the Masses* at 9; *The WPA Guide to 1930s Arkansas* 194–95, Compiled by Workers of the Writers' Project of the Works Projects Administration in the State of Arkansas (1987, originally published 1941).

8. Kilpatrick at 361. A grandfather clause would have prevented anyone from voting whose grandfather had not been able to vote before the Civil War.

9. Wiley A. Branton, "Post-War [World War II] Relations in Pine Bluff," essay submitted to Don Williams, *Pine Bluff Commercial,* 11/6/1985 (hereinafter "WAB Pine Bluff Essay"). WAB Papers.

10. Wiley A. Branton, speech addressed to Association of American Law Schools' program "Access 2000, The Challenge to Assure Diversity in the Legal Profession," 1988, pp. 3–4 (hereinafter "WAB Access 2000 Speech"). WAB Papers.

11. George Lipsitz, *A Life in the Struggle, Ivory Perry and the Culture of Opposition* 30–31 (1988) (reporting that "postal worker and chapter chairman W. B. Cloman wrote to the national office.").

12. See, e.g., Elizabeth Rauh Bethel, *Promiseland, A Century of Life in a Negro Community* 80 (1981).

13. WAB Pine Bluff Essay 11.

14. Audiotape of family history, Sterling Branton, Transcript p. 1 (hereinafter "Branton Family History").

15. John Dittmer, *Local People, The Struggle for Civil Rights in Mississippi* 147–48 (1995) (hereinafter "Dittmer, Local People").

16. Telephone conversation with Professor Tony Freyer, University of Alabama School of Law, concerning Freyer's 12/11/1979 interview with Wiley Branton.

17. 1860 U.S. Census, Series M653, Roll 1259, p. 70; 1870 U.S. Census, Series M593, Roll 1541, p. 227.

18. Branton Family History at 3.

19. James W. Leslie, *Saracen's Country* 144 (1974).

20. The 1880 Census places the family in Arkansas City, Desha County, Arkansas, and lists Ellen Wiley as "mulatto." 1880 U.S. Census, Family History Library Film 1254043, NA Film Number T9–0043, pp. 308A–309A; *http://www.familysearch.org/ Eng/Search/Census/indiv_record*, visited 7/11/2003. Photographs indicate a significant amount of Indian blood. Ellen was born in Colahja (phonetic), Alabama. Branton Family History at 3.

21. See, generally, Angela Y. Walton-Raji, *Black Indian Genealogy Research, African Ancestors among the Five Civilized Tribes* (1993).

22. Letter dated 1/22/1985, p. 3, from WAB to Professor George Lipsitz, University of Houston at Clear Lake City (hereinafter "Lipsitz Letter"). WAB Papers.

23. Warranty Deed dated 10/2/1920, from Henry H. Haizlip and Rebecca Porter Haizlip to James A. Wiley and Effie Wiley, recorded 1/26/1923.

24. See, e.g., Trina Jones, "Shades of Brown: The Law of Skin Color," 49 *Duke L.J.* 1487 (2000); Leonard M. Baynes, "If It's Not Just Black and White Anymore, Why Does Darkness Cast a Longer Discriminatory Shadow Than Lightness? An Investigation and Analysis of the Color Hierarchy," 74 *Denv. U. L. Rev.* 131 (1997); Verna M. Keith and Cedric Herring, "Skin Tone and Stratification in the Black Community," 97 *American Journal of Sociology* 760 (1991); Michael Hughes and Bradley R. Hertel, "The Significance of Color Remains: A Study of Life Chances, Mate Selection, and Ethnic Consciousness among Black Americans," 68 *Social Forces* 1105 (1990); and William M. Kephart, "The 'Passing' Question," 9 *Phylon* 336 (1948).

25. Kilpatrick at 325–26.

26. Letter dated 4/1/1980 from WAB to Mr. William Pickens III (regarding his knowledge of Pickens's grandfather, dean of Tuskegee Institute). Branton noted that his mother "was a student secretary in Booker T. Washington's office at the time of his death and she also became a great friend and admirer of Dean Pickens." WAB Papers.

27. Undated obituary published several days after her death on 3/16/1945, probably in the Eighth Avenue Baptist Church newsletter. WAB Papers.

28. Undated obituary published several days after her death on 3/16/1945, probably in the Eighth Avenue Baptist Church newsletter. WAB Papers.

29. Letter dated 4/10/1929 from J. J. Black, Branch Sec., to Mr. Bagnall, Papers of the NAACP, Part I, G13, Branch Files, Pine Bluff 1929–30.

30. George Lipsitz, *A Life in the Struggle, Ivory Perry and the Culture of Opposition* 34–35 (1988) (hereinafter "Lipsitz, *Ivory Perry*").

31. "Application for Charter of Pine Bluff, Ark. Branch of the National Association for the Advancement of Colored People," dated 11/28/1919, p. 4. Papers of the NAACP, Part I, G13, Branch Files, Pine Bluff, 1917–1922, Library of Congress (hereinafter "NAACP Papers"); *Id.* at Pine Bluff 1928–30, Membership Report 6/14/1930; *Id.* at 1935–36, letter dated 1/10/1935; *Id.* at 1937–39, letter dated 1/22/1938.

32. Letter dated 5/12/1928 from J. J. Black, Branch Secretary, to Miss Dora L.

Alston, NAACP. NAACP Papers, Part I, G13, Branch Files, Pine Bluff 1924–28, Library of Congress; Membership Report form, NAACP Papers, Part I, G13, Branch Files, Pine Bluff 1929–30, Library of Congress; Membership Report form, NAACP Papers, Part I, G13, Branch Files, Pine Bluff 1937–39, Library of Congress.

33. Lipsitz, Ivory Perry at 34–35.

34. Branton Family History at 12.

35. Warranty Deed dated 3/7/1928, James A. and Effie Wiley to Leo and Pauline A. Branton, recorded 3/14/1928.

36. Draft interview, attached to letter dated 2/13/1978 from Hollie West to WAB, p. 16 (hereinafter "WAB 1978 Interview"). WAB Papers.

37. Dr. Jane Smith, President, National Council of Negro Women, speaking at Wiley A. Branton luncheon, Sidley & Austin, September 1999 (videotape in possession of author).

38. Interview with Christopher C. Mercer, 5/21/1998, p. 3.

39. WAB Pine Bluff Essay at 4.

40. Interview with Sterling Branton, Burbank, California, 7/20/2000, p. 5.

41. Letter dated 10/11/1965 WAB to Mrs. D. S. Edwards, Merrill High School, Pine Bluff, AR. WAB Papers.

42. Transcript, p. 12, Senate Labor and Human Resources Committee Hearing, Topic: Nomination of Dr. Henry Foster to be Surgeon General, Federal News Service, May 3, 1995. [LexisNexis™ Academic—Document: *http://o-web-lexis-nexis.com.library.uark.edu/universe/*.

43. Ken Adelman, "You Can Change Their Hearts," *Washingtonian Magazine* (March 1988), 109–10.

44. Letter dated 2/14/1985, WAB to the Editor, *Pine Bluff Commercial*. WAB Papers.

45. Smith, *Educating the Masses* at 82.

46. Branton Family History at 15.

47. Wiley A. Branton, Application for Federal Employment 5, 2/15/1965, White House Central Files, Office Files of John Macy, "Branton, Wiley A.," Box 58, LBJ Library.

48. Interview with Sterling Branton, Burbank, California, 7/20/2000, p. 5.

49. Branton Family History at 8.

50. Program, Memorial Service, 12/19/1988, Washington National Cathedral, Washington, D.C.

51. Interview with Sterling Branton, Burbank, California, 7/20/2000, pp. 63–64.

52. Narrative of Leo A. Branton Jr., videotaped during Branton family reunion, 11/30/1985 (transcript in author's possession), pp. 1–3.

53. Lipsitz Letter. That firebrand was W. Harold Flowers, who challenged local custom by refusing to bring a white lawyer along when he appeared in court. Flowers went on to become a strong force in civil rights activities in Pine Bluff and Arkansas. See John A. Kirk, *Redefining the Color Line: Black Activism in Little Rock, Arkansas, 1940–1970,* at 25–33 (2002).

54. Narrative of Leo A. Branton Jr., videotaped during Branton family reunion, 11/30/1985 (transcript in author's possession), p. 3.

55. Narrative of Leo A. Branton Jr., videotaped during Branton family reunion, 11/30/1985 (transcript in author's possession), p. 3.

56. Lipsitz, *Ivory Perry* at 33–34.

57. Letter dated 10/3/1940, J. B. Watson, President, AM&N College, to Dr. W. J. Hale, President of Tennessee A&I State College. WAB Papers.

58. Lipsitz, *Ivory Perry* at 33–35. Lipsitz continued, "The Branton case illustrates the important role played by independent black businesspeople in building community resources for social contestation in southern cities. . . . Of course, the community was not monolithic and not every black business owner could or would support civil rights activity, but they did serve as a potential and sometimes an actual base of support." *Id.* at 34–35.

CHAPTER 2: Racism during World War II

1. Ulysses Lee, "The Employment of Negro Troops," *United States Army in World War II* 35 (Office of the Chief of Military History, United States Army, Washington, D.C. 1966) (hereinafter "Negro Troops").

2. Smith, *Educating the Masses* at 18–19.

3. Stanley Sandler, "Homefront Battlefront: Military Racial Disturbances in the Zone of the Interior, 1941–45," 11 War and Society 101, 103 (No. 2, October 1993) (hereinafter "Sandler"). Once the European war began, many assumed that it was only a matter of time until the United States was involved.

4. "Negro Troops" at 78–79.

5. Jack D. Foner, *Blacks and the Military in American History, A New Perspective* 146 (1974) (hereinafter "Foner").

6. Foner at 137–38.

7. Foner at 135.

8. Foner at 141.

9. George Q. Flynn, "Selective Service and American Blacks during World War II," 69 *Journal of Legal History* 14 (No. 1, Winter 1984) (hereinafter "Flynn").

10. Flynn at 19.

11. A. Russell Buchanan, *Black Americans in World War II* 72 (1977).

12. Negro Troops at 43–44, 133–34.

13. Sandler at 101, 106.

14. Foner at 157.

15. Telephone conversation with Sterling Branton, 1/4/2004.

16. Interview with Wiley Austin Branton, by Steven Lawson for the Oral History Research Office Columbia University, October 1970 in Washington, D.C., p. 50 (hereinafter "WAB 1970 Interview"). WAB Papers.

17. Wiley A. Branton, Service Record—2/25/1943 to 3/17/1946, pp. 4–5.

18. Wiley A. Branton, remarks during panel discussion, "A Historical Review of the Events of February 2, 1948," Legacy of Silas Hunt Program, 1/29–30/1988, p. 4 (hereinafter "WAB, Legacy of Silas Hunt").

19. WAB Investigation Report, File No. 3AF-19-M, p. 1 (hereinafter "Investigation Report").

20. Investigation Report at 3–4.

21. Interview with Sterling Branton, 7/20/2000, p. 64.

22. Interview with Sterling Branton, 7/20/2000, p. 64.

23. Investigation Report at 4.

24. Irving Howe and Lewis Coser, *The American Communist Party, A Critical History* 4 (1962) (hereinafter "Howe and Coser").

25. Howe and Coser at 54–55.

26. Howe and Coser at 176.

27. Howe and Coser at 234–35.

28. William Z. Foster, *History of the Communist Party of the United States* 233 (1968).

29. Howe and Coser at 212–16; William Z. Foster, *History of the Communist Party of the United States* 286–87 (1968). The charges against the men were false, but within the culture of those days, the truth had little to do with the case. Lawyers from the party's legal wing, the International Labor Defense, fought to free the nine over the course of the next nineteen years. For the complete story, see Dan T. Carter, *Scottsboro, A Tragedy of the American South* (1969); Haywood Patterson and Earl Conrad, *Scottsboro Boy* (1950).

30. Philip Foner and Herbert Shapiro, eds., *American Communism and Black Americans, A Documentary History, 1930–1934* at 36–50 (1991) (reprinted from *The Communist* IX, February 1931, 153–67) (emphasis in original) (hereinafter "Foner and Shapiro").

31. Foner and Shapiro at xxiii.

32. Foner and Shapiro at xxv; William Z. Foster, *History of the Communist Party of the United States* 287–88 (1968).

33. Investigation Report at 5–7.

34. "The need of an industrial education in an industrial democracy," in *The Middle Works, 1899–1924*, Volume 10, pp. 409–414 (J. A. Boydston, ed., 1976).

35. Investigation Report at 7.

36. Ronald B. Hartzer, "Black Aviation Engineer Units of World War II," *The CE* 20 (Winter 1998).

37. Karl C. Dod, "The Corps of Engineers: The War against Japan," *United States Army in World War II*, Appendix B (Office of the Chief of Military History, United States Army, Washington D.C. 1966) (hereinafter "Dod").

38. WAB, Legacy of Silas Hunt at 4.

39. Telephone conversation with Sterling Branton, 10/22/2003.

40. Dod at 649.

41. See generally, chapter 1, "Okinawa: The Last Battle," U.S. Army in World War II (Historical Division, Department of the Army 1948). The battle for Okinawa began on March 25, 1945, with the actual invasion a week later, on April 1. The topography was difficult and there was heavy resistance from Japanese troops. Heavy and lengthy rains beginning in May and delays in receiving supplies added to the difficulty. *Id.*

42. Wiley A. Branton, Service Record—2/25/1943 to 3/17/1946.

43. Sandler at 101, 109.

44. Flynn at 24.

Chapter 3: Citizen Activist: A New Era

1. Undated obituary published several days after her death on 3/16/1945, probably in the Eighth Avenue Baptist Church newsletter. WAB Papers.

2. Southtown Economist (Chicago), 10/25/1978 (noting his success at

overcoming white prejudice while he was "a black principal at an all-white school in the heart of the Southwest Side's anti-busing movement."). WAB Papers.

3. Branton Family History at 12.

4. Interview with Richard Branton, 9/8/2001, p. 6.

5. Speech by Wiley A. Branton delivered at Sunrise Services, Founder's Day Program, AM&N College, 4/28/1957, included in Bennie W. Goodwin, "Silas Hunt, The Growth of a Folk Hero," *Report for English* 573 (Arkansas Folklore), 5/20/1957, p. 14 (hereinafter "WAB Sunrise Services Speech"). WAB Papers.

6. Statement of Rufus McKinney, part of Interview with Eddie Williams, 9/6/2001, p. 4 (recalling that he was directed to a Branton cab by a white cab driver when he arrived to attend AM&N College).

7. Telephone conversation with Sterling Branton, 1/30/2004; Interview with Richard Branton, 9/8/2001, pp. 6–7.

8. WAB, Legacy of Silas Hunt at 4.

9. WAB 1970 Interview at 51; Ken Adelman, "Steadfast Vision of Rights," *Washington Times* 1/9/89.

10. John A. Kirk, *Redefining the Color Line, Black Activism in Little Rock, Arkansas, 1940–1970* at 31 (2002).

11. "Democrat Vote Stuns Arkansas," 11/29/1947, *Chicago Defender*, NAACP Papers, Part II, C10, Branch Files, Pine Bluff, 1940–47, Library of Congress.

12. Lawson, *Black Ballots, Voting Rights in the South, 1944–1969*, 22 (1976) (hereinafter "Lawson, *Black Ballots*").

13. 321 U.S. 649 (1944).

14. C. Calvin Smith, "The Politics of Evasion: Arkansas' Reaction to *Smith v. Allwright*, 1944," 67 *J. of Southern History* 40 (1944).

15. C. Calvin Smith, "The Politics of Evasion: Arkansas' Reaction to *Smith v. Allwright*, 1944," 67 *J. of Southern History* 40, 49 (1944).

16. WAB Pine Bluff Essay at 20. See also Calvin R. Ledbetter Jr., "Arkansas Amendment for Voter Registration Without Poll Tax Payment," 54 *Ark. Hist. Q.* 134, 138 (Summer 1995) (demonstrating that the situation had not changed by 1964).

17. WAB Interview by William A. Elwood, the Civil Rights Lawyers Documentary Project, University of Virginia, 7/15/1987, transcript p. 101 (hereinafter "WAB 1987 Interview"); WAB Access 2000 speech at 7.

18. WAB 1987 Interview at 101; WAB Access 2000 speech at 7.

19. WAB Pine Bluff Essay at p. 20; A. Stephen Stephan, "Changes in the Status of Negroes in Arkansas, 1948–50," 9 *Ark. Hist. Q.* 43 (1950) (hereinafter "Stephan").

20. Letter dated 11/4/1980 from WAB to the Editor, *Pine Bluff Commercial*. WAB Papers.

21. WAB Pine Bluff Essay at 15.

22. "Personal Memories of Thurgood Marshall," 40 *Ark. L. Rev.* 665, 666 (1987).

23. Stephan at 43 (commenting that the exact number was not known but was estimated to be about 22,600); Irving J. Spitzberg Jr., "Racial Politics in Little Rock 1954–1964," in *American Legal and Constitutional History* 33 (Harold Hyman and Stuart Bruchey, eds., 1987) (hereinafter "Spitzberg").

24. "Democrat Vote Stuns Arkansas," 11/29/1949, *Chicago Defender*, NAACP Papers, Part II, C10, Branch Files, Pine Bluff, 1940–47, Library of Congress.

25. Sidney S. McMath, *Promises Kept, A Memoir* 167–79 (2003); Stephan at 43.

26. WAB Access 2000 speech at 7, 8.

27. "Southern Lawyer," *Ebony* magazine 67, 69 (1949).

28. John A. Kirk, *Redefining the Color Line, Black Activism in Little Rock, Arkansas, 1940–1970*, 33 (2002).

29. Sec. 4873, Ch. 55., Pope's Digest, Vol. 1, Statutes of Arkansas, at 1393.

30. *Branton v. State*, 214 Ark. 861, 867–68 (1949).

31. *Branton v. Arkansas*, 338 S. Ct. 878 (1949).

32. WAB Access 2000 Speech at 8.

33. Editorial, "Throw Out a Lifeline and Repeal Jim Crow—Again," 6/4/1994, *Arkansas Democrat-Gazette*, p. 6B.

34. See, e.g., WAB Access 2000 Speech, where Branton goes into great detail about the experience.

35. Robert Mann, *The Walls of Jericho, Lyndon Johnson, Hubert Humphrey, Richard Russell, and the Struggle for Civil Rights* 152 (1996) (hereinafter "Mann").

36. Mark V. Tushnet, *The NAACP's Legal Strategy Against Segregated Education, 1925–1950* at 1–2 (1987) (hereinafter "Tushnet").

37. *Plessy v. Ferguson*, 163 U.S. 537 (1896).

38. Tushnet at 25–27.

39. Tushnet at 36.

40. *Pearson v. Murray*, 169 Md. 478 (1936).

41. *State of Missouri v. Gaines*, 305 U.S. 337 (1938).

42. 305 U.S. at 352.

43. WAB Sunrise Services Speech at 15.

44. *Sipuel v. Board of Regents of University of Oklahoma*, 199 Okla. 36 (1947).

45. *Sipuel v. Board of Regents of University of Oklahoma*, 332 U.S. 631 (1948).

46. *Sweatt v. Painter*, 339 U.S. 629 (1950).

47. 339 U.S. at 634.

48. WAB 1987 Interview at 103–4; James W. Leslie, *Saracen's Country* 210 (1974). Arkansas was within the jurisdiction of the North Central division of the Association of Colleges and Secondary Schools, and AM&N was not accredited by that body until 1950. *Id.*

49. "Negro Hopes to be Student at U. of Arkansas," 1/30/1948, *Arkansas Gazette*, p. 1.

50. "Plan to Admit Some Negroes to University," 1/30/1948, *Arkansas Democrat*, p. 1.

51. WAB Sunrise Services Speech at 15.

52. WAB 1987 Interview at 104.

53. WAB 1987 Interview at 104; WAB Sunrise Services Speech at 16–17.

54. "Hunt Was Excellent Candidate to Break Color Line," 1/27/1988, *Springdale News*, p. 1C.

55. His Service Record states he was five feet, seven inches tall and weighed 133 pounds.

56. Conversation with Stephanie Branton, daughter-in-law, 8/20/2003.

57. See descriptions of Jack & Jill organization in Lawrence Otis Graham, *Our Kind of People* (1999).

58. Obituary, 1/23/1998, *Washington Post*, p. B08; 1/17/1998, *Arkansas Democrat-Gazette*, p. B8; 1/17/1998, *Commercial Appeal* (Memphis, TN), p. A10.

59. Author's notes of interview with Richard Branton, 9/8/2001.

CHAPTER 4: Desegregating the University of Arkansas School of Law

1. Thomas Rothrock, "Joseph Carter Corbin and Negro Education in the University of Arkansas," 30 *Ark. Hist. Q.* 277, 281 (1971).

2. Robert A. Leflar, *The First 100 Years, Centennial History of the University of Arkansas* 273 (1972) (hereinafter "Leflar, *First 100 Years*").

3. Richard C. Cortner, *A Mob Intent on Death, The NAACP and the Arkansas Riot Cases* 51 (1988); Mary White Ovington, *Portraits in Color* 92 (1927). These publications state that Jones attempted to enter the Law School. However, since a law department was not authorized until 1890 and no law classes were given until 1893, John Hugh Reynolds and David Yancey Thomas, *History of the University of Arkansas* 296–97 (1910), Jones probably attempted to enroll in the undergraduate school, if at all.

4. Judith Kilpatrick, "Race Expectations: Arkansas African American Attorneys (1865–1950)," 9 *J. Gender, Social Policy and the Law* 63 (2000).

5. Guerdon D. Nichols, *Breaking the Color Barrier at the University of Arkansas,* 27 *Ark. Hist. Q.* 3, 5 (1968) (hereinafter "Nichols").

6. Bob Lancaster, "Living by the Rules," *Northwest Arkansas Times* 24, 29 (August 1986).

7. Nichols at 5–6.

8. Nichols at 6.

9. Nichols at 6.

10. Nichols at 8, 10–11.

11. Nichols at 8–9.

12. Nichols at 11–13.

13. Nichols at 13.

14. Nichols at 14.

15. Leflar, *First 100 Years* at 281.

16. "Plan to Admit Some Negroes to University," 1/30/1948, *Arkansas Democrat*, p. 1.

17. "NAACP Leader Voices His Dissatisfaction," 1/30/1948, p. 7.

18. WAB, Legacy of Silas Hunt at 7.

19. "NAACP Leader Voices His Dissatisfaction," 1/30/1948, p. 7.

20. WAB, Legacy of Silas Hunt at 8–9.

21. WAB Sunrise Services Speech 17.

22. WAB Sunrise Services Speech 17.

23. WAB 1987 Interview at 104.

24. WAB, Legacy of Silas Hunt at 9.

25. Nichols at 16.

26. A. Stephen Stephan, "Desegregation of Higher Education in Arkansas," 27 *J. of Negro Education* 243, 246 (Summer 1958).

27. Draft letter from Jackie Shropshire to University of Arkansas Alumni Association, att. to letter dated 7/24/1987 from WAB to Shropshire, p. ii (hereinafter "Shropshire Letter"). WAB Papers.

28. WAB Sunrise Services Speech at 18.

29. WAB Sunrise Services Speech at 18.

30. Wiley A. Branton, Luncheon Speech, Legacy of Silas Hunt Program, 1/29–30/1988, p. 5.

31. A. Stephen Stephan, "Desegregation of Higher Education in Arkansas," 27 *J. of Negro Education* 243, 246 (Summer 1958).

32. Chris Osher, "Couple Befriended Hunt, Gave Him Place to Rest," 2/3/1988, *Arkansas Traveler* (University of Arkansas), p. 1.

33. A. Stephen Stephan, "Desegregation of Higher Education in Arkansas," 27 *J. of Negro Education* 243, 247 (Summer 1958).

34. Jackie Shropshire, panel discussion "The Early Years," Legacy of Silas Hunt Program, 1/29–30/1988, p. 23.

35. Interview with Christopher Mercer, 5/13/2004, p. 2.

36. Interview with Christopher Mercer, 5/13/2004, p. 2.

37. Jackie Shropshire, panel discussion "The Early Years," Legacy of Silas Hunt Program, 1/29–30/1988, p. 24.

38. Shropshire Letter at iii.

39. Interview with Christopher Mercer, 5/13/2004, p. 2.

40. Jackie Shropshire, panel discussion, "The Early Years," Legacy of Silas Hunt Program, 1/29–30/1988, p. 24.

41. Jackie Shropshire, panel discussion, "The Early Years," Legacy of Silas Hunt Program, 1/29–30/1988, p. 24.

42. Shropshire Letter at iii.

43. Shropshire Letter at iii–iv.

44. Interview with Christopher Mercer, 5/13/2004, p. 19.

45. Interview with Christopher Mercer, 5/13/2004, pp. 7–8.

46. Wiley Branton, "Advice and Dissent," 6/2/1980, *Pine Bluff Commercial,* p. 4 (excerpting B's commencement address at UALR School of Law). WAB Papers.

47. Shropshire Letter at iii. He also recalled being hit by bottle caps and hearing catcalls when he refused to stand for the playing of "Dixie" by the marching band.

48. Interview with George Howard Jr., 5/28/1998, pp. 12–13 (commenting that when he arrived on campus and presented his certificate for campus housing, there was some commotion because they had not known he was Negro). Unhappy about this, Howard considered filing suit, but decided he did not want to add litigation to the pressures that would come with beginning law studies. *Id.*

49. Letter dated 2/27/2004 from the Honorable George Howard Jr. to Judith Kilpatrick. Mercer describes the group as a "clique" that included himself and George Haley. Interview with Christopher C. Mercer, 5/13/2004, p. 35.

50. Jerol Garrison, "Negro Elected Lloyd Halls Prexy," 10/10/1952, *Arkansas Traveler,* p. 1 (noting that he had received eighty votes, twenty-four more than the nearest opponent of three other candidates).

51. Interview with Christopher Mercer, 5/13/2004, p. 3. Penix later was invited by Christopher Mercer to represent the Hoxie School Board when it faced segregationist opposition to school integration in 1954. Mercer said he remembered Penix's letter to George and thought "his cap must be on right." Interview with Christopher Mercer, 5/13/2004, p. 33.

52. "2 Negroes Tell Why They Seek UA Integration," 9/5/1964, *Arkansas Gazette,*

p. 6B. Howard was the main attorney for the two, but an earlier article in the *Gazette,* 8/18/1964, title "Negroes at UA Ask U.S. [Court] to End Discrimination," p. 1, named Harold Anderson, Wiley Branton, Jack Greenberg, James Nabrit III, and John W. Walker as attorneys in the case. Both Greenberg and Nabrit were with the NAACP Legal Defense and Education Fund, Inc.

53. Interview with George Haley, 10/15/2004, pp. 3–4.

54. Interview with Christopher Mercer, 5/13/2004, p. 3.

55. Interview with George Haley, 5/5/1998, pp. 9–10.

56. Interview with George Haley, 5/5/1998, p. 10.

57. WAB, "Draft of Remarks Prepared for Delivery . . . On the Occasion of the Fortieth Anniversary of the Admission of Silas Hunt to the University of Arkansas," 1/30/1988, p. 5. WAB Papers.

58. George Haley, panel discussion, "The Early Years," Legacy of Silas Hunt Program, 1/29–30/1988, pp. 26–27 .

59. Wiley A. Branton, Luncheon Speech, Legacy of Silas Hunt Program, 1/29–30/1988, p. 7.

60. Interview with Miller Williams, 6/25/2004, p. 3.

61. Interview with Christopher Mercer, 5/13/2004, p. 25.

62. Interview with Christopher Mercer, 5/13/2004, p. 21.

63. Interview with George Haley, 10/15/2004, p. 6.

64. Interview with George Haley, 10/15/2004, pp. 6–7.

65. Interview with Eckel and Marge Rowland, 1/23/2004, p. 29.

66. Miller Williams, Transcript, Black Alumni Weekend Program, April 1988, p. 15.

67. Miller Williams, Transcript, Black Alumni Weekend Program, April 1988, p. 5.

68. Interview with Christopher C. Mercer, 5/13/2004, pp. 26–27.

69. Interview with Richard Branton, 9/8/2001, p. 9.

70. Warranty Deed by Wiley A. and Lucille E. Branton, dated 9/18/1952.

71. Interview with Christopher Mercer, 5/13/2004, p. 26 (recalling that Wiley and Lucille "had a house full of kids," and mostly "stayed at home").

72. Interview with Eckel and Marge Rowland, 1/23/2004, p. 3.

73. Christopher Mercer, Panel discussion, "The Early Years," Legacy of Silas Hunt Program, 1/29–30/1988, p. 36.

74. "Branton Traces Civil Rights Fight," 3/25/1980, *Arkansas Gazette,* p. 1B, and Interview with George Howard Jr., 5/28/1998, pp. 12–13. Branton's son, Ricky, remembers there always being people around, "work[ing] on papers, or whatever." Interview with Richard Branton, 9/8/2001, p. 17.

75. "Dr. Bunche to Discuss Peace in Talk Here," 4/30/1952, *Northwest Arkansas Times,* p. 1.

76. Interview with Richard Branton, 9/8/2001, p. 14, and Interview with Wylene Branton Wood, 5/31/2003, p. 4.

77. The dedication was made during the "Silas Hunt Symposium, Remembering the First 50 Years, 1948–1998; Laying a Course for the 21st Century," 4/17/1998. The room was rededicated in a Law School program on 2/22/2002.

78. Interview with George Howard Jr., 5/28/1998, p. 18.

79. *McLaurin v. Oklahoma State Regents for Higher Education,* 339 U.S. 637, 642 (1950) (rejecting conditional admissions and stating that "having been admitted to a

state-supported graduate school, [a student] must receive the same treatment at the hands of the state as students of other races.").

80. Robert Allen Leflar, *One Life in the Law: A 60-Year Review* 85–86 (1985).

81. Letter dated 2/16/1987, Robert A. Leflar to WAB. WAB Papers.

82. Christopher Mercer, Transcript, Black Alumni Weekend Program, April 1988, p. 6.

83. E. H. S., "'The Legacy of Silas Hunt' Wow!" 2/4/1988, *Waterman Journal*, p. 1, 4.

84. Deborah Mathis, "Rights Effort Loses a Soldier," 12/21/1988, *Arkansas Gazette,* p. 11B.

CHAPTER 5: Arkansas Practice

1. WAB, Legacy of Silas Hunt at 57–58.

2. Fred P. Graham, "Bar Groups Open Doors to Negroes," 1/16/1966, *New York Times*, p. 63. Arkansas was not the only southern state bar association that restricted membership. The Georgia State Bar Association, when Branton moved to Atlanta in 1962 to direct the Voter Education Project, also was closed to him. That organization, too, finally integrated in 1964, and Branton became a member. As late as 1965, the Jefferson County Bar Association, in Pine Bluff, still would not admit Negro lawyers. WAB, Address at the Fifty-sixth NAACP Convention, 6/30/1965, p. 5. WAB Papers.

3. WAB, "Draft of Remarks Prepared for Delivery . . . On the Occasion of the Fortieth Anniversary of the Admission of Silas Hunt to the University of Arkansas," 1/30/1988, Fayetteville, AR, pp. 4–5. WAB Papers.

4. Kilpatrick at 309–10.

5. Interview with George Howard, 5/28/1998, p. 15.

6. Kilpatrick at 340 and 386.

7. David S. Robinson, "Branton Recalled as Leader," 12/19/1988, *Pine Bluff Commercial*, pp. 1A, 2A.

8. Sandra McElwaine, "Wiley Branton and the Trials of a African American lawyer," 1/17/1984, *Baltimore Evening Sun*, sec. B1.

9. Wiley A. Branton, "Draft of Remarks Prepared for Delivery . . . on the Occasion of the Fortieth Anniversary of the Admission of Silas Hunt to the University of Arkansas, January 30, 1988, p. 6. WAB Papers.

10. Interview with Wiley A. Branton Jr., 5/22/2002, p. 36.

11. "Money taken in as shown by receipt Book," dated 4/21/1962–2/25/1963. WAB Papers.

12. Aaron Henry and Constance Curry, *Aaron Henry, The Fire Ever Burning* 79–81 (2000) (hereinafter "Henry and Curry"). Mound Bayou was a Negro community near Clarksdale in the Mississippi Delta, and Dr. Howard was nationally known as a civil rights activist, having been the subject of an article in the *Saturday Evening Post* magazine. He began the annual meetings in an effort to educate and offer support to individual Negro professionals who were isolated in small towns. In the early 1950s, Dr. Howard was instrumental in creating the Regional Council of Negro Leadership, an effort to combine the voices of individuals into an "organized voice" for Negro economic and social interests throughout the Delta. The group brought national speakers to its programs, which sometimes had thousands of attendees. *Id.*

13. Wiley A. Branton, "Personal Memories of Thurgood Marshall," 40 *Ark. L. Rev.* 665, 666–67 (1987).

14. Juan Williams, *Thurgood Marshall, American Revolutionary* 16 (1998).

15. Interview with Professor Patricia Worthy, 11/10/2004, p. 3.

16. Interview with Branton Brothers, 6/11/1998, p. 21.

17. Interview with Richard Branton, 9/8/2001, pp. 14–16.

18. *Watt v. State,* 222 Ark. 483 (1954).

19. Arkansas Statutes, General Provisions, Sec. 24–119 (providing that a prosecuting attorney, with consent of the circuit judge, may appoint a deputy where it was considered necessary).

20. "Draft of Remarks Prepared for Delivery by Wiley A. Branton on the Occasion of the Fortieth Anniversary of the Admission of Silas Hunt to the University of Arkansas, Saturday, January 30, 1988 at Fayetteville, Arkansas," p. 6. WAB Papers.

21. The (NAACP) Oracle 61 (Fall 1981), WAB Papers; Letter, 6/28/1965, WAB to Henry Lee Moon, NAACP Director Public Relations, for use in publicity for NAACP Convention. WAB Papers.

22. Wiley A. Branton, "Personal Memories of Thurgood Marshall," 40 *Ark. L. Rev.* 665, 667 (1987).

23. Wiley A. Branton, Luncheon Speech, Legacy of Silas Hunt Program, 1/29–30/1988, p. 10.

24. Interview with Beverly Branton Lamberson, 9/10/2001, p. 15.

25. Interviews with Wiley Branton Jr., 5/22/2002, p. 15; Beverly Branton, 9/10/2001, pp. 28–29.

26. "Prince Hall Masons End Session, Elect," 8/17/1956, *Arkansas State Press,* p. 1.

27. Letter dated 10/24/1972 from WAB to the Reverend Robert Dickerson.

28. Letter dated 4/5/1979 from WAB to Jay W. Dickey Jr., Esquire.

29. Letter dated 12/12/1979 from WAB to the Reverend Robert Dickerson and Rev. J. A. Wilborn, informing them of the decision.

30. Wiley Branton, Open Letter to Members, 37–38 *Boulé Journal* 3 (Nos. 4 and 1, Summer-Fall 1974). WAB Papers.

31. Hobart Sidney Jarrett, Mission Statement, *The History of Sigma Pi Phi* 3 (1995).

32. *Alford v. State,* 223 Ark. 330 (1954).

33. *State v. Alford,* Criminal Docket, Jefferson County Circuit Court, Case No. 20641.

34. Transcript of speech by WAB, Boulé National Convention, August 1970, Miami Beach, FL (attached to letter dated 8/21/1970 from the Honorable A. Leon Higginbotham Jr., U.S. District Court, Eastern District of Pennsylvania, to WAB (hereinafter "WAB August 1970 Boulé Speech"). WAB Papers.

35. WAB August 1970 Boulé Speech, p. 9.

36. *Brooks v. Burgess,* 228 Ark. 150 (1957).

37. Personal Data Questionnaire for Wiley A. Branton, undated between 1975–1976, pp. 9–10. WAB Papers.

38. *Wabbaseka School District v. Johnson,* 225 Ark. 982 (1956).

39. *Brown v. Board of Education,* 347 U.S. 483 (1954).

40. 347 U.S. at 495–96.

41. "Cherry Says Arkansas to Obey Law," 5/19/1954, *Arkansas Gazette,* p. 1.

42. "Sheridan Rescinds Integration Order; Fayetteville to Mix," 5/23/1954, *Arkansas Gazette,* p. 1.

43. "Text of the Little Rock School Board Statement," 5/23/1954, *Arkansas Gazette,* p. 2.

44. David Davies, "Remembrances, Leaders Recall Day of Landmark Ruling," 5/17/1989, *Arkansas Democrat-Gazette,* p. B1.

45. On the weekend following release of the *Brown* decision, the national NAACP held a meeting for state NAACP presidents in Atlanta, Georgia. Benjamin L. Hooks, "Birth and Separation of the NAACP Legal Defense and Educational Fund," *The CRISIS* 218, 220 (June–July 1979). Special sessions at the NAACP's annual convention in August provided additional opportunities for discussion and coordination of plans. Brian James Daugherity, "'With All Deliberate Speed': The NAACP and the Implementation of *Brown v. Board of Education* at the Local Level, Little Rock, Arkansas," M.A. Thesis, University of Montana, 1997, pp. 26–28 (hereinafter "Daugherity"). At the convention, delegates agreed that September 1955, a year later, would be the target date for school desegregation.

46. Report of the Little Rock, Ark., Branch on Desegregation Activities, file-stamped 8/30, NAACP Papers, Part III, A98, "Desegregation, Schools, Arkansas, Central High, 1956–1957 September," Library of Congress.

47. Letter dated 8/21/1954, with petition enclosed, from Wiley A. Branton to William G. Cooper, President, Little Rock School Board, Virgil T. Blossom Papers, MC1364, Box 3, File 2, Special Collections, Mullins Memorial Library, University of Arkansas (hereinafter "Blossom Papers").

48. Letter dated 8/30/1954, from Virgil T. Blossom to Wiley A. Branton, Blossom Papers at Box 3, File 2.

49. Transcript, Hearing Before the Pulaski County School Board Wherein Petitions Were Introduced by Attorneys Representing the Patrons of the Sweet Home and College Station Schools, Regarding Integration, p. 2. Blossom Papers at Box 3, File 2.

50. Transcript, Hearing Before the Pulaski County School Board Wherein Petitions Were Introduced by Attorneys Representing the Patrons of the Sweet Home and College Station Schools, Regarding Integration, p. 2. Blossom Papers at Box 3, File 2.

51. Typed notes (2 pp.) titled "Little Rock Board of Education—Legal Redress Committee, ———, Arkansas," dated 9/9/1954. Blossom Papers at Box 3, File 1.

52. Dem Price, "Banner of White Supremacy Flashes in Defiance throughout Negro South," 9/26/1954, *Arkansas Gazette,* p. 8.

53. "NAACP Meeting Deplores Lag In Desegregation," 10/24/1954, *Arkansas Gazette,* p. 4; Daugherity at 40–41.

54. Daugherity at 41.

55. Articles of Incorporation of White America, Inc., filed 2/3/1955, with the Arkansas Office of the Secretary of State.

56. Tony Freyer, *The Little Rock Crisis, A Constitutional Interpretation* 24 (1984) (hereinafter "Freyer, *Little Rock Crisis*").

57. Freyer, *Little Rock Crisis* at 72.

58. Freyer, *Little Rock Crisis* at 16–17.

59. *Aaron v. Cooper,* 143 F. Supp. 855, 860 (1956).

60. Spitzberg at 45–46.

61. Virgil T. Blossom, *It HAS Happened Here* 26 (1959).

62. *Brown v. Board of Education,* 349 U.S. 294 (1955).

63. 349 U.S. at 300.

64. Wiley A. Branton, "Personal Memories of Thurgood Marshall," 40 *Ark. L. Rev.* 665, 667 (1987).

65. Remarks prepared for delivery by Wiley A. Branton, Symposium Commemorating the Thirtieth Anniversary of the Little Rock Central High School Crisis, University of Arkansas, Fayetteville, 9/23/1987, p. 3. WAB Papers.

66. Daugherity at 66. This was not the first time the Little Rock chapter had voted to sue the Little Rock School Board. In early 1952, the chapter had engaged in negotiations with the board for gradual integration of the schools and been rebuffed. A vote to sue followed those efforts, but the national NAACP had counseled waiting until the *Brown* cases worked their way through to the Supreme Court. That advice was heeded. Wilson Record and Jane Record, eds., *Little Rock, U.S.A., Materials for Analysis* 284–86 (1960).

67. *Payne v. Arkansas,* 356 U.S. 560 (1956).

68. *Payne v. State,* 226 Ark. 910 (1956).

69. Author's notes of Interview with Leo Branton, 7/21/2000, p. 1.

70. *Payne v. State of Arkansas,* 353 U.S. 929 (1957).

71. Wiley A. Branton, "Personal Memories of Thurgood Marshall," 40 *Ark. L. Rev.* 665, 668 (1987).

72. *Payne v. State of Arkansas,* 356 U.S. 560 (1958).

73. Wiley A. Branton, "Personal Memories of Thurgood Marshall," 40 *Ark. L. Rev.* 665, 668 (1987).

74. Transcript, Argument before U.S. Supreme Court in *Payne v. Arkansas,* 3/3/1958, p. 12.

75. *Payne v. Arkansas,* 356 U.S. 560 (1956). See also "Mental-Coercion Pleas Test Court's Umpiring," 5/26/1958, *New York Herald Tribune,* p. 1.

76. *Payne v. State,* 231 Ark. 727 (1960).

77. Letter dated 9/18/1968 from WAB to Arkansas State Board of Pardons, Parole and Probation (urging that Payne receive parole). WAB Papers.

CHAPTER 6: The Little Rock "Crisis"

1. Complaint, *Aaron v. Cooper,* No. 3113, filed 2/8/1956, United States District Court for the Eastern District of Arkansas, Western Division.

2. Tushnet at 100.

3. Tushnet at 68–69.

4. Jack Greenberg, *Crusaders in the Courts* 225 (1994) (hereinafter "Greenberg").

5. Griffin Smith Jr., "Localism and Segregation, Racial Patterns in Little Rock, Arkansas, 1945–1954," M.A. Thesis, Columbia University (citing increased recreational resources for African Americans, including admission to the public zoo and museums, although only on special days); Vivion Lenon Brewer, *The Embattled Ladies of Little Rock, 1958–1963 The Struggle to Save Public Education at Central High* 4 (1998) (hereafter "Brewer") (noting that the public library was integrated, "as were the Children's Hospital, . . . the University Medical School, the bus stations, the Girl Scouts, the League of Women Voters, [and] the transportation system"); Wilson Record and Jane Cassels Record, eds., *Little Rock U.S.A., Materials for Analysis* 284 (1960).

6. Freyer at 20–21.

7. Juan Williams, *Eyes on the Prize, America's Civil Rights Years 1954–1965* at 95 (1987).

8. Complaint, *Aaron v. Cooper*, No. 3113, filed 2/8/1956, United States District Court for the Eastern District of Arkansas, Western Division.

9. An example of the mismatch between plaintiffs' and defendants' attorneys is the fact that each of the five school board attorneys were paid $5,000, plus expenses, for the trial alone, while Branton was to be paid only $300 plus expenses, for the entire case. Letter dated 2/8/1957, WAB to Robert L. Carter, LDEF, (stating that Branton agreed to assist in the appeal for $300 plus travel expenses and a per diem of $20 each day that he was absent from his office), Joseph Crenchaw Papers, Box 1, File 3, Special Collections, University of Arkansas at Little Rock.

10. "School Board Attorneys Seek to Question Naacp [*sic*] State Head," 3/16/1956, *Arkansas State Press*, p. 1.

11. "Depositions of the witnesses, Rev. J. C. Crenchaw and Mrs. L. C. Bates, taken at instance of defendants," in matter of *Aaron v. Cooper*, No. 3113, 5/4/1956, at 63, 72, 86, and 89. Daisy Bates Papers, Box 6, Folder 1, Wisconsin Historical Society Archives.

12. *Aaron v. Cooper*, 143 F. Supp. 855, 861 (1956).

13. Roy Reed, *Faubus, the Life and Times of an American Prodigal* 212 (1997).

14. WAB 1987 Interview at 111.

15. Freyer at 92.

16. Freyer at 95; Roy Reed, *Faubus, the Life and Times of an American Prodigal* 194 (1997).

17. Transcript, "Will The Circle Be Unbroken, A Personal History of the Civil Rights Movement in Five Southern Communities," Episode 12: Nine For Justice, produced by the Southern Regional Council (1997), pp. 8–9. In a talk given on February 21, 2007, Elizabeth Eckford, one of the Little Rock Nine, denied that they received any special training. Possibly, some of the students who later dropped out of the group were the focus of these efforts.

18. Virgil T. Blossom, *It HAS Happened Here* 21 (1959).

19. WAB 1970 Interview at 54–55. See also, Wiley A. Branton, "Little Rock Revisited: Desegregation to Resegregation," 52 *J. Negro Education* 250, 258 (No. 3, Summer 1983).

20. Freyer at 100.

21. Freyer at 102.

22. Transcript, "Will the Circle Be Unbroken, A Personal History of the Civil Rights Movement in Five Southern Communities," Episode 12: Nine For Justice, produced by the Southern Regional Council (1997), p. 11.

23. Transcription notes of Tony Freyer, p. 5, following 12/11/1979 interview with WAB.

24. Grif Stockley, *Daisy Bates, Civil Rights Crusader from Arkansas* 121 (2005).

25. Freyer at 104.

26. Freyer at 118–21.

27. Letter dated 8/22/1980, from WAB to Alexander DeMont, Nuffield College, Oxford, England. WAB Papers.

28. Wiley Branton, "Personal Memories of Thurgood Marshall," 40 *Ark. L. Rev.* 665, 669 (1987).

29. *Aaron v. Cooper,* 156 F. Supp. 220. Judge Davies's decision later was affirmed on appeal, with Thurgood Marshall making the argument for the plaintiffs while Branton participated in preparing the brief. *Faubus v. United States,* 254 F.2d 797, 799 (1958).

30. Proclamation 3204 (22 F.R. 7628) and Executive Order 10730 (22 F.R. 7628).

31. Wiley A. Branton, "Little Rock Revisited: Desegregation to Resegregation," 52 *J. Negro Education* 250, 264 (No. 3, Summer 1983).

32. "A Look at Dean Branton," *Barrister* (November 1979), p. 8.

33. Willie Wofford, "Little Rock Nine Return to School Where Violence Erupted 30 Years Ago," 11/9/1987, 73 *Jet* magazine 4 (No. 7).

34. A Little Rock realtor, William F. Rector, had filed a state suit in August 1957 asking that the new segregation laws and the Johnson amendment be declared unconstitutional. Roy Reed, *Faubus, the Life and Times of an American Prodigal* 196 (1997). Ten Negro ministers challenged the legislature's interposition declaration and the establishment of the State Sovereignty Commission. *Smith v. Faubus,* 230 Ark. 831 (1959). The local NAACP also sued the state attorney general Bruce Bennett and other state officials, challenging other statutes passed by the legislature in spring 1958. *NAACP v. Bennett,* 178 F. Supp. 188 (1959).

35. Wiley A. Branton, "Little Rock Revisited: Desegregation to Resegregation," 52 *J. Negro Education* 250, 255 (No. 3, Summer 1983).

36. While that appeal was pending, Bennett convinced Little Rock officials to adopt a city ordinance that would require registration of "certain groups." Daisy Bates, as state president of the NAACP, was ordered by the Little Rock city attorney to provide the information. When she refused, she was fined. This case worked its way up to the United States Supreme Court. See, e.g., *Bates v. City of Little Rock,* 229 Ark. 819, 822–23 (1958) and 361 U.S. 516 (1960).

37. Excerpt reprinted in Wiley Branton, "Advice and Dissent," 6/2/1980, *Pine Bluff Commercial,* p. 4.

38. WAB 1970 Interview at 56; "A Look at Dean Branton," *Barrister* (November 1979), p. 9.

39. Carl T. Rowan, *Dream Makers, Dream Breakers, The World of Justice Thurgood Marshall* 248 (1993).

40. Letter dated 9/29/1980 from WAB to the Editor, *Pine Bluff Commercial.* WAB Papers.

41. WAB 1978 Interview at 15. Branton's father died the next year and it was a difficult loss for him. Letter dated 11/14/1974, WAB to O. T. Wells, New York, New York. WAB Papers.

42. Elizabeth Jacoway, interview with Wiley A. Branton Jr., 5/24/2004, pp. 22–23.

43. Letter dated 9/29/1980 from WAB to the Editor, *Pine Bluff Commercial;* letter dated 8/8/1967 from WAB to Gene Foreman, Executive Editor, *Pine Bluff Commercial,* p. 3. WAB Papers.

44. Paul Greenberg, "Wiley Branton, He Was Always Part of Us," Editorial, 12/20/1988, *Pine Bluff Commercial,* p. 4A.

45. "Wiley Branton and the trials of a African American lawyer," 7/17/1984, *Baltimore Evening Sun,* B1.

46. Interview with Richard H. Branton, 3/17/2002, Atlanta, Georgia.

CHAPTER 7: Little Rock Continued

1. *Aaron v. Cooper*, 163 F. Supp. 13, 14 (1958).

2. J. J. Peltason, *Fifty-Eight Lonely Men, Southern Federal Judges and School Desegregation* 183 (1961) (hereinafter "Peltason").

3. *Aaron v. Cooper*, 257 F.2d 33, 37 (1958).

4. Graeme Cope, "'Marginal Youngsters'" and 'Hoodlums of Both Sexes'? Student Segregationists during the Little Rock School Crisis," 63 *Ark. Hist. Q.* 380, 381 (2004).

5. 257 F.2d at 37.

6. Spitzberg at 77–78. See also, Graeme Cope, "'Marginal Youngsters' and 'Hoodlums of Both Sexes'? Student Segregationists during the Little Rock School Crisis," 63 *Ark. Hist. Q.* 380 (Winter 2004).

7. Letter dated 3/21/1958, from Blossom to McCuistion, Blossom Papers at Box 3, File 4, p. 4.

8. Copy of Matthews talk marked "(Not for publication—off the record remarks)," Blossom Papers at Box 3, File 4.

9. "Court Halts Integration 2 1/2 years in Little Rock, Cites Public Opposition," 6/22/1958, *New York Herald Tribune*, p. 1.

10. "Little Rock Decision," 6/24/1958, *Chicago Daily Tribune*, p. 16.

11. "Judge Bars Stay on Segregation for Little Rock," 6/24/1958, *New York Times*, p. 1.

12. *Aaron v. Cooper*, 357 U.S. 566 (1958).

13. "High Court to Be Asked For Little Rock Session," 6/26/1958, *Washington Post*, p. 1; "Little Rock Negroes in Plea to Supreme Court," 6/27/1958, *New York Herald Tribune*, p. 3.

14. *Aaron v. Cooper*, 357 U.S. 566 (1958).

15. Greenberg at 236.

16. Greenberg at 233.

17. Greenberg at 233–35.

18. Wiley A. Branton, 1/20/1986 speech at the United Planning Organization's Martin Luther King Breakfast, p. 6. WAB Papers.

19. "Judge Won't Lift Integration Ban," 6/23/1958, *New York Post*, p. 3.

20. John A. Kirk, *Redefining the Color Line, African American Activism in Little Rock, Arkansas, 1940–1970* at 131 (2002).

21. Louis E. Lomax, "The Negro Revolt Against 'The Negro Leaders,'" in *Reporting Civil Rights, Part One* 504 (2003).

22. Letter dated 2/12/1985 from WAB to the Honorable Damon J. Keith. WAB Papers.

23. Bobbie Forster, "Judges Take School Case under Study; No Hint on Ruling Given," 8/4/1958, *Arkansas Democrat*, p. 1.

24. Bobbie Forster, "Judges Take School Case under Study; No Hint on Ruling Given," 8/4/1958, *Arkansas Democrat*, pp. 1, 2.

25. Bobbie Forster, "Judges Take School Case under Study; No Hint on Ruling Given," 8/4/1958, *Arkansas Democrat*, pp. 1, 2.

26. 257 F.2d at 37–40.

27. 257 F.2d at 40.

28. Greenberg at 236.

29. *Aaron v. Cooper,* 358 U.S. 27 (1958). The Department of Justice, along with several individuals and groups filed *amicus* briefs in the case. One of them was Arkansas senator J. W. Fulbright, who had been one of the signatories of the "Southern Manifesto" opposing the *Brown* decision and who supported the school board's position. Not until the tide had turned against the segregationists in Little Rock would he publicly comment on the situation, "finally declar[ing] that Faubus had mishandled the situation." Peltason at 207.

30. Philip B. Kurland and Gerhard Casper, eds., Oral Argument Transcript, 54 *Landmark Briefs and Arguments of the Supreme Court of the United States: Constitutional Law* 714 (1975).

31. Transcription notes of Tony Freyer, p. 6, following 12/11/1979 interview with WAB.

32. Interview with Elaine Jones, 4/15/2004, pp. 21–22.

33. Peltason at 207.

34. Memorandum, undated, from A. F. House, R. C. Butler, and John H. Haley to Little Rock School Board. Blossom Papers at Box 3, File 4.

35. Brewer at 19.

36. Peltason at 207.

37. *Cooper v. Aaron,* 358 U.S. 1, 16 (1958).

38. WAB statement in interview by Tony Freyer, 12/11/1979, notes p. 7.

39. "Brief of William G. Cooper, et al," undated, signed by Richard C. Butler, A. F. House, and John H. Haley. Blossom Papers at Box 3, File 4.

40. *Aaron v. Cooper,* 261 F.2d 97, 104 (1958).

41. 261 F.2d at 108.

42. Brewer at 57.

43. *Aaron v. McKinley,* Order dated 2/3/1959, the Honorable John E. Miller.

44. *Aaron v. Cooper,* 169 F. Supp. 325, 336.

45. *Aaron v. McKinley,* 173 F. Supp. 944, 945 (1959). The case name had changed to reflect the change in school board membership. This change in names would continue over subsequent years.

46. *Garrett v. Faubus,* 230 Ark. 445 (1959); *Fitzhugh v. Ford,* 230 Ark. 531 (1959).

47. *Faubus v. Aaron,* 361 U.S. 197 (1959).

48. Spitzberg at 99–100.

49. Spitzberg at 101–2.

50. Brewer, generally.

51. Brewer at 24.

52. Peltason at 207, 202.

53. Brewer at 158.

54. Brewer at 71.

55. Brewer at 182–83, 220.

56. *Aaron v. Tucker,* 186 F. Supp. 913, 930 (1960).

57. *Norwood v. Tucker,* 287 F.2d 798, 805 (1961).

58. 287 F.2d at 808. In deciding applications for reassignment of students to the various high schools, the board had subjected seventeen Negro students to "home investigations" and "psychological and intelligence tests," but had done so with only three white students. The Court also observed that "even a cursory examination of

the transcripts of the hearings [on reassignment applications] illustrates that white students were given a cursory examination, in contrast to extensive cross-examination of the Negro students." In discussing the Negro students, board members had referred to their features or color as being "Caucasian" or "Negroid," and deliberately avoided granting applications of students they felt did not have an acceptable "attitude." *Id.* at 807–8.

59. "Changes He Helped Spur Haven't Been All Good, A Dismayed Branton Says," 7/9/1984, *Arkansas Gazette,* 1A.

60. Wiley A. Branton, "The History and Future of School Desegregation," 31 *Ed. Law Rep.* 1075, 1081 (1985).

61. Letter dated 9/24/1958 from Thurgood Marshall to Butler T. Henderson. WAB Papers.

62. Thurgood Marshall, "The Equality Speech," 11/18/1978, at the installation of his friend Wiley Branton as dean of Howard Law School, www.phillyburbs.com/bhm/marshall/equality.

63. John Lewis, "Wiley Branton Was There for Us," 1/2/1989, *Legal Times,* p. 16. Lewis later became a U.S. congressman for Georgia.

64. Ken Adelman, "You Can Change Their Hearts," *Washingtonian* 107 (March 1988); Ken Adelman, "Steadfast Vision of Rights," 9/9/1989, *Washington Times,* p. D3.

65. Raymond Arsenault, *Freedom Riders, 1961 and the Struggle for Racial Justice* 284–85 (2006).

66. "Personal Memories of Thurgood Marshall," 40 *Ark. L. Rev.* 665, 669–70 (1987).

67. Letter dated 4/14/1970, George Rose Smith, Little Rock, AR [Justice, Arkansas Supreme Court]. WAB Papers.

68. Letter dated 11/15/1968, WAB to Mrs. J. B. Watson, AM&N College, Pine Bluff, AR. WAB Papers.

69. WAB Pine Bluff Essay.

70. Jerol Garrison, "Branton Files Suit in Behalf of 22 Leaders," 3/9/1962, *Arkansas Gazette,* p. 1A.

71. John A. Kirk, *Redefining the Color Line, African American Activism in Little Rock, Arkansas, 1940–1970* at 153 (2002).

72. "Little Rock Pool Turns Away Five Negroes," 6/28/1963, *Arkansas Democrat,* p. 1B.

73. Letter dated December 7, 1987, from WAB to Professor Gordon Morgan, UA, Department of Sociology, p. 3. WAB Papers.

74. Letter dated 7/31/1963 from WAB to the Reverend James Donald Rice, President, Hot Springs Branch, NAACP. WAB Papers.

75. Letter dated 6/14/1965 from WAB to Sara Etoria Howard, WAB Papers, Box 12, Correspondence—Personal. WAB Papers.

76. *State of Arkansas v. Paul Louis Beckwith,* 238 Ark. 196 (1964). See also, Editorial, "Justice Is Done at Clarendon, Arkansas," *Arkansas Gazette,* 9/7/1964, p. 4.

77. The first trial ended during jury selection when the prosecutor made an inappropriate statement. "Remark by Hale about Protesters Causes Mistrial," 10/31/1970, *Arkansas Gazette,* p. 13B. In a second trial of only one defendant, the jury was deadlocked 7 to 5 and the judge declared a mistrial. The newspaper stated that this was the longest criminal trial in circuit court in over two decades. "Jury Deadlock Brings

Mistrial in Rape Case," 12/19/1970, *Arkansas Gazette,* p. 12A. A third trial also resulted in a jury deadlock of 10–2. The lawyer who prosecuted that case on the third attempt recalled listening to a tape of Branton's closing argument in the second trial. He thought it was "amazing" and "incredibly effective." Conversation with the Honorable Robert Brown, Justice of the Arkansas Supreme Court, 9/23/2005.

CHAPTER 8: The Voter Education Project

1. Judith Kilpatrick, "Wiley Austin Branton and the Voting Right Struggle," 26 *UALR Law Rev.* 641, 658 (2004). (hereinafter "Kilpatrick, Voting Rights Struggle").

2. Transcript, Louis Martin Oral History Interview II, p. 60, 6/12/86, by Michael L. Gillette, Internet Copy, LBJ Library; August Meier and Elliott Rudwick, *CORE: A Study in the Civil Rights Movement, 1942–1968* 173 (1973) (hereinafter "Meier and Rudwick").

3. See Kilpatrick, "Voting Rights Struggle" at 661–65.

4. WAB 1970 Interview at 2–3.

5. Lawson, *Black Ballots* at 174–75.

6. "The Take-Over Generation, America's 100 Most Influential Negroes," 53 *Life* magazine 228 (no. 11, 9/14/1962).

7. Contract dated 9/30/1962. WAB Papers. The purchase price was payable over time and the note apparently was never fully paid off. Letter dated 7/3/1968, from WAB to Stephen A. Matthews, Bridges, Young, Matthews and Davis, Pine Bluff, AR (explaining the transaction). WAB Papers.

8. Meier and Rudwick at 175–76.

9. Henry and Curry at 115 (stating that the coalition began as a local group, the Coahoma County Council of Federated Organizations, that focused on voter registration and other racial issues (p. 107), then expanded statewide to provide a vehicle for meetings with Mississippi governor Ross Barnett (who refused to meet with the NAACP) regarding racial problems (p. 109); "Report on Voter Registration— Projected Program," dated 1/27/1962, Papers of the NAACP, Part III, A271, "Register and Vote—Taconic Foundation, VEP 1962."

10. Branton probably came to know Medgar Evers and Aaron Henry when they joined the Freedom Riders at the Greyhound Bus Station in Jackson in 1961. Henry and Curry at 108.

11. WAB 1970 Interview at 19. Aaron Henry does not mention Branton's presence when he discusses the Clarksdale meeting in his book, although his recounting of the arrests of COFO leaders for "loitering" in moving cars after the meeting, where Branton was present to provide legal representation, seems to confirm Branton's story (described later in this chapter). Henry and Curry at 130. See John Dittmer, *Local People, The Struggle for Civil Rights in Mississippi* (1995), and Charles M. Payne, *I've Got the Light of Freedom, The Organizing Tradition and the Mississippi Freedom Struggle* (1995) (hereinafter "Payne") for further information about COFO.

12. Report, "The Voter Education Project, A Concise History 1962–1979" at 4–5. WAB Papers.

13. WAB 1969 Interview at p. 40.

14. Pat Watters and Reese Cleghorn, *Climbing Jacob's Ladder, The Arrival of Negroes in Southern Politics* 7 (1967) (hereinafter "Watters and Cleghorn").

15. "News Release, Voter Education Project," NAACP Papers, Part III, A271, file "Register and Vote, Taconic Foundation, VEP 1963–64," Library of Congress.

16. Watters and Cleghorn at 59; Henry and Curry at 138–39.

17. Lawson, *Black Ballots* at 276.

18. Press Release, Voter Education Project, dated 3/1/1963; Henry and Curry at 139; NAACP Papers, Part VI, I-3, Voter Education Project Staff, Branton, Wiley A., 1962–64 (1 of 3), Library of Congress.

19. Lawson, *Black Ballots* at 276; Watters and Cleghorn at 59. Kilpatrick, "Voting Rights Struggle" at 641, 663 n145.

20. Kilpatrick, "Voting Rights Struggle" at 663, n145. See also, Michal R. Belknap, *Federal Law and Southern Order* 107 (1987).

21. W. J. Rorabaugh, *Kennedy and the Promise of the Sixties* 112 (2002).

22. "Police Loose a Dog on Negroes' Group; Minister Is Bitten," 3/29/1963, *New York Times*, p. 1.

23. "8 Negroes Jailed In Mississippi," 3/30/1963, *New York Times*, p. 8.

24. Taylor Branch, *Parting the Waters: American in the King Years, 1954–1963* at 721 (1988) (hereinafter "Branch, *Parting the Waters*").

25. Dittmer, Local People at 147–48.

26. Payne at 170.

27. Watters and Cleghorn at 60.

28. Branch, *Parting the Waters* at 721.

29. WAB 1987 Interview at 31; Payne at 173.

30. Lawson, *Black Ballots* at 278–82.

31. Lawson, *Black Ballots* at 285. Charles Payne reported that Branton "believed Mississippi Senator James Eastland had prevailed upon the administration." Payne at 173–74.

32. Claude Sitton, "Negro Queue in Mississippi Is Symbol of Frustration in Voter Registration Drive," in *Black Protest in the Sixties* at 58–59 (August Meier, John Bracey Jr. and the late Elliott Rudwick, eds., 1991).

33. Reese Cleghorn, "The Angels Are White, Who Pays the Bills for Civil Rights?" *New Republic,* 8/17/1963, at 12.

34. Nancy J. Weiss, *Whitney M. Young, Jr. and the Struggle for Civil Rights* 114 (1989) (hereinafter "Weiss").

35. Letter of invitation dated 2/4/1963 from Stephen R. Currier to Roy Wilkins, NAACP Papers, Part III, A271, Register and Vote, Taconic Foundation-VEP 1963–64, Library of Congress.

36. Letter dated 1/13/1965, from Martin Luther King Jr. to WAB (noting that another $12,000 was going to the Southern Christian Leadership Conference and $25,000 would be placed in a special fund devoted to "furtherance of education in the realm of nonviolence"). WAB Papers.

37. "7 Civil Rights Groups Choose Coordinator to Bolster Activity," 8/16/1963, *New York Times*, p. 9.

38. Memorandum dated 9/18/1963 from WAB to "All Participating Agencies" announcing Jordan's arrival as acting assistant director. Southern Regional Council Papers, Reel 173, Auburn Avenue Research Center, Atlanta-Fulton Public Library System, Atlanta, Georgia.

39. Interview with Vernon Jordan, 6/25/2001, p. 1 (stating "[Branton] was probably one of the most formidable mentors in my life . . . mentor, example, role model").

40. WAB 1970 Interview at 61; CUCRL files, WAB papers.

41. CUCRL Agenda for May 15, 1964 meeting. WAB Papers.

42. CUCRL Agenda for May 15, 1964 meeting. WAB Papers.

43. Memorandum dated 8/26/1964 from WAB to Members of CUCRL. WAB Papers.

44. Handwritten notes attached to CUCRL Agenda for June 8, 1964, meeting. WAB Papers.

45. For example, at CUCRL's January 31, 1964, meeting, Branton chided the group for not doing more on major issues. Minutes of 1/31/1964 CUCRL Meeting at p. 8. WAB Papers.

46. Weiss at 118. Lewis was one of the leaders of the Student Non-violent Coordinating Committee at that time. John Lewis and Michael D'Orso, *Walking With the Wind, A Memoir of the Movement* 236 (1998) (hereinafter "Lewis and D'Orso").

47. Telegram dated 6/15/1963 from John F. Kennedy to WAB; WAB 1963 Calendar. WAB Papers.

48. Mann at 371. During the ten weeks after he had announced his support of the bill, there had been "nearly eight hundred demonstrations in almost two hundred cities . . . [with] 20,000 arrests. And ten deaths." Lewis and D'Orso at 203.

49. Mann at 372.

50. Interview with Wiley Branton Jr., 5/22/2003, p. 19.

51. Andrew Young, *An Easy Burden* 256–57 (1996) (hereinafter "Young").

52. Branch, *Parting the Waters* at 635–36.

53. Report of Tom Scarbrough, Investigator, Mississippi Sovereignty Commission, dated 3/25–4/3/1963, pp. 3–4. Sovereignty Commission Files, No. 2–45–69, Mississippi Department of Archives and History, Jackson, Mississippi.

54. Meier and Rudwick at 179.

55. Hearings Before the United States Commission on Civil Rights, Vol. 1, Voting, p. 184.

56. Young at 256–57.

57. Young at 256–57.

58. Watters and Cleghorn at 111, n19.

59. Taylor Branch, *Pillar of Fire* 128 (1998).

60. Watters and Cleghorn at 202.

61. Carl M. Brauer, *John F. Kennedy and the Second Reconstruction* 314 (1977).

62. Memorandum dated July 6, 1964, from Lee C. White to The Files, titled "Meeting with Negro Leadership following Signing Ceremony," WHCF, President's Appointment File [Diary Backup], 7/2/1964, Box 7, LBJ Library.

63. Handwritten note on CUCRL letterhead AGENDA dated 7/2/1964, stating "Note: This meeting cancelled at 3:20 p.m. on 7/2/64 to enable leaders (C-R) to attend White House signing of C-R bill." WAB Papers.

64. Watters and Cleghorn at 45–46.

65. See exchange of letters dated 5/2/1963, from WAB to Hertz System, Inc., and 6/5/1963 from R. E. Perrine, Hertz System, Inc., to WAB. Southern Regional Council Papers, Reel 173, Auburn Avenue Research Library, Atlanta-Fulton Public Library System, Atlanta, Georgia.

66. Hearings Before the United States Commission on Civil Rights, Vol. 1, Voting, p. 188.

67. WAB Speech for United Planning Organization's Martin Luther King Breakfast, 1/20/1986, at p. 3. WAB Papers.

68. Interview with Richard Branton, 9/8/2001, pp. 6–7; Interview with Wylene Branton Wood, 5/31/2003, pp. 9–10; and Interview with Wiley A. Branton Jr., 5/22/2002, p. 3.

69. Interview with Wylene Branton Wood, 5/31/2003, p. 10.

CHAPTER 9: Burrowing from Within: Working in the Johnson Administration

1. White House Press Release dated 2/9/1965, titled "The White House Made Public Today the Following Letter from The President to The Vice President" and attaching Executive Order "Establishing the President's Council on Equal Opportunity." WAB Papers.

2. Report to the President, On the Coordination of Civil Rights Activities in the Federal Government, Submitted by the Vice President-Elect, January 4, 1965, Washington, D.C., Part II. WAB Papers.

3. Letter dated January 4, 1965, Hubert H. Humphrey to President Lyndon B. Johnson. WAB Papers.

4. White House Press Release dated 2/9/1965, p. 2.

5. John A. Salmond, *"My Mind Set on Freedom," A History of the Civil Rights Movement, 1954–1968* at 19 (1997) (hereinafter "Salmond"); Lawson, *Black Ballots* at 78.

6. Salmond at 20; Lawson, *Black Ballots* at 78. The bill failed to pass, but Truman's action led southern Democrats to create the Dixiecrat Party and present Strom Thurmond as its presidential candidate in the next election. Salmond at 20.

7. Nicholas Lamann, "Taking Affirmative Action Apart," 6/11/1965, *New York Times,* Sec. 6, p. 36.

8. Draft of speech for Annual Convention of the National Association of Intergroup Relations Officials on 10/20/1965 at p. 7. WAB Papers.

9. See, e.g., memoranda dated 5/28/1965, 6/4/1965, 6/12/1965, 6/25/1965, 7/2/1965, 7/12/1965, 7/16/1965, 7/23/1965, 8/6/1965, 8/13/1965, 8/20/1965, 8/28/1965, 9/13/1965 and 9/20/1965, WAB to the Vice President. Hubert H. Humphrey: Vice Presidential Files: Civil and Human Rights Files, Box 826, Minnesota Historical Society.

10. See, e.g., memoranda dated 6/8/1965, 6/15/1965, 6/29/1965, 7/8/1965, and 8/2/1965, the Vice President to the President. Hubert H. Humphrey: Vice Presidential Files: Civil and Human Rights Files, Box 826, Minnesota Historical Society.

11. Interview with Patricia Worthy, 11/10/2004, p. 2.

12. Interview with Beverly Branton Lamberson, 9/7/2001, p. 6.

13. "Ark. Atty. Gets Top U.S. Rights Post," 6/10/1965, *Jet* magazine, p. 10.

14. Telegram dated 5/3/1965 from Reverend Martin Luther King Jr. to WAB (attached to WAB's 5/28/1965 response). WAB Papers.

15. Address at NAACP 56th Annual Convention, 6/30/1965, Denver, Colorado. "http://cisweb.lexis-nexis.com/histuniv/DocList Document.asp?_rerch"

16. See, e.g., letter dated 7/26/1965, WAB to Frederick D. Williams, Philadelphia, PA, reporting on Branton's investigation of Williams's complaints against the Internal Revenue Service and stating that the facts of his (Williams's) treatment did not demonstrate illegal discrimination. See also, letter dated 9/22/1965, WAB to Mrs. Zeola Vaughn, DeKalb, Texas, asking for more information, and memorandum of the same date to Samuel F. Yette, Office of Economic Opportunity, asking whether there was an agency in her area. WAB Papers.

17. WAB 1969 Interview at 61.

18. John A. Andrew III, *Lyndon Johnson and the Great Society* 33–34 (1998).

19. Watters and Cleghorn at 253.

20. Telegram dated 7/5/1965 from Lawrence F. O'Brien, Special Assistant to the President, to WAB. WAB Papers.

21. Letter dated 10/8/1965, John W. Macy Jr., Chair, U.S. Civil Service Commission, to the Vice President, United States Senate. WAB Papers.

22. Memo dated 8/27/1965 from Taylor to Lee C. White, Special Counsel to the President, WAB Papers.

23. Joseph A. Califano, *The Triumph and Tragedy of Lyndon Johnson, The White House Years* 66–67 (1991). (hereinafter "Califano").

24. Califano at 65 (1991); Mann at 484.

25. Carl Solberg, *Hubert Humphrey, A Biography* 271–73 (1984) (noting that Humphrey had been the only advisor to speak against immediate retaliation against the Viet Cong for an attack that killed twenty-three Americans in early February 1965, then wrote a memorandum to Johnson that "infuriated" the president).

26. Michael Beschloss, *Reaching for Glory: Lyndon Johnson's Secret White House Tapes, 1964–1965* at 322 (2001).

27. Hubert H. Humphrey, *The Education of a Public Man, My Life and Politics* 307 (1991).

28. See, e.g., Steven F. Lawson, "Civil Rights" in *Exploring the Johnson Years* 113 (1981), and sources cited; Mann at 485.

29. See, e.g., "Rights Groups Fear Easing of U.S. Enforcement Role," 10/17/1965, *New York Times*, pp. 1, 78.

30. List dated 9/21/1965. WAB Papers.

31. "Humphrey's Negro Aide Hits Rights Agitation, Irks Leaders," *Jet* magazine, 10/7/1965, pp. 8–10.

32. Letter dated 10/4/1965 (stating that Branton's "position was that the civil rights cause is being done a disservice by repeated published reports that large numbers of Negroes are now being registered in the South when the fact is that there are many situations in which voter registration is not going well at all. He said that the civil rights organizations share part of the blame for this misleading picture by emphasizing and publicizing situations in which registration has been successful, while failing to bring detailed facts of continued discrimination and failure to register to Government authorities."). WAB Papers.

33. Letter dated 9/30/1965, WAB to Dr. Geraldine E. Wood, President, Delta Sigma Theta Sorority, DC. WAB Papers.

34. Taylor Branch, *At Canaan's Edge, America in the King Years, 1965–68,* 332 (2006).

35. Attachment to memorandum dated 9/20/65, Marvin Watson to the President,

p. 4. WHCF, Ex FG731 "President's Committee on Equal Employment Opportunity 1/1/65-__," Box 403, LBJ Library.

36. "Branton to Step Up Vote Pace," 9/25/1965, *Washington Post,* p. A7. WAB Papers.

37. Letter dated 9/30/1965 from WAB to R. A. (Reggie) Eilbott Jr., Esq., Reinberger, Eilbott, Smith and Staten, Pine Bluff, Arkansas. WAB Papers.

38. "Rights Groups Fear Easing of U.S. Enforcement Role," 10/17/1965, *New York Times,* pp. 1, 78.

39. "Bias Roles Shift," 9/24/1965, *Washington Daily News,* p. 5; "Rights Units Are Shuffled," 9/24/1965, *Washington Evening Star,* p. A1.

40. "Federal Rights Setup Revamped by President," 9/25/1965, *Washington Post,* pp. A1, A7.

41. Memorandum dated 11/16/1965, from WAB to the Attorney General. WAB Papers.

42. Interview with Ramsey Clark 11, 4/13/2004, pp. 9–10.

43. Interview by James Mosby with Wiley A. Branton, The Civil Rights Documentation Project, Moorland-Spingarn Research Library, Howard University 63 (1969) (hereinafter "WAB 1969 Interview).

44. Robert E. Baker, "Rights Coalition—Fractious, Fragmented," 1/16/1967, *Washington Post,* p. A4 .

45. One-page document titled *"My Responsibilities in the Area of Civil Rights by Wiley A. Branton, Special Assistant to the Attorney General, U.S. Department of Justice,"* undated. WAB Papers.

46. Roger Wilkins, speaking at Wiley A. Branton luncheon, Sidley & Austin, September 2000 (videotape in possession of author).

47. Robert A. Devine, ed., *The Johnson Years, Volume Three, LBJ at Home and Abroad* 97 (1994).

48. Lewis and D'Orso at 282.

49. Payne at 358.

50. Payne at 360.

51. "Branton Is Veteran of Rights Struggles," 2/7/1966, *Washington Post,* A2.

52. WAB 1969 Interview at 64.

53. "Branton Is Veteran of Rights Struggles," 2/7/1966, *Washington Post,* p. A2.

54. Remarks before the Annual Luncheon honoring members of the judiciary, United States attorneys, and states attorneys, National Bar Association, Forty-second Annual Convention, 7/25/1967, Houston, Texas. WAB Papers.

55. WAB 1970 Interview at 47.

56. WAB 1969 Interview at 66–67.

57. Califano at 160.

58. Memorandum dated 10/3/1966, from WAB to Joseph A. Califano, Special Assistant to the President. WAB Papers.

59. Memorandum dated 11/8/1966, from Califano to the President. WHCF Name File, BRANTLEYA, Box 428, LBJ Library.

60. Memorandum dated 11/8/1966, from Califano to the President. WHCF Name File, BRANTLEYA, Box 428, LBJ Library.

61. Interview with Ramsey Clark, 4/13/2004, p. 7.

62. Interview with Ramsey Clark, 4/13/2004, p. 9.

63. WAB 1966 Calendar, page for 10/10. WAB Papers.

64. Letter dated 12/2/1966, from Hubert H. Humphrey to WAB (stating, "Not knowing what your plans are for the future, may I ask that, before you make any definite plans, we have the chance to visit"). WAB Papers.

65. Memorandum dated 12/2/1966, from the Vice President to Bill Welsh. WAB Papers.

66. Interview with Ramsey Clark, 4/13/2004, p. 10.

67. Interview with Ramsey Clark, 4/13/2004, p. 15.

68. Letter dated 10/12/1967, WAB to the President. WHCF Name File, BRANTLEYA, Box 428, LBJ Library.

69. WHCF, The President's Daily Diary, 10/1/1967–12/31/1967, Box 13, and WHCF, The President's Appointment File [Diary Backup], 10/10/1967–10/19/1967, Box 79, LBJ Library.

CHAPTER 10: Last Gasp at Direct Action:
The United Planning Organization and Alliance for Labor Action

1. WAB Interview #2 with James Mosby, The Civil Rights Documentation Project, Moorland-Spingarn Research Center, Howard University, p. 2 (hereinafter "WAB 1969(2) Interview").

2. The council chair "was considered by many to represent the more militant representatives of the poor," while the board president was vice president of a chemical corporation and very much a part of the liberal establishment. WAB 1969(2) Interview at 2.

3. WAB 1969 Interview at 73.

4. Betty James, "Branton, Clark Aide, Gets Top UPO Post," 10/4/1967, *Washington Evening Star,* p. A1.

5. William Raspberry, "Successor to Banks Risks Reputation," 5/19/1967, *Washington Post,* p. C1.

6. Report of the National Advisory Commission on Civil Disorders 19 (1968).

7. See, e.g., Califano at 210–11; The Johnson Years, Volume Three, LBJ at Home and Abroad 104; Lewis and D'Orso at 361; Meier and Rudwick at 382–86.

8. Press Release, Voter Education Project, Inc. (February 16, 1972). WAB Papers.

9. UPO Internet Site: www.upo.org.

10. David Stoloff, "The Short Unhappy History of Community Action Programs," in Marvin E. Gettleman and David Mermelstein, eds., *The Great Society Reader, The Failure of American Liberalism* 233 (1967); Lyndon B. Johnson, "Total Victory over Poverty" in Marvin E. Gettleman and David Mermelstein, eds., *The Great Society Reader, The Failure of American Liberalism* 181, 183–85 (1967); Mark I. Gelfand, "The War on Poverty," in *Exploring the Johnson Years* 126, 127 (Robert A. Divine, ed., 1981).

11. John A. Andrew III, *Lyndon Johnson and the Great Society* 68 (1998).

12. Carol J. De Vita, Carlos A. Manjarrez, and Eric C. Twombly, "Poverty in the District of Columbia—Then and Now" 21 (Center on Nonprofits and Philanthropy, The Urban Institute, Feb 2000); Summary of History, Program, UPO Martin Luther King Jr. Memorial Breakfast, 1/20/1986.

13. Watters and Cleghorn at 76.

14. Carl H. Madden, "The War over Poverty," in *Anti-Poverty Programs* 57–58 (Robinson O. Everett, ed., 1966).

15. Watters and Cleghorn at 88 (commenting that "[i]t was becoming apparent that the controlled mass-protest devices of the civil rights movement were being shifted to problems of slums and urban poverty, even as violent forces threatened to intervene.").

16. Califano at 77–78.

17. "D.C. Emerges into 20th Century," 9/28/1967, *Washington Star*, p. A1.

18. Charles Conconi, "Five Negroes Selected for 9-Man Panel," 9/28/1967, *Washington Star*.

19. Paul W. Valentine and Jean R. Hadley, "Justice Aide Gets UPO's Top Post," 10/4/1967, *Washington Post*, p. 1; Betty James, "Branton, Clark Aide, Gets Top UPO Post," 10/4/1967, *Washington Afro-American*, p. A1.

20. Michael Adams, "Model City Issue Tossed to New Regime," 9/18/1967, *Washington Evening Star*, B1.

21. Carol Honsa, "Groups Clash over Unused Summer Aid," 9/28/1967, *Washington Post*, B1.

22. "FHA Record on Low-Cost Housing Hit," 9/28/1967, *Washington Post*, p. D17.

23. Michael Adams and Paul Delaney, "Poverty's War within a War," 9/24/1967, *Washington Evening Star*, p. A1.

24. "UPO 'Most Challenging' to New Director," 10/7/1967, *Washington Afro-American*, p. 3.

25. See, e.g., Jean M. White, "Billions Can't Aid City Problems without New Ideas, Hearing Told," and Robert C. Albright, "Senate Defeats Shift of Head Start Program," 9/28/1967, *Washington Post*, p. A2.

26. WAB 1969(2) Interview at 6.

27. "New UPO Director Plans to Encourage Race Pride in Poor," 10/5/1967, *Washington Post*, p. D10.

28. Address at the 152nd Anniversary of Mt. Zion Methodist Church in Old Georgetown, D.C., 10/13/1968. WAB Papers.

29. WAB 1969(2) Interview at 5.

30. Tom Parsons, "Wiley Branton, Others Climb Mountains—He Works for UPO," 9/29/1968, *Pine Bluff Commercial*, p. 11.

31. Letter dated 12/14/1967, from WAB to the Honorable Walter E. Washington, Mayor of the District of Columbia. WHCF, District of Columbia 12/1/1967–12/31/1967, FG216, LBJ Library.

32. Betty James, "Neighborhood Services Plan to Direct Poverty Centers," 1/19/1968, *Washington Evening Star*, p. B4.

33. WAB 1969(2) Interview at 8–9.

34. Carol Honsa, "D.C. Youth Corps Faces Slash in Jobs," 1/19/1968, *Washington Post*, p. B1.

35. Betty James, "Neighborhood Services Plan to Direct Poverty Centers," 1/19/1968, *Washington Evening Star*, p. B4.

36. Carol Honsa, "UPO, Not City Hall, Expected to Run Poverty Program," 1/20/1968, *Washington Post*, p. B2.

37. Ben W. Gilbert, *Ten Blocks from the White House, Anatomy of the Washington Riots of 1968* at 14 (1968). (hereinafter "Gilbert").

38. Gilbert at 88.

39. Califano at 279.

40. See, e.g., Carol Honsa, "D.C. Estimates 2500 Lost Jobs from Rioting," 4/10/1968, *Washington Post*, p. B20; Carolyn Lewis, "Relief Efforts Centralized," 4/11/1968, *Washington Post*, p. A4.

41. Gilbert at 148. "Almost 90 per cent of those arrested were Negro males." *Id.* at 149.

42. Letter dated 5/9/1968, from Patricia Saltonstall, Director of the Volunteer Services Division, to Hal Witt, Deputy Executive Director, tendering her resignation and stating reasons for it. WAB Papers.

43. WAB 1969(2) at 15.

44. Bernadette Carey, "UPO Dissidents Stop Work, Denounce Ghetto Programs," 4/19/1968, *Washington Post*, B7.

45. Memorandum dated 4/22/1968, from Joan Cole to WAB. WAB Papers.

46. Interview with Wiley A. Branton Jr., 5/22/2002, pp. 22–23.

47. WAB 1969(2) Interview at 15–16.

48. WAB 1969(2) Interview at 17.

49. WAB 1969(2) Interview at 17–18.

50. Memorandum dated 5/7/1968, from Paul Pryde to Hal Witt. WAB Papers.

51. Memorandum dated 4/22/1968, from Joan Cole to Wiley Branton, p. 2. WAB Papers.

52. "Statement of Wiley A. Branton, Executive Director, UPO, June 27, 1968." WAB Papers.

53. "Statement of Wiley A. Branton, Executive Director, UPO, June 27, 1968," p. 28. WAB Papers.

54. Lillian Cooper-Wiggins, "Wiley Branton Remembered as a Man of Many Talents," 12/22–28/1988, *Washington Informer*, p. 1.

55. "Statement of Wiley A. Branton, Executive Director, UPO, June 27, 1968," p. 28. WAB Papers.

56. Califano at 287.

57. Steven F. Lawson, "Civil Rights," in *Exploring the Johnson Years* 106 (Robert A. Divine, ed., Austin 1981) (commenting that "[m]uch of the sympathy for the [1968 civil rights] bill prompted by the slaying [of Dr. King] gave way to anger.").

58. Gilbert at 216.

59. Califano at 287.

60. Mark I. Gelfand, "The War on Poverty," in *Exploring the Johnson Years* 133 (Robert A. Divine, ed., 1981).

61. Memorandum dated 12/3/1968, from Dick Fullmer to Bob Emond, OEO (attached to Memorandum for the Record), 1/10/1969, from Joseph A. Califano Jr., WHCF, "United Planning Organization," FG 808, LBJ Library.

62. Memorandum for the Record, 1/10/1969, from Joseph A. Califano Jr., WHCF, "United Planning Organization," FG 808, LBJ Library.

63. Tom Parsons, "Wiley Branton, Others Climb Mountains—He Works for UPO," 9/29/1968, *Pine Bluff Commercial*, p. 11.

64. Betty James, "Rights Lawyer Sees Peril," 5/26/1969, *Washington Star*, p. B2.

65. "Branton Says U.S. Unwilling to Fight Poverty," 7/10/1969, *Washington Post*, p. B3.

66. Carol Honsa, "UPO Chief Branton Delays Resignation," 6/15/1969, *Washington Post*, p. D2.

67. "A Look at Dean Branton," *Barrister* (November 1979), p. 9.

68. Interview with Wiley Branton by Dennis C. Dickerson, 2/8/1984, p. 3 (hereinafter "WAB 1984 Interview").

69. John Barnard, *Walter Reuther and the Rise of the Auto Workers* 8 (1983).

70. Frank Cormier and William J. Eaton, *Reuther* 47 (1970).

71. National Automobile, Aerospace, Transportation and General Workers Union, *Walter Reuther, 1907–1970, Hopes and Aspirations* 14 (1995).

72. Biographical statement, Walter P. Reuther Library, Wayne State University, www.reuther.wayne.edu/exhibits/wpr.html.

73. Henry and Curry at 188.

74. Walter P. Reuther by Tom Featherstone http://www.reuther.wayne.edu/exhibits/wpr.html.

75. Carl H. Madden, "The War over Poverty," in *Anti-Poverty Programs* 59 (Robinson O. Everett, ed., 1966).

76. Karl F. Treckel, "The Rise and Fall of the Alliance for Labor Action (1968–1972)" at 6 (Labor and Industrial Relations Series No. 3, Center for Business and Economic Research, Graduate School of Business Administration, Kent State University, 1975).

77. WAB 1984 Interview at 6.

78. "Branton Joins New Labor Alliance," 7/15/1969, *Washington Post*, p. C4.

79. WAB Interview at 6; "A Look at Dean Branton," *Barrister* (November 1979), p. 9.

80. "Branton Joins New Labor Alliance," 7/15/1969, *Washington Post*, p. C4.

81. Karl F. Treckel, "The Rise and Fall of the Alliance for Labor Action (1968–1972)" at 15 (Labor and Industrial Relations Series No. 3, Center for Business and Economic Research, Graduate School of Business Administration, Kent State University, 1975) (concluding, however, that the social programs work was a secondary goal).

82. "Branton Decides against Going into Private Practice," 7/21/1969, *Pine Bluff Commercial*, p. 3.

83. 115 *Congressional Record*, 8/5/1969, S9154, No. 132.

84. Wiley A. Branton, "Report of Community and Social Action Division," Alliance for Labor Action, 10/11/1969. WAB Papers.

85. Report, "Social Action Grants Awarded during First Year of A.L.A.," 5/26/1969–5/31/1970. WAB Papers.

86. WAB 1984 Interview at 6.

87. Memorandum—Confidential dated 5/28/1970, from WAB to Leonard Woodcock, Chair, Committee on Community and Social Action (citing his administrative experience). WAB Papers.

88. Memorandum dated 8/6/1971 from Leonard Woodcock to Wiley A. Branton. WAB Papers.

89. Letter dated 4/25/1977 from WAB to Joseph Aragon, The White House. Wiley

Branton Papers, Moorland-Spingarn Research Center, Howard University, Box 2, folder 9.

90. WAB 1984 Interview at 6.

CHAPTER 11: Private Practice Again: A Respite

1. Paul R. Webber III, *Enjoying the Journey, One Lawyer's Memoir* 46 (2003).
2. Interview with Wiley A. Branton Jr., 5/22/2002, p. 17.
3. Personal Data Questionnaire for Wiley A. Branton, undated c.11/1974, p. 5, WAB Papers.
4. *United States v. Kramer,* 286 A.2d 856 (1972).
5. *Jones v. Safeway Stores, Inc.,* 314 A.2d 459 (1974). Branton lost both trial and appeal.
6. Questionnaire dated 5/14/1975. WAB Papers.
7. *Flack v. Laster,* 417 A.2d 393 (1980).
8. *Beer v. United States,* 374 F. Supp. 357 (1974).
9. *New York State v. United States,* 65 F.R.D. 10 (1974).
10. *Lee v. Kelley,* No. 76–1185 (D.D.C. 1/31/1977) and *Southern Christian Leadership Conference v. Kelley,* No. 76–1186 (D.D.C. 1/31/1977).
11. Interview with Professor Patricia Worthy, Howard University School of Law, 11/10/2004, pp. 4-5.
12. Interview with Professor Patricia Worthy, Howard University School of Law, 11/10/2004, p. 4.
13. "Controversial Democratic Fund Tapped," 4/12/1972, *Washington Post,* A1. The funds became controversial when Republicans accused the Democrats of violating a law prohibiting corporate contributions to political organizations. By 1972, such contributions were permitted only if used "specifically" for "nonpartisan voter registration purposes." *Id.*
14. "Final Report of the Voter Registration Fund, Or 'What ever happened to the Greatness Fund?,'" Wiley A. Branton, pp. 4–5, 1976. WAB Papers.
15. "Final Report of the Voter Registration Fund, Or 'What ever happened to the Greatness Fund?,'" Wiley A. Branton, Appendix, p. v, 1976. WAB Papers.
16. Letter dated 9/16/1981 from WAB to Michael R. Winston, director, attaching a signed Agreement of Deposit. WAB Papers.
17. Personal Data Questionnaire for Wiley A. Branton, undated, p. 16. WAB Papers.
18. Interview with Elaine Jones, director-counsel, NAACP LDEF, 4/14/2004, p. 2.
19. Interview with John Crump, executive eirector, National Bar Association, 11/10/2004, pp. 15, 18–19.
20. Interview with John Crump, executive director, National Bar Association, 11/10/2004, p. 16.
21. Wiley Branton, "Open Letter to Members," 37–38 *Boulé Journal* 3 (No. 4 & 1, Summer-Fall 1974).
22. Interview with Eddie Williams, president, Joint Center for Political and Economic Studies, Washington, D.C., 9/6/2001, p. 8.

23. See, 37–38 *Boulé Journal* 51 (No. 4 & 1, Summer–Fall 1974); Hobart Sidney Jarrett, *The History of Sigma Pi Phi*, Vol. II, pp. 190–94 (1995).

24. "Racism, Violence, Injustice: From 1960 Study Commissions to 1970 Massive Results," Remarks of Archon Wiley A. Branton during panel discussion July 28, 1970, pp. 2–4. WAB Papers.

25. "Racism, Violence, Injustice: From 1960 Study Commissions to 1970 Massive Results," remarks of Archon Wiley A. Branton during panel discussion, 7/28/1970, p. 5. WAB Papers.

26. Hobart Sidney Jarrett, *The History of Sigma Pi Phi*, Vol. II, pp. 194, 242 (1995).

27. "A Proposed Social Action Program for Sigma Pi Phi," Submitted by the Social Action Committee and approved by the Executive Committee of the Grand Boulé, 1975, p. 1. WAB Papers.

28. See Dr. J. Ernest Wilkins Jr., "Report of the Grand Sire Archon to the 1974 Grand Boulé," 37–38 *Boulé Journal* 8 (No. 4 & 1, Summer-Fall 1974). WAB Papers.

29. Statement attached to letter dated 8/19/1974 from WAB to Matthew G. Carter, Grand Grapter, Sigma Pi Phi Fraternity. He also wrote a letter to the man he replaced, asking for his ideas on what was needed. Letter dated 8/23/1974 from Dr. Percy L. Julian to WAB. WAB Papers.

30. "A Proposed Social Action Program for Sigma Pi Phi," Submitted by the Social Action Committee and approved by the Executive Committee of the Grand Boulé, 1975, p. 1. WAB Papers.

31. Memorandum dated 11/26/1975 from WAB to Grammateus of Boulés Which Have Not Responded to Social Action Program. WAB Papers.

32. See, e.g., letter dated 5/11/1976 from Albert N. Whiting, chancellor, North Carolina Central University, to Archon George N. Redd (the Boulé's secretary). WAB Papers.

33. "Official Minutes, 1976—Thirty-Third Grand Boulé, 1976," 7/24–28/1976; handwritten list titled "Boulé Visits." WAB Papers.

34. "Report of the Grand Sire Archon to the 1974 Grand Boulé," Cincinnati, Ohio, July 29, 1974, p. 1 (attached to letter dated 9/18/1974 from J. Ernest Wilkins Jr., Past Grand Sire Archon, to Matthew G. Carter, Grand Grapter. WAB Papers.

35. See, e.g., letters dated 9/2/1975 from WAB to Dr. William McAllister, Omicron Boulé, Minneapolis, MN, and to Franklyn W. Taylor, Phi Boulé, Montgomery, AL. WAB Papers.

36. "Pi Initiates 13 in Little Rock," News Release to *Boulé Journal,* 7/9/1975. WAB Papers.

37. "Official Minutes, Meeting of Grand Boulé Executive Committee," 11/12–13/1976, p. 2. WAB Papers.

38. Letter dated 2/24/1977 from WAB to the Honorable A. Leon Higginbotham Jr. WAB Papers.

39. Interview with Eddie Williams, 9/6/2001, p. 14.

40. Remarks delivered at the Divinity School, Vanderbilt University, 12/1/1977, Nashville, Tennessee. WAB Papers.

41. Paul R. Webber III, *Enjoying the Journey, One Lawyer's Memoir* 47 (2003).

42. See handwritten note, undated c. 11/13/1974 from WAB to A. Leon Higginbotham, enclosing the application form and thanking Higginbotham for his help. WAB Papers.

43. "6 Names for 2 D.C. Judgeships," 5/9/1975, *Washington Post*, p. C7.

44. Letter dated 7/9/1975 from WAB to the Honorable A. Leon Higginbotham Jr. WAB Papers.

45. Letter dated 7/9/1975 from WAB to the Honorable A. Leon Higginbotham Jr. WAB Papers.

46. Letter dated 9/8/1975 from WAB to the Honorable Carleton Harris, chief justice, Arkansas Supreme Court. WAB Papers.

47. See, e.g., *In re Vogel,* 382 A.2d 275 (1978) (indicating Branton was vice chairman at the time).

48. Draft of Remarks Prepared for Delivery by Wiley A. Branton at the Honors Day Program, University of Arkansas-Fayetteville, April 24, 1979. WAB Papers.

49. Letter dated 1/7/1977 from WAB to Edward C. Mazique, M.D. WAB Papers.

50. Conversation with Wiley A. Branton Jr., 12/7/2005, Little Rock, Arkansas.

51. Letter dated 4/28/1976 from WAB to Debra E. Branton, Spelman College. WAB Papers.

52. Paul R. Webber III, *Enjoying the Journey, One Lawyer's Memoir* 53 (2003).

53. Interview with Professor Patricia Worthy, Howard University School of Law, 11/10/2004, p. 5.

54. "Howard Names New Law Dean," 12/6/1977, *Washington Post*, p. A1.

55. Letter dated 10/10/1977 from WAB to Wiley A. Branton Jr. (congratulating him on the achievement and enclosing forms for admission in the District of Columbia). WAB Papers.

56. Interview with Wiley A. Branton Jr., 5/22/2002, pp. 24–25.

57. Memorandum dated 11/10/1977 from WAB to Family and Friends (attaching a news article from the *Washington Star*). WAB Papers.

CHAPTER 12: Dean at Howard Law School: Training Future Civil Rights Lawyers

1. "A Mission Lost; Glory Days over for Howard?," 7/25/1988, *National Law Journal,* p. 1.

2. Genna Rae McNeil, *Groundwork: Charles Hamilton Houston and the Struggle for Civil Rights*, 117–18 (1983).

3. "A Mission Lost; Glory Days over for Howard?," 7/25/1988, *National Law Journal,* p. 1. See also, Genna Rae McNeil, *Groundwork: Charles Hamilton Houston and the Struggle for Civil Rights*, Ch. 6 (1983).

4. "Howard University School of Law: A Brief History," a publication of the school.

5. Program, Investiture of the Dean, Dedication of the Moot Court, Howard University School of Law, 11/18/1978. WAB Papers.

6. "A Look at Dean Branton," *Barrister* (November 1979), p. 9.

7. WAB 1978 Interview at 11.

8. Letter dated 1/4/1978 from Joseph D. Tydings, commission chairman, to WAB responding to Branton's request to have his name withdrawn from consideration and stating, "You know how seriously the Commission considered your candidacy; your inclusion on the court would have added a dimension of quality." WAB Papers.

9. Interview with Richard Branton, 9/8/2001, p. 23.

10. See, e.g., "Lawyer Son Follows Footsteps of Father in Desegregation," 9/3/1982, *West Memphis Times.*

11. "Howard Names New Law Dean," 12/6/1977, *Washington Post*, p. A1.

12. Branton represented Rougeau during the Baton Rouge, Louisiana, sit-in cases in the early 1960s, and Rougeau thought of Branton as a "second father," giving Branton credit for encouraging Rougeau to attend law school. Interview with Weldon Rougeau, Washington, D.C., 11/9/2004, pp. 1–3.

13. "Branton Named Howard Law School Dean; Howard Names New Law Dean; Attorney Wiley Branton," 12/6/1977, *Washington Post*, p. A1.

14. "A Mission Lost; Glory Days over for Howard?," 7/25/1988, *National Law Journal*, p. 1.

15. "Branton Names Howard Law School Dean; Howard Names New Law Dean; Attorney Wiley Branton," 12/6/1977, *Washington Post*, p. A1.

16. "Wiley A. Branton Named Dean of Law School," *Congressional Record,* 12/7/1977, S19435–37.

17. Branton's Challenge," 1/24/1978, *Washington Post*, p. B1.

18. "A Look at Wiley Branton," 2 *District Lawyer* 30, 31 (April/May 1978, no. 4).

19. WAB 1978 Interview at 4.

20. "Branton Leads School Toward Positiveness," 2/3/1978, *Hilltop*; "A Look at Wiley Branton," 2 *District Lawyer* 30, 35 (April/May 1978, no. 4).

21. "Branton Leads School toward Positiveness," 2/3/1978, *Hilltop.*

22. Program, Investiture of the Dean, Dedication of the Moot Court, Howard University School of Law, 11/18/1978; "The Equality Speech," 11/18/1978, www.phillyburbs.com/bhm/marshall/equality.

23. "NAACP Attorney Test Case [*sic*] Before Howard Faculty," The Barrister (Nov. 1979), p. 3. A similar exercise was held at the school toward the end of Branton's tenure when William T. Coleman Jr., LDEF board chair and a partner at the O'Melveny & Myers law firm, practiced the arguments he would present to the Supreme Court in a case challenging federal tax benefits for Bob Jones University, a private school that practiced racial discrimination. "A Civil Rights Tally; Hugs and Hurrahs for Coleman at Legal Fund Dinner," 5/26/1983, *Washington Post*, p. B1.

24. "On the Circuit: Scenes from Four Washington Parties; The Commemoration," 5/16/1979, *Washington Post*, p. B3.

25. "The Celebration and the Vigilance; Vigilance," 5/18/1979, *Washington Post*, p. C1.

26. "A Look at Dean Branton," *Barrister* (Nov. 1979), p. 9.

27. Photocopy of certificate. WAB Papers.

28. Interview with Professor Patricia Worthy, 11/10/2004, p. 5.

29. "A Look at Wiley Branton," 2 *District Lawyer* 30 (April/May 1978, no. 4).

30. "Branton Sees Change, But Need for More," 9/21/1980, *Pine Bluff Commercial*, p. 29.

31. Interview with Vernon Jordan, 6/25/2001, p. 1.

32. "People," 3/1/1979, *Washington Post*, DC, p. 2.

33. "A Brief History of Conrail" at www.conrail.com/history.html.

34. Memorandum dated 2/12/1979 from WAB to Dr. Lorraine A. Williams, Vice President for Academic Affairs. WAB Papers.

35. "Conrail Board Announces Election of Two New Directors," 2/15/1989, PR Newswire (announcing Branton's replacement).

36. The Washington Lawyers' Committee for Civil Rights Under Law, Annual Report, 1980–81, p. 1.

37. Interview with Roderic V. O. Boggs, Executive Director, Washington Lawyers' Committee for Civil Rights Under Law, 11/10/2004.

38. Interview with Roderic V. O. Boggs, Executive Director, Washington Lawyers' Committee for Civil Rights Under Law, 11/10/2004, pp. 2–3.

39. Annual Report, 1981–82, Washington Lawyers' Committee for Civil Rights Under Law, p. 1. WAB Papers.

40. Committee Report (newsletter), vol. 1, no. 4, Fall 1987, p. 2.

41. Program, Wiley A. Branton Awards Luncheon, Washington Lawyers' Committee for Civil Rights and Urban Affairs, 6/3/2003, p. 2.

42. Branton also was elected to serve as a member of the Board of Columbia Federal Savings and Loan in March 1978, "Branton elected director of Columbia Federal S-L," 3/18/1978, *Washington Afro-American,* p. 11; to the board of directors of Arkansas's Winthrop Rockefeller Foundation in 1980; and with the group *Africare,* a private organization that helped develop self-help programs in rural Africa, "Helping Africa Realize Its Potential," 6/16/1988, *Washington Post,* p. D3.

43. "Draft of Remarks Prepared for Delivery by Wiley A. Branton at the Honors Day Program, University of Arkansas-Fayetteville," 4/24/1979, p. 6. WAB Papers. He continued with this theme more directly in January 1983, when Branton chastised city officials and other D.C. leaders, stating that the lack of civility and ambition among a proportion of D.C.'s youth resulted from the role models presented to them. He encouraged those in attendance to "put forth a special effort to present a good image." Wiley A. Branton, "Continuing Challenges for Washington, the City-State," 1/3/1983, pp. 11–12.

44. "Advice and Dissent," 6/2/1980, *Pine Bluff Commercial,* p. 4.

45. Transcript attached to letter dated 12/18/1980 from the Honorable Barrington D. Parker, Judge of the U.S. District Court, to WAB, p. 10. WAB Papers.

46. Letter dated 2/2/1982 from the Reverend Herbert H. Eaton, pastor, St. John Baptist Church, Columbia, MD, to Dr. Lorraine A. Williams, Howard University. WAB Papers.

47. Interview with Professor Patricia Worthy, 11/10/2004, pp. 1–2.

48. "The FTC's Private War on Lawyers," *American Lawyer* 75, 76 (January–February 1990).

49. *Federal Trade Commission v. Superior Court Trial Lawyers Association,* 493 U.S. 411 (1990).

50. Lillian Wiggins, "Attorney Wiley Branton—A Special Person," 12/29–1/4/1989, *Washington Informer,* p. 11.

51. "Tribute to Wiley Austin Branton," Program, Annual Law Day Dinner, Washington Bar Association, 4/28/1978. WAB Papers.

52. Quoted in Myles V. Lynk, "Appreciation, Wiley Austin Branton," Equal Access to Justice, Law Day 1989, Washington Bar Association.

53. Letter dated 5/5/1978 from WAB to Dr. Herman B. Smith Jr., chancellor, UAPB. WAB Papers.

54. "U of A to Honor Poet, Law Dean," 4/13/1980, *Arkansas Gazette,* p. 8A.

Branton would receive an honorary doctorate, posthumously, from the University of Arkansas in 1989.

55. For example, Alexander DeMont, a history student at Nuffield College, Oxford, England; George Lipsitz for *A Life in the Struggle, Ivory Perry and the Culture of Opposition*; and Tony Freyer for his book *The Little Rock Crisis: A Constitutional Interpretation*.

56. "Rift: NAACP and legal arm," 4/3/1979, *News World* (New York). *See also,* "NAACP, Defense Fund Rift Threatens Unity," 56 *Jet Magazine* 15 (No. 2, 3/29/1979).

57. Unsigned copy of NAACP Resolution dated 6/28/1979. WAB Papers.

58. Letter dated 7/9/1979 from Benjamin L. Hooks, executive director, and Margaret Bush Wilson, chairman of the board, to William T. Coleman Jr. WAB Papers.

59. Letter dated 10/9/1979 from William T. Coleman Jr., Julius LeVonne Chambers, and Jack Greenberg to Benjamin L. Hooks, executive director, and Margaret Bush Wilson, chairman of the board. WAB Papers.

60. "NAACP Is Suing Legal Fund to Keep the Initials for Itself," 5/25/1982, *Washington Post*, p. 2B.

61. "Two Top Civil Rights Groups Battle over Right to Use Initials NAACP," 1/24/1983, *Pine Bluff Commercial*, p. 12.

62. *National Association for the Advancement of Colored People v. N.A.A.C.P. Legal Defense & Educational Fund, Inc.,* 559 F. Supp. 1337 (1983). Order dated 3/28/1983, by the Honorable Thomas Penfield Jackson, U.S. district judge for the District of Columbia (attached to memorandum dated 3/31/1983 from Jack Greenberg to board of directors (stating that LDEF would appeal the decision). WAB Papers.

63. *National Association for the Advancement of Colored People v. N.A.A.C.P. Legal Defense & Educational Fund, Inc.,* 753 F.2d 131 (1985).

64. One said that formal battle had been delayed by the presence of Roy Wilkins, who "had strong personal ties in both organizations" and when he died, "we lost the bridge." "Two Top Civil Rights Groups Battle over Right to Use Initials NAACP," 1/24/1983, *Pine Bluff Commercial*, p. 12.

65. "Two Top Civil Rights Groups Battle over Right to Use Initials NAACP," 1/24/1983, *Pine Bluff Commercial*, p. 12.

66. Letter dated 2/2/1983 from WAB to the Editor, *Pine Bluff Commercial*. WAB Papers.

67. Carl T. Rowan, "Race, Justice and Howard University," 5/6/1983, *Washington Post*, p. A27.

68. Letter dated 7/11/1983 from WAB to Dr. James E. Cheek, president, Howard University. WAB Papers.

69. Letter dated 7/1/1983 from James E. Cheek, president, to WAB. WAB Papers.

70. Letter dated 7/11/1983, WAB to Dr. James E. Cheek, WAB Papers.

71. "Branton Resigning as Dean of Howard U. Law School," 7/29/1983, *Washington Post*, p. B1.

72. "Branton Resigning as Dean of Howard U. Law School," 7/29/1983, *Washington Post*, p. B1. Branton also had criticized the University's decision "to expel the undergraduate editor of the student newspaper." "Branton Resigning as Dean of Howard U. Law School," 7/29/1983, *Washington Post*, p. B1. The editor had given prominent coverage to a sex discrimination suit by a white male attorney against the

university that had "sparked student unrest for several months." "Howard U.???," 7/30/1983, *Washington Post*, p. B1.

73. "Leaving With Honor(s)," 8/4/1983, *Pine Bluff Commercial*, p. 4.

74. "Howard U.???," 7/30/1983, *Washington Post*, p. B1.

75. "National Roundup," undated, unattributed, p. 8. WAB Papers.

76. "Just Thinking; Why Branton Is Leaving Howard—$64 Question???," 8/20/1983, *Washington Afro-American*, p. 4.

77. Interview with Professor Werner Lawson, Howard University School of Law, 9/13/2002, pp. 9–10.

78. Annual Report, 1982–1983, School of Law, to the President of Howard University from Wiley A. Branton, Dean, 7/1/1983. WAB Papers.

79. They included the need for more scholarship and financial aid for students, funding support for legal scholarship by the faculty, and funding for increased faculty salaries. Branton was most concerned about student aid, as he recalled how helpful the G.I. Bill had been during his own law school education. He pulled money out of his pocket to aid students in several instances, always with the understanding that it was not a gift (although he sometimes "forgave" a debt). See, e.g., letters dated 4/4/1984 and 12/5/1984 from WAB to C. Lamont Smith and letter dated 9/25/1984 from WAB to Fred Gant. WAB Papers.

80. Annual Report, 1982–1983, School of Law, to the President of Howard University from Wiley A. Branton, Dean, 7/1/1983, Appendix 8. WAB Papers.

CHAPTER 13: Sidley & Austin: Elder Statesman

1. S&A announcement, 7/29/1983. WAB Papers. The term, "Of Counsel," has no specific meaning. In Branton's case, it indicates he would be paid by the firm, but not have the position of either associate or partner. This arrangement is frequently made to bring a noteworthy lawyer to a firm.

2. David Lauter, "A Unique 'Culture' Aids Sidley's Boom," 8/6/1984, *National Law Journal*, p. 56.

3. Interview with Richard Branton, 9/8/2001, p. 27.

4. *Southern Pacific Communications Company v. American Telephone and Telegraph Company*, 556 F. Supp. 825 (U.S.D.C, D.C 1982).

5. Interview with Richard Branton, 9/8/2001, p. 27.

6. 556 F. Supp. 825 (1982).

7. Interview with Richard Branton, 9/8/2001, p. 27 (stating that he was told it was almost an ultimatum of the company).

8. Interview with George Jones, 9/10/2001, pp. 13–14.

9. "A Look at Dean Branton," *Barrister* (November 1979), p. 11.

10. "Comings and Goings," 2/4/1985, *Washington Post*, p. D2.

11. Interview with Richard Branton, 9/8/2001, p. 27.

12. Interview with George Jones, 9/10/2001, p. 14.

13. Interview with William T. Coleman, 9/2/2001, pp. 6, 7. Coleman also had worked closely with Branton in civil rights matters over the years, when both were members of the NAACP LDEF Board of Directors.

14. "Friendly Spirit Lures Families to North Portal," 9/15/1990, *Washington Post*, E1 (quoting Lucille Branton).

15. Interview with Wiley A. Branton Jr., 5/22/2002, pp. 23–24; Interview with Debra Branton, 3/16/2002, pp. 11–12.

16. *Lee v. Kelley,* No. 76–1185 (D.D.C. 1/31/1977) and *Southern Christian Leadership Conference v. Kelley,* No. 76–1186 (D.D.C. 1/31/1977).

17. *Lee v. Kelley,* 99 F.R.D. 340 (1983). The D.C. Circuit affirmed the decision in 1984. *Southern Christian Leadership Conference v. Kelley,* 747 F. 2d 777 (1984).

18. Some matters were begun prior to his joining the firm, e.g., the representation of a lawyer fighting for an award of attorney's fees. *Murray v. Weinberger,* 741 F.2d 1423, 239 U.S. App. D.C. 264 (1984). Others came to him as a result of prior associations, e.g., he worked with lawyers from LDEF on new litigation in the "old" Little Rock school integration case. *Sidley & Austin Practice Bulletin,* vol. 3, no. 8 (August 1986). He also undertook the task of reviewing grant applications for the Taconic Foundation, with which he had developed a close relationship during the VEP years. Letter dated 3/8/1984 from WAB to Mrs. Jane Lee J. Eddy, executive director Taconic Foundation, Inc. WAB Papers.

19. Letter dated 2/1/1985 from WAB to the Honorable Charles R. Richey. WAB Papers.

20. Quoted in Judith Kilpatrick, "Wiley Austin Branton, A Role Model for All Times," 48 *Howard Law Journal* 827, 837 n48 (Spring 2005).

21. Remarks, Wiley A. Branton Luncheon, September 1998, sponsored by Sidley & Austin. [videotape at 50:51, in author's possession.]

22. Opening Remarks, Wiley A. Branton Luncheon, September 1990, sponsored by Sidley & Austin, Washington, D.C. (videotape in author's possession).

23. For example, he spoke at D.C.'s Twelfth Annual Commemorative Luncheon honoring Dr. Martin Luther King Jr., "Area Events Mark King Birthday," 1/14/1984, *Washington Post,* Sec. B6; gave two talks on twentieth anniversary celebrations of the 1964 Civil Rights Act (one for the Chicago Lawyers' Committee for Civil Rights Under Law, letter dated 3/20/1984 from WAB to Kathleen C. Yannias, associate director and one for Harvard University's Kennedy School of Government, letter dated 2/7/1985 from WAB to Jeffrey Bartel and Leah Dickerman accepting the invitation).; spoke with Vernon Jordan at the Fiftieth Annual Southern Governors Meeting, "GOP Urged to Seek Black Vote; Southern Governors Assess Civil Rights," 7/9/1984, *Washington Post,* Sec. A4; and one for the Judicial Conference of the Eighth Circuit Court of Appeals. Letter dated 4/1/1985 from Donald P. Lay, chief judge, to WAB. WAB Papers.

24. "Branton Elected Chairman of D.C. Judicial Nomination Commission," 2/1/1984, *Daily Washington Law Reporter,* p. 1. D.C. mayor Marion Barry Jr. had appointed Branton a member of the commission in November 1982. Letter dated 11/22/1982 from Marion Barry Jr., mayor, to WAB. WAB Papers.

25. "Chief Judgeship Hangs in the Balance; D.C. Commission to Weigh 2 Candidates," 10/17/1988, *Washington Post,* p. E1.

26. See 1/9/1984, *Washington Post,* Sec. D2 and 2/13/1984, *Washington Post,* Sec. D2.

27. 2/13/1984, *Washington Post,* Sec. D2.

28. "100 Seeking New D.C. Judgeships," 4/9/1984, *Washington Post,* Sec. C1.

29. See "5 GOP Senators Oppose Reagan Court Nominee," 8/16/1984, *Washington Post,* Sec. C1, and "A Crisis Averted," 3/25/1985, *Washington Post,* Sec. B2.

30. See "Four on D.C. Superior Court Are Nominees for Chief Judge," 5/8/1986,

Washington Post, Sec. D3, and "Judge Fred Ugast Selected to Head D.C. Superior Court," 5/28/1986, *Washington Post*, Sec. C1.

31. "9 Nominated for 3 D.C. Judge Vacancies," 9/13/1987, *Washington Post*, p. B3.

32. See, e.g., Remarks of Wiley A. Branton, Esq. Before the Senate Judiciary Committee, February 2, 1988, Regarding the Available Pool of Women and Minorities for Judicial Appointment in the District of Columbia, p. 2. WAB Papers.

33. See letter dated 2/15/1985 from Jim Burnley, deputy secretary of transportation, to WAB and letter dated 4/2/1985 from Congressman Parren J. Mitchell to WAB. WAB Papers.

34. Letter dated 3/10/1986 from WAB to Dean Lawrence H. Averill Jr., UALR School of Law; letter dated 2/12/1986 from WAB to Jimmy McKissic. WAB Papers.

35. Letter dated 3/26/1986 from WAB to Juanita Jackson Mitchell. WAB Papers.

36. Letter dated 3/13/1987 from WAB to the Honorable Gladys Kessler. WAB Papers.

37. Letter dated 3/20/1986 from WAB to the editor, *Pine Bluff Commercial*. WAB Papers.

38. Letter dated 5/7/1986 from Bill Clinton to WAB. WAB Papers.

39. Memorandum dated 3/26/1986 from WAB to Benjamin W. Heineman Jr. WAB Papers.

40. Memorandum dated 5/20/1086 To All Personnel, Sidley & Austin. WAB Papers.

41. Interview with Wylene Branton Wood, 5/31/2003, p. 30.

42. Interview with Richard Branton, 9/8/2001, p. 11.

43. Interview with Richard Branton, 9/8/2001, p. 11; Interview with Wylene Branton Wood, 5/31/2003, p. 32.

44. Interview with Wylene Branton Wood, 5/31/2003, p. 32.

45. Interview with Wylene Branton Wood, 5/31/2003, p. 31.

46. Branton did not attend the program but, afterward, Governor Bill Clinton wrote a note condoling Branton on his daughter's death and reporting that Branton "would have been proud of" the anniversary program. Note dated 6/17/9186 from "Bill," Governor's Mansion, to WAB. WAB Papers.

47. "Wiley A. Branton to Be Honored at Banquet as 1986 Lawyer of the Year," December–January 1987, *Bar Leader*, p. 1. Notice of the award appeared in the Sidley & Austin Practice Bulletin, vol. 4, no. 1 (January 1987), WAB Papers; "D.C. Bar Wants a New Code of Ethics," 12/1/1986, *Washington Post*, p. D2.

48. Sidley & Austin Practice Bulletin, vol. 5, no. 2 (February 1987). WAB Papers.

49. Transcript, WAB comments on Segment 2, *Eyes on the Prize*, from Henry Hampton Collection, Film and Media Archive, Washington University Libraries, St. Louis, Missouri, 1986.

50. Letter dated 7/1/1986 from Henry Hampton to WAB. WAB Papers.

51. Sidley & Austin Practice Bulletin, vol. 4, no. 2 (February 1987). WAB Papers.

52. "Civil Rights Lawyers Revisited," *Ebony* magazine (December 1986), p. 76.

53. Letter dated 12/3/1986 from WAB to the editor, *Ebony* magazine. WAB Papers.

54. Letters dated 8/20/1986 from WAB to the Honorable David Pryor and the Honorable Dale Bumpers. WAB Papers.

55. *Congressional Record*, 9/17/1986, p. 23803.

56. Letter dated 1/20/1987 from WAB to Dr. David J. Garrow. WAB Papers.

57. Letter dated 1/20/1987 from WAB to Mrs. Coretta Scott King (referring to the letter to Brown). WAB Papers.

58. "Didn't Say King Engaged in Extramarital Affairs, Lawyer Sues For $6 Million," 73 *Jet magazine* 36 (No. 22, 2/29/1988).

59. Conversation with Wiley A. Branton Jr., 12/7/2005.

60. Letter dated 3/13/1987 from WAB to the Honorable Gladys Kessler, Superior Court of the District of Columbia. WAB Papers.

61. Letter dated 3/13/1987 from WAB to the Honorable Gladys Kessler, Superior Court of the District of Columbia. WAB Papers.

62. Letter dated 6/12/1987 from WAB to Dean John Robson, School of Business Administration, Emory University. WAB Papers.

63. Letter dated 4/28/1987 from WAB to Dean J. W. Looney, University of Arkansas School of Law. WAB Papers.

64. Conversation with Wiley A. and Stephanie Branton, 12/7/2005.

65. Interview with Wylene Branton Wood, 5/31/2003, p. 11.

66. Early in 1988, Branton received the first Martin Luther King Jr., Leadership Award from the District of Columbia Public Library. In June, on its twenty-fifth anniversary, the VEP presented Branton with an award for his work with the organization. Letter dated 6/9/1987 from Clarence D. Coleman, interim executive director, to WAB. WAB Papers.

67. Letter dated 7/1/1987 from Rowena Pon to WAB confirming interview date of July 15. WAB Papers.

68. "Awed Crowd Hears Faubus, Branton Argue," 9/25/1987, *Arkansas Gazette,* p. 1.

69. Transcript, The Crisis at Central High: A Thirty-Year Perspective on "Little Rock" and the Constitution, 9/23–25/1987, Session #2.

70. "Editorial omits judge's record," letter to editor from Mark Johnson, appearing 2/5/2006, *Arkansas Democrat-Gazette,* p. 5J.

71. Letter dated 1/20/1988 from WAB to Dean J. W. Looney, School of Law. WAB Papers.

72. Letter dated 6/14/1988 from Carol H. Allie, executive vice chancellor, to WAB. WAB Papers.

73. "Making Marshall's Night; An 80th Birthday Appreciation for the Justice," 9/15/1988, *Washington Post,* p. C1.

74. Letter dated 9/19/1988 from Donald L. Hollowell to WAB. WAB Papers. In what was his last public appearance with Marshall, on December 3, Branton would present a special award to Marshall on behalf of the Bar Association of the District of Columbia. Wiley A. Branton, "Remarks, Tribute to Justice Thurgood Marshall," 12/3/1988. WAB Papers.

75. Program, Washington Committee of the NAACP Legal Defense and Educational Fund, Inc., *Pro Bono* Awards Luncheon, 11/10/1988. WAB Papers.

76. Letter dated 11/21/1988 from Daniel E. Ferritor, chancellor, to WAB. WAB Papers.

77. Letter dated 11/22/1988 from [] to WAB. WAB Papers. Note: Branton's papers include only the first page of the letter.

78. News Release, Federal City Council, dated 11/29/1988. WAB Papers.

Epilogue

1. David Pryor, "Tribute to Howard University Law School Dean Wiley Branton," 3/16/1989, 135 *Congressional Record,* p. 4644 (March 16, 1969).

2. Paul Greenberg, "What Wiley Branton Left Us," 8/31/2003, *Arkansas Democrat-Gazette,* p. 4J.

3. William Raspberry, "A Few Thousand Close Friends," 12/23/1988, *Washington Post,* p. A19.

4. John Lewis, "Wiley Branton Was There for Us," 1/2/1989, *Legal Times,* p. 16.

5. Sandra Hope, "Wiley Branton Remembered as One Who Touched Many," 12/21/1988, *Pine Bluff Commercial,* pp. 1A, 2A.

6. Opening Remarks, Wiley A. Branton Luncheon, September 1991, sponsored by Sidley & Austin, Washington, D.C. (videotape in author's possession).

7. Opening Remarks, Wiley A. Branton Luncheon, September 1991, sponsored by Sidley & Austin, Washington, D.C. (videotape in author's possession). In September 2005, the evening after the Sidley & Austin luncheon, now held in conjunction with the Law Review of the Howard University School of Law, Mrs. Cecilia Marshall, Thurgood's widow, said his feeling of loss remained with Marshall until he died in 1993.

8. WAB Pine Bluff Essay at 23.

INDEX

A

Aaron v. Cooper
  See Cooper v. Aaron
Abernathy, Ralph, 131, 135
advocacy efforts, 28, 60–62, 104–5,
  114–18, 151
African American population
  See black population
Alford, Samuel, 60–61
Alliance for Labor Action, 133–36
American Civil Liberties Union, 139
American Federation of Labor and
  Congress of Industrial
  Organizations (AFL-CIO), 132–33
anti-integration efforts, 66, 75–78, 84,
  87–92
anti-lynching laws, 29
anti-poverty programs, 111, 122–27,
  130–36
A. Phillip Randolph Education
  Fund, 139
appellate courts, 75–76, 85–92, 143, 154
Arkansas Agricultural, Mechanical and
  Normal College (AM&N), 2, 13,
  23, 32, 152
Arkansas Baptist Convention, 5, 7
Arkansas Branch Normal School, 2, 37
Arkansas State Bar Association, 53–54
Arkansas State Conference (NAACP)
  awards, 57
  purpose, 28, 71–72
  school desegregation, 64, 66–67
Arkansas Supreme Court, 29, 68–69,
  82, 165
armed forces, 15–22
army investigation experience, 18–19, 21
arrest and conviction, 29–30
AT&T, 157
awards and recognition
  Arkansas State Conference, 57
  civil rights activism, 144, 150–53,
  162–64
  Little Rock Nine, 86

memorials, x
military service, 18, 21

B

ballot forms, 26
Baptist student groups, 45
Bar Association of the District of
  Columbia, 143, 162
Barry, Marion, x
Bates, Daisy, 64, 74–75, 77–78, 81, 86
Bates, L. C., 81
Beals, Melba Pattillo, 80, 92
Beckwith, Paul Louis, 96
Bennett, Bruce, 80
birth of Wiley Branton, 8
Black Cherokees, 5
black population
  Communist Party, 19–20
  educational system, 30–33, 62–63
  light-skinned population, 5–6, 8,
    18–19, 61–62
  middle class, 6
  organized labor, 132–35
  Pine Bluff, Arkansas, 1–3
  protest riots, 116–17, 122, 127–28,
    131
  voting rights, 2, 25–30, 97–108, 122
  See also segregation
Black Power movement, 117, 122, 129
Blackwell, Randolph, 99
Block, Sam, 100
Blossom, Virgil T., 64–66, 75–77, 84, 90
board memberships, 139–43, 149–50
Bond, Mildred, 64
Booker, J. R., 38–39
Boulé, 60, 139, 140–42
boycott of clothing store, 13
Branch, Taylor, 114
Branton, Beverly, 110
Branton, Debra, 81, 144
Branton, Estelle, 3
Branton, James L., 3–4, 7, 11, 23
Branton, Julia, 8, 23

color in black community, 5–6, 8, 18–19,
   61–62
   See also black population
Committee for Citizen Participation in
   Model Cities, 124
Committee for Public Justice, 139
Committee for Welfare, Education and
   Legal Defense (WELD), 102
   See also Council for United Civil
   Rights Leadership (CUCRL)
Committee on Community and Social
   Action, 133
Committee on Organizing and
   Collective Bargaining, 133
Communist Labor Party, 20
Communist Party, 18, 19–20
Community Action Programs, 122–24
Community Improvement Corporation
   (CIC), 124
community involvement, 58–60,
   94–95, 165
Conference on Graduate and
   Professional Education for the
   Negro Population of Arkansas,
   32–33
Congress on Racial Equality (CORE),
   93, 98–99, 102
Consolidated Rail Corporation
   (CONRAIL), 149–50, 160–61
Consumer Action Programs, 130
Cooper v. Aaron, ix, 71, 76–77, 83–84, 89,
   101, 154
Cooper, William G., 64
Council for United Civil Rights
   Leadership (CUCRL), 102–3, 107
Council of Federated Organizations
   (COFO), 99, 102
Council on Community Affairs
   (COCA), 95
Court of Appeals, 75–76, 85–92, 143, 154
Crenchaw, J. C., 74
cross burnings, 81–82
Currier, Stephen, 102, 113–14

D

Davies, Ronald N., 78–79, 83
Davis, Clifford, 33, 38–40
Davis, Lawrence, 32
Davis, Wylie, 43
Dawson, Richard A., 1
deanship of Howard University Law
   School, 144–56
death of Wiley Branton, x, 166, 168
death threats, 57
Delta Sigma Theta, 35
Democratic Party
   fund distribution, 138–39
   Mississippi Democratic Freedom
   Party, 102–3
   organized labor, 132
   voting rights, 25–26, 28–29
Dennis, David, 104
Dewey, John, 21
discrimination
   armed forces, 15–22
   educational system, 30–33, 37–51,
      62–63
   federal programs, 110–12
   hospital care, 48–49
   housing issues, 41–44, 95
   legal practice, 54–69
   Little Rock school crisis, ix, 71–93
   personal experiences, ix, 10–14, 18,
      46–47, 81–82
   personal philosophy, 154–56, 167
   voting rights, 2, 25–30, 97–107
   See also civil rights activism;
      segregation
Distinguished Alumni Citation
   award, 152
District of Columbia, 122–31, 137–43,
   157–60
Dollarway High School, Pine Bluff,
   Arkansas, 95
Doll League, The, 35
Downie, Tom, 65
Du Bois, W. E. B., 6
Due, John, 105
Dunaway, Edwin, 53
Dunn, Fay, 64

Justice Department
  civil rights activism, 113–17
  criminal investigations, 131
  Little Rock school crisis, 81
  voting rights, 97, 100–101, 118–19

K

Katzenbach, Nicholas deB., 113–15, 118
Kennedy, Edward, 162
Kennedy, John F., 97, 103–4
Kennedy, Robert, 99–100, 101
Kerner Commission, 122
Kessler, Gladys, 161
King, Coretta Scott, 159, 163–64
King, Martin Luther, Jr., 86, 98, 102, 111,
  113–14, 127–28, 138

L

labor unions, 132–35
Laney, Ben, 32, 37, 39–40
law practice
  civil rights cases, 55, 57, 60–69,
    93–96, 104–5, 138
  clientele, 54–55, 137–38
  District of Columbia, 137–43
  as independent counsel, 157–59
  Little Rock school crisis, ix, 71–82
  nonconfrontational approach, 61
  Pine Bluff, Arkansas, ix, 53–69
  Sidley & Austin law firm, x, 157–59
law schools
  desegregation efforts, 31–34, 37–51
  Howard University Law School,
    31, 38–39, 144–56
  U.S. Supreme Court decisions, 31
Lawson, Steven, 153
Lawyers' Committee, 150
Lawyers' Committee for Civil Rights
  Under Law, x, 157, 159
League of Women Voters, 139
Leflar, Robert A., 38–39, 41, 43, 46, 50
LeFlore, Greenwood, 4, 100
LeFlore, Julia, 4
Legal Defense and Education Fund, Inc.
  as board member, 139–40
  civil rights cases, 138

Council for United Civil Rights
  Leadership (CUCRL), 102
  Little Rock school crisis, 71–73,
    79–80, 85–89
  rift with NAACP, 153–54
  school desegregation, 63, 66, 154
  See also NAACP (National
    Association for the
    Advancement of Colored
    People)
Lemley, Harry T., 83–87
Lewis, John, 94, 103, 117, 168–69
light-skinned colored population, 5–6,
  8, 18–19, 61–62
Little Rock Nine, 79, 83–84, 86, 101
Little Rock School Board, 63–66,
  71–80, 83–84, 86–92
Little Rock school crisis, ix, 71–93
Looby, Z. Alexander, 163
Lorch, Grace, 78
loyalty oaths, 25–26
Lucas, John Grey, 1

M

Macy, John W., Jr., 112
Mahon, L. M., 95–96
Manpower Programs, 131
March on Washington, 103–4, 133
marriage to Lucille McKee, 34–35
Marshall, Burke, 97
Marshall, George C., 16
Marshall, Thurgood
  civil rights cases, 31–32, 67–68
  Freedom Riders case, 94
  friendship with Wiley Branton,
    x, 28, 56–57, 72, 93, 147,
    165, 168–69
  Howard University Law
    School, 145
  Little Rock school crisis, 79–81,
    85–89
Martin, Louis, 97, 113
Masons, 1, 3, 59, 139
maternal grandparents, 4–5
Matthews, Jess W., 84
Mayevski, Ziegman, 28

Negroes
  See African American population;
  black population; light-skinned
  colored population
Negro press, 24
Neighborhood Development Program,
  128, 130
Neighborhood Legal Services Project,
  130
Neighborhood Planning Councils, 124
Neighborhood Services Program, 126
Nimitz, Chester W., 16
1908th Engineer Aviation Battalion, 21
Nineteenth Street Baptist Church,
  Washington, D.C., 59
Nixon, Richard M., 122, 143

O

obituaries, 168–69
Okinawa, 22
Oral History Research Project,
  Columbia University, 153
organized labor, 132–35
out-of-state tuition, 38

P

"passing," 18–19, 61–62
paternal grandparents, 3–4
patriotism, 151
Pattillo, Melba
  See Beals, Melba Pattillo
Payne, Charles M., 100, 117
Payne, Frank Andrew, 68–69
Payne v. Arkansas, 68–69, 82
Pearson v. Murray, 31
Penix, Bill, 42, 44
personal character, 56–57, 61–62, 93,
  106, 149–52, 158–60, 165–69
personal safety, 57, 82, 94
Phase Plan, 66–67, 73–76, 83–88
Phillips, Carter, 159
Pigskin Club of Washington, 139
Pine Bluff, Arkansas
  colored community, 1–3
  educational system, 1–2

law practice, ix, 53–69
long-term affiliation, 94–95
racism, 11–14
segregation, 2–3, 8
Plessy v. Ferguson, 30, 32
poll tax, 26, 29
Ponder, Annelle, 105
Poor People's March on Washington, 131
pop-calls, 59–60
Pratt, Jack, 105
Presbyterian student groups, 45–46
President's Council on Equal
  Opportunity, 107-8, 109–13
Private School Corporation, 89
protest riots, 116–17, 122, 127–28, 131
Pryde, Paul, 129–30
Pryor, David, 163, 168

R

racism
  armed forces, 15–22
  personal experiences, ix, 10–14, 18,
    46–47, 81–82
  voting rights, 97–107
  See also discrimination; segregation
Raspberry, William, 122, 168
Reagan, Ronald, 160
Redmond, S. R., 31
Regional Council of Negro Leadership,
  181n12
Rehnquist, William, 163
Reid, Herbert O., 155
religious beliefs, 59
Republican Party, 25
Reuther, Walter, 132–36
Robinson, George, 4–5, 59
Robinson, Mary, 4
Rougeau, Weldon, 147
Rowland, Eckel and Marge, 46

S

school desegregation
  closures, 88–92, 101
  law schools, 31–34, 37–51
  Little Rock school crisis, ix, 71–93

U

Union Baptist Church, Atlanta, Georgia,
107-8
United Auto Workers (UAW), 132-33
United Planning Organization, 119,
121-34
United States Youth Council, 139
University of Arkansas at Little Rock
School of Law, 151
University of Arkansas at Pine Bluff
See Arkansas Agricultural,
Mechanical and Normal College
(AM&N)
University of Arkansas School of Law,
33, 37-51, 151
University of Maryland School of
Law, 31
University of Missouri School of
Law, 31
University of Oklahoma School of
Law, 31
University of Texas School of Law, 31-32
U.S. Commission on Civil Rights, 104-6
U.S. Supreme Court decisions
Little Rock school crisis, 82, 85-91
Payne v. Arkansas, 68-69
school desegregation, 30-32, 37-38,
50, 63-67, 85-91
voting rights, 25

V

veterans
career opportunities, 28
civil rights activism, 24
educational system, 45, 49
Veterans and Citizens League for Better
Government, 24
Veterans Good Government
Association, 24
violence
armed forces, 17
Freedom Riders case, 94
intimidation incidents, 46-47
Little Rock school crisis, 78-80,
83-84

protest riots, 116-17, 122, 127-28,
131
voting rights, 99-101, 112
Voter Registration Fund, 138-39
voting rights
Arkansas, 2, 25-26
black population, 2, 25-30, 97-108,
122
federal protection, 99-101, 112
harassment, 99-101, 112
Johnson administration, 112, 115
legal cases, 138
U.S. Supreme Court decisions, 25
Voter Education Project (VEP),
97-107, 125-26, 139
Voting Rights Act (1965), 112
white opposition, 99-101
See also civil rights activism

W

Walden, A. T., 163
Walker, John W., 93, 96, 147
Walker, Sonny, 77
War on Poverty, 111, 122-27, 133
Washington Bar Association, 152
Washington, Booker T., 3, 6, 9
Washington Center for Metropolitan
Studies, 139
Washington Home Rule Committee,
139
Washington Lawyers' Committee, x, 150
Washington Urban League, 139
Washington, Walter, 123-24, 126, 128
"Waste of Manpower" pamphlet, 18, 21
Waterman, J. S., 37
Watson, John, 13
Watt case, 57, 60, 72
Webber, Paul R., III, 143, 144, 168
White America, Inc., 66
Whitfield, George, 95
Whitney North Seymour Award,
150, 162
Wiley A. Branton Award, 150-51
Wiley, Effa Louise Lavinia Emily
Rosetta Armstrong Stewart, 4-9, 23
Wiley, Ellen, 5

Wiley, Frank, 7, 19
Wiley, James Austin, 5, 7, 12
Wiley, Joe, 7
Wiley, Julia, 7
Wilkins, Roger, 116
Wilkins, Roy, 72, 98, 134
Williams, Eddie, 142
Williams, Miller, 45, 46–47, 50, 152–53
Williams, Thaddeus, 65
Wilson, Henry Hall, 138–39
Wofford, Harris, 97
Women's Emergency Committee to
    Open Our Schools, 91–92
Woodcock, Leonard, 136
Wood, Wylene Branton
    See Branton, Wylene
Worthy, Patricia, 56, 138, 144, 148,
    151–52

Y

Young, Andrew, 105, 113
Young, Jack H., 163
Young, Whitney, Jr., 98, 113–14, 132, 135

Z

Zinn, Leo, 34, 35
Zinn, Richard
    See Branton, Richard (Zinn)

JUDITH KILPATRICK is professor and associate dean at the University of Arkansas School of Law. She has written several articles about Wiley Austin Branton. *There When We Needed Him* is her first book.